## *Insider Quotes: The Blind Man's Elephant*

"...we'd have to classify the Christianity we experience today as a different species of elephant compared to our first century predecessor."

"If we can't explain the reasons for our beliefs, we don't have any beliefs. We have someone else's beliefs."

"It is better to be sure of one truth you have proven than ninety-nine others for which you take someone else's word."

"Ultimately, though, our unchallenged fears bully us, making our lives smaller. They garner control shrinking our world imperceptibly until we end up cloistered in dark cubbyholes fearing even the faintest hint of unfamiliar light."

"When we look at time's relativity and it being a singularity, Einstein, Feynman, Hawking and our Biblical non-physicist 3000 years ago have reached the same conclusion about the construction of our universe, but from two different, though, complementary routes."

"One gets the distinct feeling that today's concept of heaven is a place no longer inhabited by harp playing angels, but rather by angel chauffeured SUV's that take you from mall to mall with unlimited credit on your plastic key to heaven."

"The Ottoman Empire... came to an end exactly 2520 years after the Babylonian king had his dream, as foretold in the Book of Daniel in absolute violation of the psychological arrow of time thus proving the validity of the theological arrow of time."

"While all the "anti-Christ of the day" sentiment has raged on over the millennia, the real identity, according to the Biblical record, has remained steadfast and unchanged. The events of the apocalypse were set in motion at least four thousand years ago by the very characters involved today."

## Dedication

This book is for all those who have, as Einstein put it, a holy curiosity.

Michael J. Miller

# The Blind Man's Elephant

*A unique, fresh insight into science and the Biblical record regarding evolution, beginning of life, creation in six days, the apocalypse and the key to the 4000 year old identity of the antichrist of Revelation*

If the shoe fits, wear it.

New book by Michael J. Miller
**The Hijacked Elephant**

Copyright © 2007, 2008 Michael J. Miller

All rights reserved under International and Pan-American Copyright Conventions. No part of this book may be reproduced in any form or by any means whatsoever without prior written permission of the publisher except in the case of brief quotations embodied in critical articles, reviews or books when properly credited.

ISBN 978-976-8212-13-9

Second printing.

A redshoebooks publication www.redshoe.com

Cover design: Blue-Concepts GmbH
              www.blue-concepts.com

The redshoebooks bookmark and redshoe graphics are trademarks of redshoebooks.

**Table of Contents**                                                          **Page**

| | |
|---|---|
| Preface: Finding The Elephant | 11 |
| Prologue: The Blind Man's Elephant | 19 |
| Chapter One: Three Creations Of Life: A Bridge To Understanding | 47 |
| Chapter Two: Did The Second Man Marry His Sister | 81 |
| Chapter Three: If Life Begins At 40 Where Does That Leave Conception? | 105 |
| Chapter Four: Creation in Six Days, But Who's Counting? | 131 |
| Chapter Five: I'd Like An Ottoman To Go With That | 157 |
| Chapter Six: The Genesis Birthright | 185 |
| Postscript: Seeing The Elephant | 261 |
| Appendix: Chapter Endnotes | 267 |
| Endnotes Chapter One | 268 |
| Endnotes Chapter Two | 279 |
| Endnotes Chapter Three | 283 |
| Endnotes Chapter Four | 287 |
| Endnotes Chapter Five | 291 |
| Endnotes Chapter Six | 297 |

# The Blind Man's Elephant

## Preface: Finding The Elephant

I still remember the hot, cloudless day in August when I first stepped foot on campus even though it was more than thirty-five years ago. I had turned down a full scholarship to Yale for a Master's degree in finance. Now here I was at a small bible college to get a degree in theology. While some viewed my choice of bible college over Yale as a great lapse in judgment, I felt quite the opposite. To me a choice between a degree in finance versus theology was the classic choice between mammon and God.

Even as a child I had questions about God, creation and life. Our great kosmic [the theological kosmos versus the scientific cosmos] puzzle, life, had begun creeping into my consciousness, enlarging my global awareness. My first notable recollections of the world outside my neighborhood and elementary school occurred when I was about nine years old. When the sisters teaching Sunday school said that God was everywhere at once, I wanted to know how that was possible. The sisters couldn't explain except to say, "It's a mystery." If the adults couldn't figure it out, what was I to do? My young mind wrestled with that one for a long time.

It was about the same time that I learned nothing traveled faster than the speed of light in our universe. Naturally, I wanted to know what would happen if I turned on a flashlight at the back of the spaceship going that fast. Would the light just pile up inside the flashlight until we slowed down when it would explode out all at once? Or if we slowed down to just one mile an hour less than the speed of light, would the light just come out v-e-r-y s-l-o-w-l-y? And what would happen to a fly buzzing around inside the spaceship if, while it was flying forward just at the moment we attained the speed of light, would it just freeze in mid-air? And while I was traveling on this spaceship, how was it possible I would age more slowly than my friends back on Earth? The universe I heard about seemed much stranger than the one I experienced everyday. Why did God make the cosmos this way?

I don't know if other nine-year-old kids thought about these things because we only talked and played neighborhood football, basketball or baseball depending on the time of the year. But those questions and a lot more grew with me until I felt I just had to know the answers. I'm still this way today. I want to know the answers to the many questions my mind still pops out for me to think about. The Prologue and chapters in this book are answers to some of them.

Walking on campus to classes the first day was very exciting for me. I was, in hindsight, very naïve in some ways about my "true believer" expectations. In my twenties, I had formed ideas and opinions about many theological issues. And I thought I had the answers to many of my questions. Getting into bible college and getting my degree in theology would surely provide the missing answers to all my questions. But what I hadn't counted on was that spiritual growth and understanding are a personal lifelong process not found within the confines of a ready-made package handed out by organizations. It isn't something that mysteriously appears in toto when they hand you the piece of paper that is your degree. In fact, by the time graduation rolled around I had more questions than answers. This was a blessing in disguise. For had I walked off campus for the last time thinking I knew the answers, I would have missed out on the adventure of a lifetime.

## Preface: Finding The Elephant

One big lesson I learned wasn't in any of our textbooks. Namely, it is entirely possible to spiritually outgrow the organization to which you belong. Like many others, I always looked upon "my" church as the provider of all answers in a sea of other churches who hadn't gotten it right. But as Christ said, some grow ten fold, some thirty fold, some sixty and others one hundred. While most people probably believe their church is the one hundred-folder, in fact, no organization is that. The reason is the larger and more successful a religious organization becomes, the less it is open to change, which equates to the lifelong process that is spiritual growth.

Plus organizations, by definition, run on money. Become successful enough to grow large and financial overhead becomes a major concern. Supporting it is an even bigger concern. With churches, too often financial success is equated with spiritual success when in fact it's very likely the opposite. It's the God and mammon equation. Thus organizations tend towards stability at the point they reach their greatest growth in numbers rather than continually challenging beliefs in order to grow spiritually. The largest numbers are found at the bottom of the spiritual growth pyramid.

Organizations, and churches are organizations, do not have a spirit as opposed to human beings. Thus any organization cannot grow more than its human leader. Organizations tend to be a reflection of their leadership especially when it comes to religion. In order to remain a true believer, one's spiritual growth cannot exceed the church's understanding. However, spiritual growth, contrary to indoctrination efforts, is not found on an organizational chart. Thus, the decision to leave a religious organization can be a very tough time in a Christian's life. After all, why would anyone seriously join a church to begin with if they felt it was the wrong one?

Some organizations have put the fear into its members that if they leave the organization, they leave their opportunity for salvation and will surely suffer in everlasting hell fire or some other eschatological Hades. This is done it appears, mostly to protect the organization rather than out of a genuine concern for the individual. God holds no such sword over our heads. He is concerned for our salvation not our damnation. We are told to seek first his kingdom, not seek first a religious organization especially as there are more than 30,000 Christian denominations that sincerely believe they are the way to salvation. How many Christs are there?

When we get to that proverbial fork in the road of life, do we accept God at his word and walk the narrow path set before us or do we stay in the sheltered protection of the organization? Much to their credit, some church organizations try to grow and change as they learn. But too often, their organizational inertia makes this a slow and difficult process often resulting in compromises ultimately made for the well-being of the organization. Thus the decision to challenge one's beliefs and leave an organization is a major turning point in any Christian's life.

We cannot grow spiritually beyond the head of a church unless we leave the organization, which I did. Interestingly, after I left the church, members with whom I was very close sincerely asked me if I still believed in God. To them, the organization and its leadership had become synonymous with, and was the portal to, God. I'm sure this is common to very many denominations. While I can understand their feelings and see their point of view, I replied that it was because I believed in God rather than the church organization that I left. I had spiritually outgrown the church and its leadership.

I was grateful for the education and learning experience. But when I discovered, along with many others, that certain tenets of the church were indeed plainly incorrect in relation to the Biblical record due to our growth in spiritual understanding, and the church refused to implement the changes, I was left with one of two choices. Stay or continue to grow spiritually. This decision was arduous at the time because I was viewed as a heretic, a pariah by many still in the church and whom I considered friends. Yet there really was no choice. My faith is in the living God, our Father in heaven and in his son, Jesus Christ as it should be for every Christian serious about their faith. No organization can be your spiritual surrogate.

There is a verse, 1 John, 2:27, that every believer should live by. "But the anointing which you have received of him abides in you, and you don't need any man to teach you: but as the same anointing teaches you of all things and is truth and is no lie, and even as it has taught you, you shall abide in him."

Some people have asked me "Why don't you start your own church?" While I do miss the regular fellowship the organization provided, the answer is very simple. The church began by Christ is still in existence today. But it is a spiritual entity not a physical one. It is found in God's Spirit within us, not inside an organization or within a building as magnificent as it might be. Ultimately, it is an intimate spiritual relationship between God the Father, Christ the mediator and each of us individually. That's it. No one else is necessary or even possible for that matter. Beware of anyone who tells you different especially someone who answers you, "Yes, but...."

While we may have "soul mates" as traveling companions through life, and I am blessed to be in such a situation, the journey of the spirit is one we all walk for ourselves. The challenges in life are directed at us through the spirit within us. It is through this filter that we experience the symmetries of life: suffering, pain, sorrow as well as joy, love, and passion. And it is different at different times for each of us. Our mountain may be a spiritually stronger person's molehill. None of us, however, knows all the answers. Some are just a bit further down the spiritual road in life.

This book definitely is a product of thinking outside the box we call Christianity today. Thus it presents a picture much different from modern day organized, institutional Christianity. The Biblical record is used as a primary reference text as well as many sources from physics, cosmology, biology and history. I do expect that many will take exception to what they will find here.

In addition to the verse in John, the apostle Paul admonishes all of us to prove all things and hold on to that which is good or of God. This has been my guideline in writing this book. The main purpose is to get each person reading this to think and question the reasons for their own beliefs, not an organization's beliefs, in a constructive way. Can you explain to someone the exact reasons for each of your beliefs? Or have you trusted that to the professionals? Our faith is to be our profession. There aren't any

# Preface: Finding The Elephant

piggyback rides into the kingdom of God. There are no coattails to ride on. If we can't explain the reasons for our beliefs, we don't have any beliefs. We have someone else's beliefs.

Christianity today has changed from what we can read plainly in the Biblical record. We can examine one part [denomination] of the elephant, but it doesn't tell us about the elephant [Christianity] as a whole. If we examine Christianity as a whole, it tells us nothing about a specific denomination. Thus referring holistically to Christianity today is somewhat misleading in that there are somewhere between 20,000 to nearly 34,000 denominations [we aren't certain exactly] representing about 1.7 billion Christians worldwide all based on one Bible, more or less. As all these denominations can't be in exact agreement with the Biblical record, we don't know exactly where Christianity is today.

While attempting to shed light on the basics as set forth in the first century AD, I may have added one more view to the growing list that describes Christianity. I am uncertain which it is at this point in time. But I am certain most will be quite surprised by what they find just in the Prologue. Don't take my word for it, however. Go beyond just reading. Search out the answers for yourself until you are sure. Ultimately, we are all accountable for our lives and the decisions we make. It is better to be sure of one truth you have proven than ninety-nine others for which you take someone else's word.

I fully expect some of you to react angrily to this book, yell at it, maybe even jump up and down on it. To my way of thinking, this would be good, unless, of course you are reading this on your computer or media player. Why? It shows you are thinking and taking your faith and spirituality seriously. Better to be hot or even cold in your faith than to be lukewarm. When you're lukewarm, what is written here becomes nothing more than just words. Remember, faith requires works. We need to do our due diligence when it comes to the Word of God.

Michael J. Miller
October 2007

## Prologue

## The Blind Man's Elephant

*"So oft in theologic wars, The disputants, I ween,*
*Rail on in utter ignorance Of what each other mean,*
*and prate about an Elephant Not one of them had seen!"*
*-- John Godfrey Saxe*

The title of this book is, The Blind Man's Elephant. It is an analysis of science and the first century AD understanding of Christianity's big picture compared to Christianity's understanding today particularly that of the religious right. You may be familiar with the story of the six blind men describing their encounter with an elephant for the first time in John Godfrey Saxe's 19th century poem. That experience is similar to what we have in Christianity today. Among the six, the blind men came away from their experience with very different descriptions of an elephant. The first blind man said the elephant was like a very strong rope. One other blind man said, "No, I ran my hands over it, an elephant is like a massive wall. "Well," said another, "I'd have to disagree. It is like a sturdy tree trunk that my arms could not reach around." The last blind man said, "I believe you're all mistaken for an elephant is like a thick and powerful snake." Taken individually, one can understand how these descriptions would be seen as accurate and sincere by each of the blind men for a elephant's leg would certainly be like a tree trunk and it's tail like a rope especially when they had no big picture of what an elephant looked like or where it came from. But it would produce an incorrect view of what an elephant actually looked like and yet each blind man would depart believing he and he alone had the true picture of what an elephant was like. This approach applied to Christianity, would have resulted in the establishment of a Church of the Holy Rope, a First Wall Church, the Living Tree Trunk Church and perhaps thousands of variations on these themes. But no matter how sincere and honest in their beliefs, none of these churches would have had the accurate big picture from the beginning. Such is the case with Christianity today as ludicrous as it may first sound. By the time you finish reading the last chapter, this analogy will become extremely clear in its veracity.

While Christianity as a whole rejects the concept of biological evolution, ironically it is Christianity itself that has theologically evolved and mutated from one entity [elephant] into more than 30,000 denominations [varying descriptions] over the past two millennia. And it has morphed into an entity, when looked at holistically that is barely recognizable when compared to its theological genome ancestor in the first century AD. In fact, we'd have to classify the Christianity we experience today as a different species of elephant compared to our first century predecessor.

To get a clearer understanding of just how much modern day Christianity has evolved, this Prologue will examine five simple questions and compare the answers of today directly with those in the Biblical record from the time of Adam to the time of the second Adam, Christ. Upon completely reading this book, and surveying our contemporary world, you may find yourself wondering, "What is this religion we call Christianity?"

Therefore we are going on an adventure. It is an adventure in theological genetics if you will. We want to discover those quantum principles, those elementary points, the theological markers that were part and parcel of Christianity in the first century. In other words, we are going on an adventure, a spiritual safari, to discover the big picture rather than big game. We're going to find out if the elephant described by Christianity is really out there.

There is a deliberate reason for choosing the word adventure in our context. Adventure is defined as an unusual and exciting experience. Now this may be an odd way to describe a book about Christianity, but when you arrive at the end of this Prologue I believe you will have found it to be unusual and more than likely exciting in a visceral as well as thought provoking way. So think of the adventure in this book as an exhilarating journey making our way to a mountain summit with new discoveries waiting for us around each bend in the trail before eventually making our way back to our jumping off point here in the Prologue. The view from the summit, however, will provide us with an extraordinary view of our theological wanderings over the past two thousand years. It will provide us with a clear view of that first century elephant.

And like climbing any mountain, along the way we will discover a second, more profound journey. It is a journey to the core of our existence, a journey into the covert known only to God and us. We will discover as we climb the mountain that we are exploring the fortitude of our own personal faith. It is a different person who returns from the summit than the one who began the climb. As Sir Edmund Hillary reflected upon climbing Mt. Everest, "It is not the mountains that we conquer, but ourselves."

Theologically speaking then, there are two journeys in this book.

One is the mountain of information presented here. Any person literate in English who will spend the time can read it. The other is the second journey that is the more vital path. For within each of us lies the secret, hidden world in which passage is denied to all others. In it are the mountains we must conquer on our own. With child-like abandon, we can run for the peaks. Or, we can refuse to climb them and no one else will know. Ultimately, though, our unchallenged fears bully us, making our lives smaller. They garner control shrinking our world imperceptibly until we end up cloistered in dark cubbyholes fearing even the faintest hint of unfamiliar light.

By controlling the course of action in our lives, facing new challenges head-on, fear gives way to strength and confidence, a new respect for our lives. We climb the mountains within us rediscovering a lost sensation upon reaching the summit. We are bathed in light of renewed curiosity, experiencing the rewards of an unencumbered vista. It provides a refreshing perspective in life known only to those who've reached the top. It gives us the opportunity to see the elephant. There are few opportunities in life to summit a previously unscaled peak. Yet within each of us, new peaks wait to be conquered. The adventurous journey in this book, as you are about to discover, is one of them.

Like any adventure, climbing requires proper gear or kit. The Biblical record, our trustworthy map from the first century, tells us to stand up and strap on the "whole armor of God" for our journey. At minimum, you will need a helmet, shield and a sword to slay some falsehoods. As we begin our journey up the mountain, we will discover some wonderfully surprising things that we didn't learn in Sunday school.

## Prologue: The Blind Man's Elephant

Speaking of Sunday school, it's quite likely most people who are Christians would consider that they have a pretty good understanding of the basic tenets of Christianity. But do we? Or have we, ever so slowly, exited the straight gate and walked off the narrow path leading to the summit to wander among the enticingly broad pastures sheltered by our fears?

There's only one way to find out. Strap on your helmet and let's explore five simple questions. Keep in mind, the answers are five quantum principles of theology, the theological markers that define our faith. They are predicated on what we will plainly discover in the Biblical record.

First, Adam and Eve were created in the garden of Eden. True or false?
Second, the wise men brought gifts to Christ as a baby in a manger. True or false?
Next, Israelites are not the Gentiles. True or false?
Fourth, Christ is the savior of mankind. True or false?
And finally, Christ came to bring peace on earth. True or false?

These are pretty simple straightforward questions. Got all your answers? Good. For those of you who answered "True," to all the questions above, congratulations. You got a perfect score. You got every question... wrong!

WHAT!!! No way. How can this possibly be? See, you got whacked on the head right off the bat. Good thing you were wearing your helmet. These are basic tenets. I mean every Christian knows Adam and Eve were created in the garden of Eden, right? Christ is the savior of mankind isn't he? Before getting too worked up here and you throw this book in the trash, let's begin our ascent towards the summit and discover the answers together. As we'll see, the common cliché, the truth is stranger than fiction, holds forth once again.

The purpose of these five questions is to provide some easily verified points in the Biblical record, a few spoken directly by Christ, to show us that what we've assumed to be so, even with the most simple points of fact, isn't always the case. Should you be sufficiently adventurous to keep on climbing with an open mind, watch out for falling dogmas. Keep your helmet on.

When confronted with information that challenges our closely held beliefs, our first reaction normally is to put up our defenses, our swords and shields. Then we usually make one of two available choices. One choice is to remain in the broad, wildflower field of deceit at the base of the mountain. Most people would choose this option although not without self-rationalizing justifications. The other is to seek the unfamiliar light of the higher path leading to the summit, which requires a certain amount of fortitude on many levels. This book is, after all, an adventure in discovery.

## Adam and Eve were created in the garden of Eden?

For those of you suitably geared up or kitted out for the occasion, be bold. Open the Biblical record to Genesis, chapter two, verses seven and eight. It is different than the common misperception. Read it out loud if you prefer. "And the LORD God formed man of the dust of the ground, and breathed into his nostrils the breath of life; and man became a living soul." Next what happened? "And the LORD God planted a garden eastward in Eden…." Then

Prologue: The Blind Man's Elephant

what? "...and there he put the man whom he had formed."

You see, God created Adam, then he planted the garden eastward in Eden and then God put Adam in the garden. Adam wasn't created in the garden of Eden as we commonly assume but west of it, in Eden. This isn't just a word game here. The garden of Eden and Eden were two very different places perhaps not unlike heaven and hell at least from Adam's perspective.

Now continue in Genesis to chapter three. Read verse twenty-three. "Therefore the LORD God sent him [Adam] forth from the garden of Eden, to till the soil from which he was taken." Plainly, Adam was not a fruit of the garden.

Eve, on the other hand, was created in the garden of Eden which you can read about in chapter two, verse twenty-two. Thus, Adam and Eve weren't created in the garden of Eden, just Eve. How about that? Mountain climbing isn't so bad after all.

## The wise men brought gifts to Christ as a baby in a manger?

Now what about the wise men? Surely they were in Bethlehem at the time of the birth of Christ. We've all seen the nativity scenes in front of churches every December and the Christmas cards showing the star, the wise men, the manger and their camels bundled with gifts in Bethlehem. Let's go back in time to Matthew chapter two, verse eleven.

Again, read it out loud to yourself. "And when they [an unknown number of wise men from the east] were come into the house, they saw the young child with Mary his mother and fell down, and worshipped him: and when they had opened their treasures, they presented unto him gifts: gold, frankincense and myrrh."

The wise men weren't at the nativity at the time of Christ's birth when the shepherds in the fields came to visit without gifts. One of Raphael's large tapestries hanging in the Vatican has the nativity depicted correctly. No wise men, just shepherds. And even the Archbishop of Canterbury, Dr. Rowan Williams recently stated publicly that the "Nativity" is a legend. The wise men visited Christ as a young child in a house up to two years after his birth. In fact, the account here in Matthew, in only the second chapter of the New Testament, refers to Christ as a young child [Greek, paidion] six times in seven verses and not once as a newborn infant [Greek, brephos]. Thus, the gifts they brought weren't birthday presents, but were gifts presented to a king. The fact is Christ was never in what is celebrated today as Christmas.

How is it then that Christians have come to celebrate December 25th as Christmas by giving each other gifts supposedly on Christ's birthday when he didn't get any gifts on his day of birth? He didn't receive the gifts until he was a young child living in a house. And the gifts were presented to Christ the king, not Christ the birthday boy. Christmas is the product of theological evolution.

While we're bursting bubbles, now is as good a time as any to pop another one with the tip of our swords. Christ wasn't born in December either. The 25th of December celebration date was chosen by an emperor of the Roman Empire, Constantine, which was the first day of winter [solstice] back then in the fourth century due to the precession of the Earth's rotation around its axis. Lest we think he knew something we don't, Constantine also picked the 25th of December as the date for the celebration of Osiris, the Egyptian goddess of the dead [winter is the dead season of the year] and also Mithris, the Roman sun god as the days [winter solstice] begin to get longer once again in late December. It must have made analogous sense to Constantine. Christians said Christ is the son of God who rose from the dead. The 25th was a perfect tie in with both the Roman sun god and the Egyptian goddess of the dead.

At the time, Constantine was having religious trouble in the empire caused by different factions not unlike what we see in the Middle East today. In his attempt to put an end to this, he made a political decision. He lumped these religious celebrations into the 25th of December as the day for Christians to celebrate their religion along with the Egyptians and the Romans. It was a take it or leave it proposition. It had nothing to do with the reality of Christ's birthday. First century Christians didn't celebrate Christmas. They were still on the path to the summit.

All this raises the question, then, what in the world are "Christians" doing celebrating a false birth date for Christ established by a Roman emperor, in a retail orgy frenzy exchanging gifts [most often not gold, frankincense and myrrh] with each other, in front of an evergreen tree, a superstitious symbol used in pagan winter celebrations, when the shepherds in the fields, who didn't bring any gifts with them to the birth day of Christ, had long since packed it in for the autumn by the end of October as it was too cold to keep sheep out in the fields with nothing for them to graze on in December? Granted this is one long question, but the short answer to the long question is, "Everybody does it. It's tradition." More correctly, it's theological evolution resulting in a species of Christianity much different than the one found in the first century.

You should have a few questions yourself about the Christmas celebration at this point. If so, there is a wealth of information on websites about the pagan origins of the Christmas celebration that you can explore as you like. Last time I googled this subject, there were more than 750,000 results. After this, also read chapter ten of Jeremiah. One caveat. The idea that holidays of pagan origin, as opposed to the holy days set aside by God in the Biblical record, can somehow be appropriated by modern man for "good" to promote Christianity is a false and evil perversion. The theological significance of the Christmas celebration is that it seduces us away from the days that have great significance and purpose for us today deliberately put in place by God to act as sign posts marking the narrow path to the summit rather than celebrating a day marked by an emperor of Rome. Christ said, "a corrupt tree cannot bring forth good fruit." Christ didn't say, probably can't or might not. Keep this in mind next time you head out to buy a Christmas tree. This distinction made by Christ is a key waypoint on our journey. But we digress a bit here. Let's move on to question three.

### Israelites are the Gentiles?

Christians, by and large, though not all, consider themselves to be Gentiles and not Israelites. I use the word Israelites because the Jews are descended from only one of the twelve sons of Israel, Judah, mentioned in the Biblical record. Jews descended from Judah are the people of the Old Testament, but only one-twelfth of them.

In fact, the first time in the Biblical record the word Jews is used [2Kings 16:6] Rezin, the king of the north or Syria and Pekah, the king of Israel came up to Jerusalem to make war against Ahaz, the Jewish king of the House of Judah. Israel and Syria were at war with the Jews! As we are told, Rezin drove the Jews out of Elath. So it's important to understand that the Jews are not all Israel. They are just a part of Israel, a one-twelfth part.

Christ's first coming is commonly taught by modern day Christianity to be to the Gentiles rather than to Israel. The "Christian" thinking is that the Old Testament [the Tanakh, or Jewish Bible which is comprised of: one, the Law [Torah]; two, the Prophets [Neviim] including both the Former Prophets and the Latter Prophets; and three, the Sacred Writings [Ketuvim]] which include the Poetic Books, the Megilloth or Festival Books, and the Restoration Books] is for the Jews and the New Testament [which is comprised of: one, the Gospels and Acts; two, the Universal and Paul's Epistles; and three, Revelation, paralleling the Law, Prophets and the Writings of the Tanakh] is for the Gentiles. This is partially correct in one very narrow sense as we'll discover in detail in Chapter Six, but not in the way we currently understand it to be. Thus, Christians, for the most part, consider themselves to be Gentiles and not Israelites. However, the followers of Christ have come to be called Christians. Therefore, if Christ said he was sent only to the Gentiles, then Christians indeed would be Gentiles. And it would stand to reason if he said he was sent only to Israel, then Christians would be Israelites. The logic seems rather simple.

Let's see to whom Christ himself says he is sent. We can read his straightforward answer in Matthew chapter fifteen, verse twenty-four: Christ plainly says, "I am not sent but unto the lost sheep of the House of Israel." Put another way, "I am sent only to the lost sheep of the House of Israel." There is no mention of "the Gentiles of the world." This is the quantum theological root principle of the New Testament. It is the Biblical record equivalent of $E = MC^2$. It is the key that unlocks the mystery and provides understanding of the events taking place in the world around us as we'll read in Chapter Six, our final ascent to the summit.

How can it be like that? This can't be right! An entire book could be written on this subject, but we'll just hit the highlights as it were. Read it again out loud this time. There is a very simple explanation. The lost sheep of the House of Israel, the descendants of Israel's twelve sons, except those from the House of Judah, the Jews, and the priests of Levi, were divorced from God. They lost their national identity, they lost their inheritance and all the promises given to Abraham, Isaac and Israel more than 700 years before Christ's first coming.

How did this come about? Turn to Jeremiah chapter three, verse eight, "And I [God] saw, when for all the causes whereby backsliding [House of] Israel committed adultery I had put her away, and given her a bill of divorce; yet her treacherous sister [House of] Judah feared not, but went and played the harlot also." While the House of Judah was not divorced because of promises God had made with Israel and David, she was punished in captivity for seventy years in Babylon. You can read about what led up to this in Jeremiah chapter seven. In essence, the House of Israel failed to live up to their end of the agreement they had with God. They missed the mark and lost their share of the promises and inheritance.

God caused all the nations of Israel, except the Jews and the Levite priests, to be taken captive by the Assyrians in the early eighth century BC. They were divorced and scattered among the gentiles or countries by the Assyrians, "their ways scattered to the strangers." This is commonly referred to as the "dispersion" or the Diaspora. The promises and blessings given by God to Abraham passed down to Israel were no longer theirs. Their brothers in Israel, those of the House of Judah or the Jews, referred to their cast off brothers as "goyim," which simply means of the nations or gentiles as those of the House of Israel were now scattered among the peoples of the world without their own national identity. It's as if the nations of the United States and Britain and Germany no longer existed and all their citizens were scattered among other nations and peoples. They had become gentiles, the nations divorced from God, disinherited from the birthright promises, a dispersed people. The word used for gentiles in Hebrew or Greek is simply the same word as nations or people. The English word gentiles, however, has come to take on a religious subjective connotation not originally associated with the Hebrew gowy or the Greek ethnos.

The House of Israel remained in this condition until Christ's first coming. Turn to Matthew chapter four. Let's take a look at verses twelve through sixteen. Christ is about to begin his ministry bringing the gospel [meaning good news] to the gentiles. In fact, this is the first mention of the gentiles in the New Testament. Who are these gentiles? What was the good news? The Biblical record defines itself. Let's see who it says are the gentiles.

"Now when Jesus had heard that John was cast into prison, he departed to Galilee: And leaving Nazareth, he came and lived in Capernaum, which is upon the sea coast, in the borders of Zebulon and Nephthalim: That it might be fulfilled which was spoken by the prophet Isaiah saying, The land of Zebulon and the land of Nephthalim, the way of the sea, beyond Jordan, Galilee of the Gentiles; the people that sat in darkness saw great light; and to them which sat in the region and shadow of death, light is sprung up."

The Biblical record tells us that the land of Zebulon and Nephthalim is part of the land of the Gentiles, Galilee of the Gentiles to be precise, and are the people who "sat in darkness." So what does the Biblical record tell us about the identity of the gentiles? Turn back to Genesis, chapter forty-nine. Here is a list of the sons of Israel, with their national identities, who are told what would befall them in the last days meaning they are identifiable nations once again today. If you look down to verse eight, you will see Judah, the Jews mentioned. Then go over to verse thirteen and twenty-one and you will see Zebulon and Nephthalim mentioned here along with all of their other "gentile" brothers, all who are the sons of Israel just like Judah.

Why was Christ, a blood descendant of King David of Judah, born in Bethlehem, Judea beginning his earthly ministry in Galilee, the northern area of Palestine, in the historical lands of the House of Israel? Why was he delivering the good news to these gentiles who, according to the Biblical record from the first century, turn out to be the descendants of the House of Israel, the people who sat in great darkness? What is the significance of Christ beginning his ministry to the "Gentiles" in this place? This is a simple fact that every Christian should know. But its significance has been lost to modern day Christianity over two millennia of theological evolution.

Christ began his ministry from this area of Galilee because this was the first area from which the Assyrians took captive the House of Israel after their divorce from God nearly seven and a half centuries earlier. Though this is an imprecise comparison, it would be somewhat like a descendant of the Confederate president Jefferson Davis, who was born in South Carolina, moving to the area of Lexington and Concord, running for the US presidency, and kicking off his campaign with a speech about George Washington. There is an unmistakable symbolic meaning.

The location, Galilee of the Gentiles, or nations, would symbolically remind all the lost gentiles, or the divorced people of the House of Israel who sat in darkness that where their House of Israel ancestors were first taken captive more than seven centuries earlier is where the beginning of the redemption and restoration would take place as well. Thus, Christ, their savior, would deliver the good news to them first in this place. They were to be reinstated into their former relationship with God, no longer in the shadow of death, but of life through Christ as savior of the world. To clarify, the word world, as used in John's gospel ["For God so loved the world..."], is the Greek word kosmos, meaning a harmonious, orderly arrangement. It does not refer to mankind which is the Greek word anthropos. Nor does it refer to oikoumene which is the Greek word translated as world that means the inhabited earth.

Christ restored order to the lost House of Israel putting them back into their arrangement with God. They were reconciled. No other people needed redeeming. No other people were put away for their sins. Our ancestors in the first century understood the purpose of Christ's first coming. We read in the New Testament Book of Acts, chapter five beginning in verse thirty, "The God of our fathers [the Old Testament House of Israel] raised up Jesus... Him has God exalted with his right hand, a Prince and a Savior, for to give repentance to Israel, and forgiveness of sins." As Christ plainly spoke, "I am not sent but unto the lost sheep of the House of Israel."

When Christ began his ministry in Galilee, he traveled throughout the cities and villages of the land of the House of Israel, not Judea, teaching, preaching the gospel, again meaning the good news of the kingdom, healing every sickness and disease among the people. And of his performing of miracles, it was said, "It was never so seen in Israel." When he saw the tired and weary multitudes of the people following him, Christ took compassion on them. Why? "Because they were scattered abroad, as sheep having no shepherd." This was a direct reference by Christ to the ten nations of the House of Israel to whom he was sent.

Jeremiah, son of a Levite priest in the land of Benjamin, made the same point in the Old Testament when he wrote, "[The House of] Israel is a scattered sheep...the king of Assyria has devoured him." Christ is our shepherd who came to redeem his lost sheep as John quoted him, "I am the good shepherd: the good shepherd gives his life for the sheep." The House of Israel was a scattered people, divorced from God. In this divorced state according to Paul's writing to the Roman Christians, they were hated of God, but the House of Israel was "reconciled to God [the Father] by the death of his Son…"

By Biblical definition, Christians are the lost sheep of the House of Israel. Christ plainly said, "I am not sent but unto the lost sheep of the House of Israel." Christ said what he meant and he meant what he said.

Stop here. Turn to Luke, chapter fifteen, starting in verse eleven, read the story of the prodigal son. Perhaps not surprisingly, the parable of the lost sheep precedes the parable of the prodigal son in Luke. If you think about this as a Christian, it should hit home. The prodigal son, the divorced House of Israel, is welcomed back by his Father, those put away under the first or old covenant are now recipients of an eternal inheritance as we read in Hebrews, chapter nine, verse fifteen. In chapter eight, verse eight the day comes when the Lord will make a new covenant with the House of Israel and the House of Judah. Rather than being called the Old Testament or covenant and the New Testament or covenant in English, it might be clearer to understand our relationship if they were referred to as the First Arrangement and the Second Arrangement as the Greek word, diatheke also means.

The Bible is one book written to the same people. Through Moses, God made the First Arrangement with Israel. Christ's first coming fulfilled the terms of the First Arrangement and set in motion the events that will lead to the fulfillment of the Second Arrangement at his return. The story of how and why this all came about is explored in detail in Chapter Six, The Genesis Birthright.

We have many other specific references in the New Testament

to the House of Israel. When Christ sent out his twelve apostles [the fact that there were twelve is not a coincidence], he sent them to the lost sheep of the House of Israel and no one else. He told them, in Matthew ten, verses five and six: "Go not into the road of the Gentiles [or nations as the Apostle Paul was a chosen vessel specifically to travel the road to the far reaches of the Roman Empire that extended to England and preach Christ to the dispersed descendants of the House of Israel. The apostle to the "Gentiles" in Asia Minor stood up addressing the "Men of Israel," saying "God according to his promise has raised unto Israel, a savior, Jesus...."], and into any city of the Samaritans, do not enter, but go rather to the lost sheep of the House of Israel." It was to the many descendants of the House of Israel who, having been in captivity, had migrated back into the nearby traditional homeland in the early years of the Roman Empire that the apostles were sent initially.

The Biblical record in Matthew four tells us that when Christ began his ministry preaching in Galilee of the Gentiles, it fulfilled an Old Testament prophecy regarding Israel in Isaiah, chapter nine, verses one and two. In Isaiah, however, it reads Galilee of the nations, not Gentiles. Which Old Testament nations? It's referring to the divorced nations, the lost sheep, of the House of Israel. The entire context of Isaiah nine is Israel. "The Lord sent a word into Jacob, and it has lighted upon Israel" as it says in verse eight. Interestingly, Paul, "the apostle of the Gentiles," was of the House of Israel being an "Israelite, of the seed of Abraham, of the tribe [or nation] of Benjamin" as he said in Romans chapter eleven. Benjamin was the youngest of Israel's twelve sons. The House of Israel, in their divorced or alienated state, were outsiders or gentiles, and therefore disqualified as lawful heirs under the terms of the old covenant. Christ dramatically changed all this for the House of Israel, as we'll read about in detail in chapter six.

Read Paul's explanation of this mystery found in Ephesians, chapters two and three. Paul was sent to deliver the good news, the gospel. Paul tells the "Gentile" Ephesians that they "were without Christ, being aliens from the commonwealth of Israel." The word aliens used by Paul is not a noun in the original Greek meaning a foreigner or one who was not of Israel. It is a verb, apallotrioo. It means to be shut out from fellowship and intimacy. Who was shut out from the fellowship of the commonwealth of Israel? Even non-Israelites were provided a means under the old covenant or testament to become legally incorporated into the fellowship of Israel. Who was divorced, put away from their intimacy, having no hope and without God in the kosmos, the orderly arrangement? There is only one correct answer. It's the lost sheep, or lost nations, of the House of Israel.

Of all the churches that the apostle Paul wrote letters to, the church at Corinth in Greece would certainly be considered a "Gentile" church. Yet even here the apostle to the "Gentiles" says very plainly at the beginning of chapter ten, "Moreover brethren, I would not have you ignorant, how that all our brothers were under the cloud and all passed through the sea; and all were baptized unto Moses in the cloud and in the sea; and all ate the same spiritual meat; and all drank the same spiritual drink: for they drank of that spiritual Rock that followed them: and that Rock was Christ." The very clear point made by Paul here is that the Corinthians were Israelites. We just need to keep in mind when reading the New Testament that while all the lost sheep of the House of Israel were "gentiles," not all gentiles, nations or people were of the House of Israel.

In the New Testament, James, the son of Alphaeus, the apostle of Christ wrote in the first sentence of his epistle, "James, a servant of God and of the Lord Jesus Christ, to the twelve tribes which are scattered abroad, greeting." The word tribes is phule in Greek and refers to all persons descended from one of the sons of Israel as some of Judah and Levi were also scattered abroad after the Babylonian captivity. Isn't it just possible that James, in the first century, knew that Christ was sent to the lost sheep of the House of Israel and that Christ directed James to them when he wrote these words?

In the very first book of the New Testament, Matthew chapter nineteen, Christ says to the twelve apostles, including James, "… Verily I say unto you, That you which have followed me, in the regeneration when the Son of man shall sit in the throne of his glory, you also shall sit upon twelve thrones, judging the twelve tribes of Israel."

Ask yourself, in which nations is Christianity "indigenous" in these last days? Which nations compiled our Bible today, not just the Old or the New Testament? Look at which nations put it in print, which nations are the "Christian nations" of the world today? Who did it? It's very important. Now, re-read what Christ said, "I am not sent but unto the lost sheep of the House of Israel." And where did Christ first preach the gospel, the good news? In Galilee of the Gentiles, in the coasts of Zebulon and Nephthalim, who are the sons of Israel.

Those scattered among the nations or gentiles, those descended from the sons of Israel who were dispersed among the nations without identity, without inheritance, without hope until Christ's first coming, were the divorced House of Israel of the Old Testament. Yet these same sons do have national identities in the last days according to Jacob/Israel in Genesis forty-nine. And it is to them only that Christ said he was sent. Is it not possible that Christ knew of what he was speaking? This was common knowledge in the first century. Where is that elephant today?

Isn't it amazing what we've discovered along the narrow path on the way to the summit in Genesis and Matthew, the first books of the Old and New Testaments respectively? Imagine what other unusual and exciting finds we might unexpectedly uncover in the Biblical record! Still have your helmet in place? Good, don't go weak now. Let's keep climbing.

## Is Christ the savior of mankind?

Question three leads us nicely to question number four, "Is Christ the savior of mankind?" as is so commonly, but mistakenly thought by just about every one of the 30,000 or so Christian denominations. Before we examine the Biblical record on this matter, let's look at a very simple example of a logic equation. If plumber A is a father, and plumber B is the son of plumber A, and a father is head of the plumber's association, which plumber, A or B, could be the head of the plumber's association? Of course, it's plumber A. Anyone, just about, would get this right.

As the Biblical record defines itself, let's see what it tells us concerning the identity of the savior of all men. If you like, open your Biblical record to 1Timothy, chapter four, verse ten and read it for yourself.

The apostle Paul is writing and he says, "For therefore we both labor and suffer reproach, because we trust in the living God, who is the savior of all men, especially those that believe." Paul, the apostle to the "Gentiles," is saying that he and others were laboring and suffering reproach because they trust in the living God, the savior of mankind or all men.

All we need to do is to let the Biblical record tell us if Christ is the living God. For whoever is the living God that the "apostle of Jesus Christ by the commandment of God our Savior, and Lord Jesus Christ" trusted, he is the savior of mankind.

Okay, let's go back to Matthew chapter sixteen. Let's begin in verse thirteen and go through to verse seventeen. "When Jesus was come into the coasts of Caesarea Philippi, he asked his disciples, saying, "Whom do men say that I, the Son of man, am?"

It is important to note that Jesus is deliberately asking about his identity here.

"And they said, some say you are John the Baptist: some say Elijah, some say Jeremiah or one of the prophets. He [Jesus] said to them, But whom do you say that I am? And Simon Peter answered and said, 'You are the Christ [Messiah], the Son of the living God.'"

Now did Christ chastise Peter, did he tell him, haven't you read John 3:16, haven't you seen a football game lately Peter? How could you get this wrong!? No he did none of that. Instead Jesus Christ said to Peter, "Blessed are you, Simon Bar-jona: for flesh and blood has not revealed it to you, but my Father which is in heaven."

Who is the savior of mankind, the living God? It is God the Father. Jesus Christ is the Son of the living God. And the Son of the living God says he is not sent but unto the lost sheep of the House of Israel, not mankind. God the Father is the savior of all men especially those who believe. In this God the Father, Jesus Christ and the apostle Peter are in agreement. Maybe we should be too.

Does Christ not instruct us that when we pray, we are to pray, "Our Father who is in heaven, hallowed be your name, your kingdom come, your will be done on earth as it is in heaven, give us this day our daily bread....?" Stop and think about what Christ is saying here. First we are to address our Father in heaven, not Christ. His name is to be held sacred. Whose kingdom do we pray to come? God the Father's, the savior of all men. Whose will do we ask to be done here on earth? Again it's our Father's in heaven. Who do we ask to provide us our daily bread? Again, it is our Father the living God as Christ said. Christ is the mediator between God and mankind. But our Father is the savior of mankind.

In all the apostle Paul's introductory salutations to the churches in his epistles, he continually makes the point he is an apostle of Jesus Christ by the will of God our Father. Paul always puts God the Father ahead of our Lord Jesus Christ. Christ does the same thing. And the other two major Abrahamic religions of the world, Islam and Judaism, recognize only God the Father. Christ was sent, by God the Father, the savior of all men, to the lost sheep of the House of Israel. More than half the world's religious believers are said to be descendants of Abraham. Christ wasn't sent to them at his first coming but only to the lost House of Israel. God the Father is the savior of all men. The Biblical record is clear on this point.

## Christ came to bring peace on earth?

Your mind might be reeling somewhat about now, and rightly so. The air continues to get thinner the closer we get to the summit. We don't want you keeling over from High Attitude Sickness. But certainly, Christ did come to bring peace on earth! Sorry. In fact it's quite the opposite. I know there is no rest for the weary of mind here. Just flip a few more pages back to Matthew chapter ten, verse thirty-four and down to verse thirty-nine. It must be hard to believe all this excitement and adventure is packed into the first gospel in the New Testament.

"Think not that I [Christ] am come to send peace on earth: I am come not to send peace, but a sword." You can read the rest down to verse thirty-nine. And the gospel of Luke says just about the same in chapter twelve, verse fifty-one. "Do you suppose that I am come to give peace on earth? I tell you, No: but rather division." Christ deliberately caused division, breaking the bonds of brotherhood at his first coming. Again, we'll read more about this in The Genesis Birthright in Chapter Six.

Despite the peace salutation of the apostles to individuals or churches, it is at Christ's second coming that he will bring peace, or harmony and agreement on earth which is pictured by the millennium or a thousand years of peace. If Christianity had stayed on the narrow path and held sacred the holy days, rather than the false pagan holidays, which have evolved over the millennia, then all this would be old news.

From the time between his first coming and until his second coming, has Christianity experienced peace or a sword, unity or division? Very clearly, once again, Christ knew of what he was speaking. So much for showing a shining star above the wise men at the nativity on Christmas cards emblazoned with "Peace on Earth."

What has the Biblical record told us? Adam wasn't created in the garden of Eden, the wise men came to visit Christ as a young child in a house, Israelites are the Gentiles, God the Father is the savior of mankind, Christ isn't, and Christ came not to bring peace on earth, but a sword, and division.

This certainly paints a picture of an elephant much different than the perception most have of Christianity's elephant. How can it be like that? How can our common perception of what Christianity is be so far off the mark? For the answer, you'll have to keep on heading for the summit. By the way, how are you holding up? If you're still standing at this point, that's a good sign. The chapters, where matters are more complex, are even more exciting. This is why it's critical that we have a keen awareness of what the Biblical record actually tells us.

Modern day Christianity is, in large part, made up of the traditions and commandments of men that have slowly crept into mainstream religion. We've evolved eyes that don't see and ears that don't hear what the Biblical record tells us plainly as we've just seen with these very basic and simple examples. Because of this, Christianity today has lost much of its relevance. In many cases, it's the errors that have relevance in our daily lives rather than what the Biblical record teaches us. Society and our quality of life suffer as a result. Are we willing to get off our collective pews and make changes? My collective guess is probably not, some individuals, most certainly.

At this juncture, we have reached a fork in the road. For those of you with a keen awareness, it may feel like a pitchfork in the derriere, which is what happens when we don't have our "loins girt about with truth."

What do we do now? How do we react to this? One reaction might be "So what? Who cares? What difference does it really make if Adam was created in Eden and not the garden or that the wise men saw Christ in a house as a young child rather than as a baby in the manger?" Fair enough. Some may react angrily defending their traditional beliefs arguing that this can't be correct because it conflicts with what they've learned since they were a child in Sunday school. Another reaction might be, "Hmmm, if these simple points are this far off, what else might be this way too?" Obviously these are paths that lead to different places on the mountain. The question is, "Which one gets us to the summit?"

For anyone serious about his or her Christian faith, there is a very important principle we need to consider. In Luke sixteen, verse ten. "He that is faithful in that which is least is faithful also in much: and he that is unjust in the least is unjust also in much."

Unjust here is adikos in Greek. It also means to be unrighteous, or one who deals fraudulently or deceitfully. If those who would be our teachers deal fraudulently with the least, then we will be deceived in much. If we are not faithful to these simple points, how can we be faithful to the facts stated in the Biblical record in the larger matters of Christianity? The point is if we don't get

# Prologue: The Blind Man's Elephant

these simple points correct, the bigger points will be wrong too at least if Christ is to be believed. If we don't have what it takes to make the climb to the first base camp, how can we expect to make it to the summit?

The question arises naturally, then, have you known these five simple Christian truths that we've just read in the Biblical record or have you been ignorant of them? And if the answer is the latter, then chances are you have been deceived in the larger noteworthy matters as well. That's what the adventure in this book is all about, rediscovering our theological genome ancestor from the first century AD in the Biblical record to set straight larger matters in the face of some very traditional institutionalized beliefs.

And you'll also discover one other very important principle. Christ was right when he said, "Because straight is the gate and narrow is the way which leads unto life, few there be that find it...enter you in at the strait gate: for wide is the gate, and broad is the way, that leads to destruction, and many there be which go in thereat."

To answer the question then, what difference does it make that we portray the wise men at the nativity or believe that Adam was created in the garden of Eden or we don't understand that God the Father is the savior of all men? None, if the way to life is broad and wide is the gate that leads to our understanding of God.

Christ gave us a parable. He likened the kingdom of God to a grain of mustard seed, the seed that is least of all. Yet when it is grown, it is the greatest among herbs so that birds come and lodge in its branches.

If the way that leads to life is narrow, then maybe it's important that we don't veer off the path set before us, that we remain faithful even to the least matters. Yet we can't remain faithful to even the little things that lead us on our adventure to the summit of the mountain of God unless we know them. The greatest deceit, therefore, is the least truth unknown.

# Chapter One: Three Creations of Life: A Bridge To Understanding

Bare feet are wonderful things. And when school was out for the summer, my fifth grade feet never saw the inside of my cowhide insulators [aka shoes] until the first day of the new school year. Well, not at least without a lot of complaining to my parents anyway. Every tract house in our neighborhood had wonderful manicured, dark green lawns perfectly suited for running on with bare feet when the adults weren't watching. Sometimes my parents would walk the neighborhood in the evening, usually two or three blocks over, checking out the competition, looking for ideas to make our front yard nicer. The competition was friendly, but fierce for the unofficial title of best lawn on the block. Nary a weed lasted more than a day with my weekly twenty-five cent allowance on the line. Such was the summer of '57 in suburbia.

Grass was especially great for bare feet in the summer. You could tell what kind of grass our neighbor's had for a lawn just by walking on it barefooted. Dichondra, St. Augustine, Kentucky blue grass, it all felt different. The Kentucky blue grass always came up green though and it even felt green on my bare feet. It's still a mystery although the folks at Boise State may have finally figured it out.

You knew when a lawn had been freshly mowed by waking on it barefooted, provided the hint of new mown grass didn't give it away first especially when the early morning Sun was drying up the dew. St. Augustine grass was rough and tickly to walk on while Dichondra, which really isn't a grass, felt really cool, but thin on bare feet tender still the first week in July. Kentucky blue grass felt like, well, grass.

Grass was an excellent organic cleaning agent for bare feet that had stepped in Fido's Finest Canine Lawn Fertilizer. You knew instantly it was Fido's Finest and not an imitation, mud. With shoes insulating you against nature, it could take minutes to make the unpleasant discovery. By that time, I could have tromped it half way across mom's newly Simonized Vista One Step Cleaner/Wax'd linoleum kitchen floor. It was bad enough if even one clean barefooted toe touched mom's shiny linoleum before it was dry much less stenciling aromatic patterns of you know what across it.

Bare feet also helped a young boy discover the world he lived in. It didn't take long on a hot summer day, probably by 10 am at the latest, to experience the difference that black asphalt driveways were much hotter than white sidewalks or Dichondra. I even cooked an egg, sunny-side up, on our driveway once just to see that it was hot enough to cook an egg like the radio disc jockey said. None of the kids in the neighborhood would dare eat the egg even though I took care to find a relatively clean patch of asphalt. When I learned in school about heat radiation and absorption, I had my bare feet, and the egg, to thank.

On a different level, my bare feet, compared to wearing shoes, gave me a connection to the world not unlike going from black and white television to color. Our bare feet connect us to the dirt, the earth from which our bodies were formed. Maybe it's not an accident that nerve endings for our body parts are found in our feet. It's as if bare feet interfacing with the dirt enlivens those nerves some special way. It's a shame that some city people's bare feet never touch the earth even once for months at a time. I think this disconnect affects us too in other ways that we perhaps aren't cognizant of in our daily routines. It's as if technology has placed a barrier between life and our souls, our spiritual roots. I think everyone should walk barefooted on the dirt and grass an entire day at least once a month just to keep life in perspective given our air conditioned, wall-to-wall carpeted digital world of computers, MP3 players and game consoles.

The world feels different when you walk barefooted. Even dangling my bare feet in the water during summer camp at the edge of the lake's dock provided me an experience with the earth and creation that felt much different from swimming or running through sprinklers on a hot afternoon. It was more contemplative, even spiritual, although I didn't know that's what it was at the time. There was a connection with my feet in the water between creation and me. It set me to thinking. First just about little things like were we going to have bar-be-qued hamburgers for dinner tonight. Then, I would wonder about what my friends Walt and Jim Bob were doing. Eventually, it got me to thinking and asking questions about why water is so important to life. It seemed so ordinary. It was hard to believe more than 70 percent of my body was water because I didn't feel I was mostly water or mostly ordinary. Besides weren't we formed from the dust, the dry dirt of the earth? If I was 70 percent water, how much of me was dirt? I didn't feel much like dirt either, but what ten year-old boy does? The only dirt my mom was obsessively concerned about was on the outside of me and I had to wash that off with water! To protect myself, at times, I would run the shower but not actually get in it. My note to moms of the world: we boys figure we've got enough water on the inside, so what's a little dirt on the outside? We played hard to get it, and we'd just as soon keep it there at least until we jump into our neighbor's swimming pool!

Dirt and water. The Biblical record says we are made from the dry dirt of the earth and my science teachers said we are mostly water. I didn't realize the seeds of controversy concerning our origins were this basic. Even as a kid this got me to thinking that I had stumbled upon another one of those Sunday school "mysteries" the nuns talked about. I didn't know what to believe because when I got cut, I got blood not water. When I blew my nose, well it wasn't dust coming out of there. I mean how would it read that God formed man of the boogers of the earth!? Of course, this would have cleared up many childhood mysteries in my neighborhood.

As I got older, I realized there was a lot of discussion about lots of mysteries just like the water and dirt but the words were different...creation and evolution. People seemed pretty much settled on the dirt and water thing. The great debate was how we got the dirt and water to start with. Some folks said God created them. Others said the dirt and water evolved into people. It seems to me that if dirt and water get along just fine in our bodies without turning to mud [another mystery], then creation and evolution should get along just fine without creating another mystery.

So, I decided to take off my shoes and walk around on this subject barefooted for a while. Creation and evolution felt differently barefooted just like those grassy lawns. I realized the answer was a lot like my childhood. Being barefooted did connect you to life in a different way. And just like life, creation and evolution don't get you into trouble as long as you don't step in Fido's Finest and track it onto someone's newly waxed kitchen floor.

While exploring the subject of creation and evolution in my bare feet, I came across this statement of hope. "...Perhaps Adam and Eve were the first Homo sapiens to walk the Earth. I hope that in my lifetime the theories of evolution and creation will merge, because the truth in each is overwhelming." This is from a letter to the editor in National Geographic's Forum March 2005 regarding the November 2004 article "Was Darwin Wrong?"

Can this hope ever be fulfilled? Does evolution and creation have the chance of merging or at least respecting each other for what they are? Is the truth overwhelming for both? And if so, how can it be like that? Well, the answer to these questions has been right in front of us all along. It's one of those "can't see the lawns for the grass" situations. For the record, there is no contradiction between evolution[1] and the creation of man. Very likely, at this moment, you are probably thinking, "Yeah, right, and weeds don't grow in lawns." Either that, or you are sure I am in a great state of something obviously not of this planet induced by smoking, rather than walking bare foot on, the grass.

For the record, I soberly discovered that Charles Darwin, author of the famous or infamous, depending on your point of view, legendary 1859 work, "On the Origin of the Species by Means of Natural Selection, or the Preservation of Favoured Races in the Struggle for Life," [commonly called the Origin of the Species], did not find a conflict between his revolutionary observations and his belief in God as the Creator of life.[2] By the time he finished

Descent of Man in 1871, however, he was expressing doubts about creation compared to religious teachings of the time.

Interestingly, an on-line word search of the Origin of the Species shows that Darwin never once used the word evolution! He used the word revolution a few times as he was cognizant of the disturbance his work might cause. In Chapter 14, titled "Recapitulation and Conclusion, he stated, "When the views entertained in this volume on the origin of species, or when analogous views are generally admitted, we can dimly foresee that there will be a considerable revolution in natural history." He didn't foresee or expect that his work would stir up such a revolution between science and Christianity. Darwin believed that the Creator was the primary cause of life. It was from this primary cause of life that secondary causes brought forth the species. Origin of and change within the species is addressed by evolution. Origin of life is addressed by creation.

The fact that he didn't use the word evolution in Origin of the Species doesn't prove anything one way or the other, just that the term that has become the rallying cry for those on both sides of the issue was not used by Darwin in Origin of the Species. In his work, Darwin does acknowledge the existence of a Creator, using this term on several occasions throughout his text. Yet in Descent of Man, Darwin is using the term evolution saying "Man is descended from a hairy quadraped...." Where does this leave us? Square one would be an appropriate answer. So let's start there.

Ask any theologian or religious layperson in the western world who was the first man and the answer will be Adam. Ask just about any scientist the same question and the reply likely will be they don't know except the answer goes back perhaps 160,000 or more years, long before Adam was created 6000 years ago. I am using 6000 years as it is the commonly accepted date for the creation of Adam. Although, if the actual date for Adam's creation were 16,000 or 160,000 years ago rather than 6000, the principle here would still apply. Ever since Darwin's revolutionary theory took hold, science and Christianity have been on opposite sides of a great chasm with no apparent answer to this conundrum in sight.

It's almost impossible nowadays to think that prior to Darwin's published work hardly anyone would dispute the claim that Adam was the first man. But herein lies the crux of the dilemma. The definition of the "first man" has shifted in the past one hundred plus years. The Hebrew word used in the Biblical record for man is adam. So, asking who was the first man is really asking, who was the first adam? Uh, Adam? By definition, you really can't get this one wrong at least when speaking Hebrew.

Scientifically speaking, hominids are primates of the family Hominidae including Adam and the rest of us, which more specifically are known as Homo sapiens. Before Homo sapiens, Neanderthals, Homo erectus and Homo habilis were hominids that roamed the Earth. Adam in this case would be just another guy in a long line of guys. So how is it Adam was the first man but not the first Homo sapiens or the first hominid?

The difficulty arises when both scientists and Christians look at the hominid/man conundrum solely from a physical point of view. Those who side with natural science, by definition, can only approach this subject from the physical vantage. Perhaps most Christians would argue that Adam was the first man and was created 6000 years ago. [Obviously not all Christians share this view. But for purposes of this book, Christians refers to those holding the particular views discussed in each chapter] All we have to do is add up the genealogies in the Biblical record and we get about 4000 BC as the creation date for Adam, the first man. Scientists will say not so, as the fossil and DNA [deoxyribonucleic acid] sequences unique to the Homo sapiens species is unquestionably far greater than 6000 years old. The first Homo sapiens appeared maybe as far back as 200,000 years ago. And so the battle rages on between these two extremes.

Was Adam the first adam? Yes. Was Adam genetically similar to those predecessor Homo sapiens that lived on earth up to perhaps 150,000 to 200,000 years ago? Yes. Was Adam was the first man, but not the first hominid? Yes. Was the first Homo sapiens the first man? No. Can we reconcile Darwin's theory with the Biblical record's account of the creation of Adam? Yes.

But what about the creation of mankind being about six thousand years ago versus the recent dating of the Omo River fossils found in Ethiopia in 1967 that scientists now claim Homo sapiens were alive nearly two hundred thousand years ago? Can we reconcile these two seemingly contradictory points? Yes we can. Scientists, by definition and through no fault of their own, are dealing with physical comparisons only. God's distinctions, however, are of the spirit that gives life, not the container in which it is placed. Christians, on the other hand, are ignoring the significance of Adam's creation by merely adding up the years of Biblical genealogies. They also need to respect the discoveries of empirical science for these findings give us greater understanding of the Biblical accounts especially in Genesis. As we'll discover, it takes both science and theology joining together to see the entire picture.

By March 2000, a privately funded company called Celera Genomics had mapped the genes of the common fruit fly, Drosophila, and found that the fly had many genes in common with humans. As it turns out, some trees have traits in common with humans too. In fact, man shares 66.7% of his amino acid chain with corn [maize]. And no, eating popcorn is not considered cannibalism. Can we assume from this, however, that corn and trees and flies are part human or that man evolved from trees and flies and corn and just about everything else? Or does it mean that the basic building blocks of our carbon based physical life, as we know it on our planet, have some related common denominators thus implying a common origin?

In DNA The Secret of Life, James Watson, the Nobel Prize winning co-discoverer of the double helix DNA molecule, says that all humans today are 99.9% genetically alike. According to various DNA studies, it's interesting to note that chimps are claimed to be 99.6% genetically like man. This genetic closeness, no doubt, makes many in the religious community very nervous. Perhaps joyously, it provides impetus to those who claim that man has evolved from lower primates at the expense of a Creator.

Regardless of the exact genetic percentages, all human life today has a common genetic ancestor, according to a study of mtDNA by Cann and Wilson, estimated as "recently" as 150,000 years ago. In a parallel study of the male Y chromosome by Peter

Underhill, his estimation of "mankind's genetic family tree" goes back about the same 150,000 years. Therefore, the in-common genetic building blocks of Homo sapiens physical container, the body, according to these studies, have been around at least 150,000 years and maybe as long as 200,000 years.

While reasonable scientific arguments can be made for drawing the line at just about any point, the physical containers, the genetic building blocks of Adenine and Thymine, Guanine, and Cytosine [A & T, G & C] that make up the nucleotide bases of DNA are the determining factors for similarities, but are not the determining factor for life differences. Chimpanzees are closer genetically to humans than they are to gorillas. But chimps are chimps and humans are humans. While chimps are very close to man genetically, they are vastly different in significant ways as Darwin acknowledged.

Let's say we have the bones of three nearly identical Homo sapiens side by side. Scientists could determine that the three are 99.9% genetically identical. If DNA evidence says one of them is 150,000 years old, another one 3000 years old and the other one 100 years old, then this proves that mankind has been around a lot longer than what Christians claim the Genesis account says. This is an erroneous deduction but not because scientists are necessarily wrong about the genetic DNA dating comparisons.

Both scientists and Christians are in disagreement because both see only one side of the issue. Imagine a ball painted white on one half and black on the other. Show one side to the scientists and they will say it is black. Simultaneously, Christians see the other side and say the ball is white. They will argue all day long that each is correct. The truth only comes into focus when both parties see the entire ball or in our case, the entire elephant.

Science and religion are polarized. In reality, they should be complementary. Neither, by itself, contains the truth of our existence. Therefore, constant battling between these two extremes produces nothing more than animosity and solidifying of each other's intransigence. When it comes to the creation of "man," we need to examine the duality of man's nature scientifically and spiritually. Anyone who entirely excludes the other will never see the complete picture. Thus our goal should be consensus on the part of the stakeholders, i.e., mankind. We need to determine our points of agreement and work outwards from there.

The basic underlying difficulty concerning the origin of "man" is that we assume the word "man" to mean all those in the flesh who, physically or genetically, were nearly identical to what we see in the mirror when we shave. While hominid and Homo sapiens are scientifically more accurate terms than man, many scientists and media accounts misapply the term man for all Homo sapiens because today man is the only Homo sapiens still standing. But this wasn't always the case. It's the old saw, all men are Homo sapiens, but not all Homo sapiens were men.

The cover of the January 2000 Scientific American magazine shows two beings. One is a man, the other a creature. Yet an interesting question was posed. "Our species had at least 15 cousins. Only we remain. Why?" Scientific American continued, "Homo sapiens is the only hominid that still walks the earth. Yet over the past four million years, 20 or more types of creatures similar to us and our ancestors may have existed...." Confusion on this point of man vs. hominid, however, has clouded the issue for non-scientists, particularly Christians.

We will see, like the black and white ball, both scientists and Christians are right and wrong about the entire picture. In the eyes of the Creator, the bones of our three "humans" side by side would be completely different or completely the same depending on what exactly was being determined. Which part of the elephant, in other words, is being evaluated? This is an important principle. Scientists would say all three essentially are the same except for their age differences. Christian theologians would argue that if they are the same, then the scientists must be wrong about their dates because man was created about 6000 years ago.

Let's use an example of something else by way of analogy that might help us to clarify the picture. If we have three cars, all identical on the outside, we could say all three are the same. But let's say we open the hoods [or bonnets for you English folks], to look at the power plants or engines. Under the hood, in the same space for all three, one car has a steam engine, another a diesel turbocharged engine and the third a computerized hydrogen fuel cell power plant. One could hardly say the three are identical or were invented at the same time. Though when we put the hood down, they would look the same just as certain A, T, G & C sequences look the same.

If we removed the power plants from each car and all vestiges of them and then brought in car experts to examine the three cars, they could conclude that all three are 99.9% alike. In essence, they would all have the same "DNA." They reasonably could

# Three Creations of Life: A Bridge To Understanding

deduct that all were very likely from the same manufacturer yet differing in age due to the rate of oxidation. We know that steam engines powered cars, such as the famous Stanley Steamer, in the early years. Later, the internal combustion engine supplanted steam. Now as we look at alternative power sources, some day hydrogen fuel cells may replace the internal combustion engine. Because we have the advantage of knowing the power plants for each of the three vehicles, we know that they were different and were built over a period of 100 years or so even though the cars in all other respects may look alike.

The same is true for us mortals. If the power plants are missing, as they are for archeologists, biologists and other scientists looking at fossil remains, bone fragments or DNA sequences, then they are missing some key information.

In the pages of the Biblical record, we are told there are three spirits that interface with mortal bodies. One is the spirit of creatures. The other is the spirit of man. The other is the Spirit of God. Theologically speaking, there have been three creations. At the first creation of life, the spirit common to beasts or creatures, too, was created. Later, with Adam in Eden, came the spirit of man. With Christ, came the Spirit of God. All three spirits make physical bodies alive. When the spirit leaves the body, the body is dead.

In the New Testament Book of Romans[3] we read, "But if the Spirit of Him [God] that raised up Jesus from the dead dwell in you, He that raised up Christ from the dead shall also make alive your mortal bodies by His Spirit that dwells in you...For as many as are led by the Spirit of God, they are the sons of God."

For those who have God's Spirit dwelling in them, it is this Spirit that makes alive our mortal bodies as opposed to the spirit of man that did this before we were baptized and received his Spirit. Please keep in mind, the resurrection is not to a mortal, but immortal 'body.' It is in this life, prior to the resurrection, that God's Holy Spirit makes alive our mortal bodies if his Spirit dwells in us. It does not mean mankind has an "immortal soul" as is commonly thought. It does mean mankind has this potential for immortality however. Creatures do not.

This is why Christ said to Nicodemus "except a man be born again...." [or born from above]. Only Christ had the Spirit of God during the time of his mortal ministry. And continually in the Biblical record we see Christ referred to as the only begotten son[4] of God. Begotten means born. At that time, the only one "born from above" was Christ. It wasn't until Pentecost, 50 days after the resurrection of Christ, when the disciples were filled with the Holy Spirit.[5]

However, mankind began with Adam. God placed a spirit in man that is different from that of Adam's predecessors or creatures outside of Eden. These are the hominids that scientists have discovered proof of in archeological studies. The fact that they existed 6000 years or more years ago is proven. Very likely there were inhabited villages just outside the confines of Eden as rivers were popular sites for water whether it was for wild animals to drink or for areas to develop villages. It is possible that Adam, Eve, Cain and Abel saw these Homo sapiens across the river boundaries of Eden perhaps from even little as a few hundred feet away. What might they have seen exactly?

About 4000 BC, they certainly wouldn't have seen any dinosaurs. They had long since vanished along with Raquel Welsh draped in loincloth. What did exist outside Eden in 4000 BC might surprise many religious people. The area of Mesopotamia, or the area between the rivers [Tigris and Euphrates] was beginning to see the emergence of cities by 4000 BC. These grew from villages that were able to provide irrigation for agricultural purposes. Life had progressed beyond the hunter-gatherer phase that we tend to associate with "cavemen." Farmers were growing irrigated crops.

In 4000 BC, it was the Late Chalcolithic period or the copper-stone age. Copper artifacts were being made by this time. The melting point of copper is 1083 C or nearly 2000 degrees F. This would take some rather sophisticated knowledge of metallurgy and tools to work with copper. By this time, that's exactly what Homo sapiens were doing.

Ceramics were in use by 5000 BC and some rather elegant, fine examples of ceramic work have been found in Tell Halaf in northern Syria that dates to about 4000 BC. Craftsmen or artificers, who did not have to work out in the fields, were in evidence by this time demonstrating that society outside Eden was fairly well progressed beyond Maslow's physiological tier hierarchy of food and shelter.

Sometime between 4000 and 3500 BC, the city of Uruk was founded along the banks of the Euphrates River. Uruk is considered the first city in Mesopotamia and it was the hometown, so to speak, of Abraham about 1500 years later. The year 3500 BC marks the beginning of the Early Bronze Age. Some estimates place the population of Uruk at 40,000 by 3000 BC.

This is hardly the Sunday school picture most religious people have of the world at the time of the creation of Adam and Eve. We need to realize that Adam and Eve weren't created on a deserted, relatively sterile planet. The opposite is more likely the case as Genesis shows them to be the last of creation on day six. Most probably the Earth was teeming with life, including hominids, by time Adam and Eve made their appearance. Their isolated existence, first in the garden, then in Eden, however, marked a turning point and initiated a new age, the age of man.

Read the creation of life in day five and day six in Genesis chapter one. Two notable facts stand out. First, God said, on day five, let the waters bring forth moving creatures that have life and fowl[6] that may fly above.... Where then would we expect to find evidence of life, just in Eden? No, because we read at the end of the day five account that "And God blessed them saying, Be fruitful, and multiply, and fill the waters in the seas, and let the fowl multiply in the earth." This surely indicated that the entire Earth was involved not just the area within the confines of Eden.

Next we read on day six, "And God said, 'Let the earth bring forth the living creature after his kind....'" Were living creatures then just to be found in Eden? Of course not. The entirety of the Earth was filled with fish of the sea, fowl in the air and creatures on land, particularly in the area between the Tigris and Euphrates rivers. And all of them were created before adam was put in the garden of Eden. For those of you who will raise the point that there is no way that the fish of the sea, the fowl of the air and the creatures could fill the Earth in a current 24 hour "Earth day," you'll have to read the chapter "Creation in Six Days, But Who's Counting?" for the answer.

God said, "Let the earth bring forth the living creature...." It is not surprising then that from Darwin's premise of secondary causes, and from those who have followed in his footsteps that they would notice a commonality among creatures brought forth from the earth. Did not God say let the earth bring forth the living creature after his kind? If so, wouldn't this also mean that the earth itself would be the common origin for creatures? Yes, it would. And was not Adam, the first man, created from of the "dust of the earth?"[7] Yes, of course. So why then should we be surprised that there are common traits between the physical bodies of man and other creatures including hominids? The earth is the place of common origin for them both. Our fleshly bodies are all from the same pile of dirt called earth. We can't get away from the fact that physically, it's only about the dirt. We come from the dirt. We sustain ourselves with food from the dirt. And when it's all said and done, all physical bodies go back to being dirt.

Above we noted that villages and communities were beginning to be formed along the areas adjacent to rivers about the time of Adam's creation. Much of this development, according to archeologists and other scientists, is traced to the development of irrigation. Now this is an interesting and important point. In the timeline of Adam's creation, we know then that these Homo sapiens were farming by 4000 BC. It was the advent of irrigation that led to the development of farming. And farming as we know involves tilling of the ground. Wooden plows can do the job, but farming would become much more efficient when wooden plows were covered with copper or other metal which, in time, would lead to solid metal plows as communal prosperity increased. Thus the rise of irrigation coupled with the use of metal farming tools would greatly bolster the formation of village and communities. Again this is in evidence at the time of 4000 BC.

But notice the statement in the Biblical record, "And every plant of the field before it was in the earth, and every herb of the field before it grew: for the LORD God had not caused it to rain upon the earth, and [there was] not a man [adam] to till the ground."[8] What we are seeing then is that irrigation was needed for farming because rain had not yet fallen on the earth. Therefore, rivers would be the primary source of water for irrigated farming purposes. Secondly, we're told there was no man to till the ground. Adam, originally, was put in the garden of Eden to dress it and keep it with apparently no tilling of the ground involved. But we know there were Homo sapiens farming at this point using irrigation. Irrigation allowed for concentrations of populations as opposed to small, scattered groups being gatherers of wild food sources that were made possible in that "there went up a mist from the earth and watered the whole face of the ground."[9] This mist would be sufficient for plants to grow, but not sufficient to provide enough water to grow sustainable food supplies for a concentrated population in one area over a prolonged period.

Homo sapiens tilling the ground as farmers at the time of Adam's creation would lead us to believe that these hominids were considered to be different than mankind as indicated in the Biblical record. There was no man, no adam to till the ground at this point. It isn't until Adam is kicked out of the garden in Eden that mankind is first known to till the ground.

The Biblical genealogies and related information indicate that Adam was created about 4000 BC. This is the commonly accepted date. Adam lived to be 930 years old according to the Biblical record. This means Adam lived until 3070 BC or thereabouts. The Early Bronze Age, 3500 BC, equates with Adam's middle age years. This fits in exactly about what the little glimpse the Biblical record says it was like outside of Eden.[10] The Biblical record tells us that Cain left Eden and built a city. This is the period in Homo sapiens history as determined by archeologists during which cities were first being built. Excavations throughout Mesopotamia stand in evidence of this.

By the time of the creation of Adam, and Eve in the garden of Eden, Homo sapiens were establishing societies in transition from villages and communities into larger, more concentrated entities. It is very likely that Adam and Eve had seen some indication of this while cloistered in the confines of Eden. Their lives, and the lives of their descendants, with the exception of Cain, were kept separate for a good reason. The spirit that gave them life was not that of creatures, but rather the spirit of man.

By definition, the spirit is not traceable through any DNA studies because the spirit is not made of nitrogenous base pairs [AT and GC], sugar and phosphoric acid molecules. Physically man and creature's containers have the same destiny, the same breath and the same basic genetic DNA components. This is why scientists conclude that man's genetic ancestors include apes or trees or flies. This is why Darwin's theory is connected to mankind today. Scientists can't detect any trace of the spirit. They never will. It is beyond the scope of physical science. This is not so with our breath or mortal bodies.

We read in the Old Testament, "For that which befalls the sons of men, befalls creatures; so even one thing befalls them: as the one dies, so dies the other; yes, they have all one breath; so that a man has no preeminence above a beast: for all is vanity [transitory]. All go to one place; all are of the dust and all turn to dust again."[11] It all goes back to the dirt both for creature and man.

The Biblical record plainly makes the point that scientists have made for quite some time. The fleshly bodies of both man and creatures, including non-adamic Homo sapiens, are no different either in terms of origin [the dust of the earth] or in terms of finality [both return to dust]. We all have one breath. Our human body is not superior to a creature's body in terms of origin or destiny. This is a vital point. DNA is DNA. Spirit is spirit.

In fact, Charles Darwin in his book Descent of Man in 1871, a dozen years after his Origin of the Species, came to the very same conclusion. Darwin was able to discern that man's body has the same breath as beasts. He could see both the bodies of man and animal die and return to the dust of the Earth. Our physical bodies are transitory. Life comes from the life before it. It breathes and lives in a fleshly body. Then the body dies alike for man and creature.

When an animal dies both its body and spirit transition back into the dirt. When man dies, however, his spirit transitions back to God who gave it. But Charles Darwin was not able to discern this fact with his enormous physical powers of observation.

The spirit of man actually raised up man above the animal kingdom. Therefore, I would beg to differ with Darwin's conclusion in the Descent of Man, namely that Adam, rather than delineating the descent of man onto a level with other Homo sapiens and creatures, marked the ascent of man over other Homo sapiens and creatures. Darwin's observation was from the physical side of the coin and is correct if only the physical aspect of man is considered. God's creation of man, however, adds a new dimension when viewed from the spiritual side. Darwin was able to discern notable facts that correlate with the Book of Genesis. Man has qualities that are noble as Darwin puts it. These noble qualities are not found among animals. Darwin includes qualities such as sympathy, benevolence and "god-like" intellect. Was not man made in the image and likeness of God?

In chapter 21 of Descent of Man, Darwin's General Summary and Conclusion, he, in fact, echoes the point made in Ecclesiastes, "We must, however, acknowledge, as it seems to me, that man with all his noble qualities, with sympathy which feels for the most debased, with benevolence which extends not only to other men but to the humblest living creature, with his god-like intellect, which has penetrated into the movements and constitution of the solar system- with all these exalted powers- Man still bears in his bodily frame the indelible stamp of his lowly origin."

This precisely is the point made in Ecclesiastes. Man has no preeminence in his bodily frame over any creature. Darwin therefore, most likely unwittingly, makes the same point found in the Biblical record, that while man has noble qualities that set mankind apart from animals or beasts, our fleshly bodies are not the differentiating point. The physical body, in and of itself, is of lower origin coming from the dust of the Earth. Mankind's superiority comes not from the flesh, but from the spirit, the spirit of man, from God above. One could argue, then, that Darwin makes a strong case for the superiority of man, "with all these exalted powers," but not when it comes to the "bodily frame." Darwin is acknowledging that man does have something that makes him different from beasts or animals, but it isn't his body. Mankind is not superior to animals, nor the vanished Homo sapiens, when one looks solely at the body. In fact, mankind's body ties him in with all the fleshly bodies of creatures or animals as Darwin noted.

Without realizing it, Darwin discovered after writing the Origin of the Species and the Descent of Man including a dozen years of study in between one the most important theological quantum points of understanding: Life similarities are of the flesh. Life differences are of the spirit.

Attempts by religious people to use man's physical genealogy to account for theological differences with scientific discoveries regarding physical similarities, and timelines are building their houses on sand. Nothing destroys religious credibility like a creation museum showing Adam and Eve cavorting among dinosaurs! It demonstrates a complete lack of understanding of the subject. If we can't understand the simpler matters of the flesh, how can we hope to understand those things of the spirit?

Religion by definition should focus on the spiritual aspects of man's creation and existence not his physical ones. "For they that are after the flesh do mind the things of the flesh; but they that are after the Spirit the things of the Spirit."[12]

Scientists have been very diligent about their discoveries and methodology in documenting the past history of physical life here on Earth. They do not have expertise in the realm of man's non-physical existence. This is where Christian and religious leaders need to put their attention. Once both scientists and religious leaders learn to respect each other, realizing they have essentially the same goals, and work together to find answers to questions about life, then all mankind will be the beneficiary.

When does life begin for the flesh? "For the LORD God formed man of the dust of the ground, and breathed into his nostrils the breath of life; and man [adam] became a living soul."[13] This is about as simple and straightforward as a statement of fact can get. When does God say man becomes a living soul, a living physical entity? When do we take our first breath? When do we start life? The answer is the same. Life begins with breath both for man's bodies and creature's bodies alike. It is the same breath for both man and creature.

It should be noted that the breath common to creatures and man alike is not a spiritual essence. It is 100% pure physical. It maintains the fleshly habitat of our respective spirits. We breathe in molecules of nitrogen, oxygen and a few minute amounts of other inert gases as far as metabolism is concerned. A gas transfer takes place at the alveoli and hemoglobin trades off the by-products through respiration, mostly $CO_2$ and nitrogen, for a new supply of oxygen rich air. Cut off this physical supply of molecules long enough and the physical body dies. These metabolic processes are very well documented and are completely in the realm of common biochemistry and physiology, neither of which deals in the spiritual.

We see from the Biblical side of the coin that physically, man and Homo sapiens are the same, well, at least for the last 150,000 years or so. Neither has preeminence over the other. Life begins with a breath. Science and the Biblical record agree.

In the past, religious doctrine did not agree with Galileo's telescopic observations of the planets and their relative motions that showed we lived in a heliocentric system, not a geocentric system. Condemned by the Catholic Inquisition in the 1630s for this heretical truth, Galileo was put under house arrest for the remainder of his life.

The question we need to ask today is how open-minded are we to new understandings that challenge our accepted set of beliefs? Are we willing to consider new concepts that challenge tradition? Or do we retreat into doctrinal caves shunning the light no different than our ancestors in the Dark Ages? For most, the answer, quite honestly, would be to run back into the cave where we have the safety and comfort of the familiar. To paraphrase Marianne Williamson, it is the unfamiliar light, not the familiar darkness that we fear the most.

Our physical bodies, according to the Biblical record, are not the discerning factor in life. It makes no difference whether or not a chimp is less than half a percent different in gene sequence from man or that mankind has 3 billion base pairs in our genome compared to the "simple life form" amoeba dubia that has 670 billion. This is why scientists see no differences when looking at dead bones. There is a difference not left behind in the fossilized dust.

In the Old Testament Book of Ecclesiastes, a significant point is made. "Then shall the dust [physical bodies] return to the earth as it was; and the spirit [of man] shall return to God who gave it." "Who knows that the spirit of man goes upward, and the spirit of the beast that goes downward to the earth?"[14]

This is the critical significance of what took place in Eden and with Eve in the garden of Eden. Mankind was given the spirit of man that sets us apart from creatures. This is a noteworthy quantum theological point. God created a difference on that day about 6000 years ago. He set mankind apart from creaturekind. He started with a new patch of dirt. Adam was not the direct descendant of a creature. He did not evolve from hominids or chimps. When it comes to the creation of adam, mankind, God did not say as he did up to this point on "day six" with the creatures on land, "let the earth bring forth" implying secondary causes for the formation of species as Darwin surmised. Instead God said, "Let us make man..." The creation of adam, therefore, was a primary cause, an independent creation. It was not a secondary cause as Darwin noted with other species, and as would have been the case if Adam was indeed a descendant of preceding hominids. While Adam's fleshly body was of the same earth as all other physical creatures, his was a separate creation.

The Creator gave adam virtually the same DNA[15] being of the same earth as other Homo sapiens though he set Adam physically apart in Eden. The key to man's creation is that God gave adam a different spirit, one that made Adam different from every creature on Earth until that time. This was the second creation, the kingdom of mankind. It set man apart and above the animal kingdom.

Let's take a prime example. When God said "Let us make man in our image and likeness" in the first chapter of Genesis, a commonly held belief is that he was referring to making man physically in the image of God as opposed to all the cattle and fowl and fish as well as any "caveman" type creature. Many religious people believe the difference between Neanderthals or other hominids and Adam was only a fleshly difference that made man like God in his physical appearance. But, differences are of the spirit not the flesh.

The Hebrew word for image is tselem and means to shade or a shadow. Likeness comes from d'muwth and means a similitude or likeness. Thus God said let us make adam a shadow of our likeness. Now simply ask yourself, is God of the spirit or of the flesh? Spirit of course. And did Adam receive the same spirit of life as did the Homo sapiens outside Eden? No, he received the spirit of man that returns to God who gave it. Thus, knowing that it is those things of the spirit that makes man different from creatures and that God made man a shadow of his spiritual likeness, then what was it that made man, Adam, like God, his flesh or his spirit? Of course, the answer is simple. It is the spirit of man. And the spirit of man is the shadow of the spirit of God.

Remember, it wasn't just Adam and Eve who were created on day six according to the account in the first chapter of Genesis, but all living creatures made from the dust of the earth. "Let the earth bring forth the living creature after his kind...." Day five concerns itself with life from the oceans and the air or "fowl that may fly above the earth in the open firmament of heaven" as it says in verse twenty. It appears that man was last in line in terms of physical creation, which fits perfectly with life on Earth outside Eden. It's quite possible that the "Cambrian Explosion" found in the fossil record dating from 570 to 530 million years ago actually corresponds to day five and early day six in the Genesis account. More about this in Chapter Four, "Creation in Six Days, But Who's Counting?"

The Creator gave Adam a potential not afforded to other Homo sapiens, the other living breathing creatures outside the confines of Eden as well as the beasts therein. While our physical bodies, our genetic DNA, might be 99.9% identical to other Homo sapiens, our potential for life after physical death is light years apart because God made adam in his image and likeness through the spirit of man.

In the prestigious medical journal, The Lancet, December 2001, Pim van Lommel, a cardiologist who has extensively studied Near Death Experiences [NDE] wrote an article titled, "Near-Death Experience in Survivors of Cardiac Arrest: A Prospective Study in the Netherlands" in which he said that mankind has a "soul" or a non-physical component to his life. This is a very bold statement coming from a scientist in this context. Dr. van Lommel made a very clear point that a non-breathing man that is clinically dead has a living consciousness apart from the body. While this shook up the scientific community that an article of this sort would appear in such an esteemed science journal, it is completely in line with the creation of mankind according to the Biblical record.

For our purpose, his record of NDE goes to the very core of the point made in Ecclesiastes about 3000 years ago, namely that the spirit of man goes upward at death. In the case of NDE, a common occurrence is the "deceased" in the spirit above looking down on their dead physical body. "I was looking down on my body and I could see my friends and family in the hospital room…." In other cases, they experience rising up towards a great white light often described as peaceful or loving. Perhaps the most notable recent account of an NDE was Bob Woodruff's account in his book "In An Instant" resulting from an exploding IED in Iraq. The events of NDE, according to van Lommel, are similar worldwide regardless cultural differences. This should not be surprising in that the spirit of man is common to every human being.

One NDE individual related that the experience was a blessing for him as it provided him with first-hand experience that body and spirit are separated, and that a form of life continues after death. It convinced him that consciousness exists past the physical death of the body. He came to the understanding that physical death is not finality, but a transition to another form of life as related in the Biblical record. It is a form of life that separates adamkind from creatures whose spirits return to the earth at death as does their physical bodies including their entire genome no matter how close or similar they are to mankind genetically.

While NDE are somewhat controversial, and all experiences are by no means identical, it does lend credence to what the Biblical record states. Man has a spirit that returns to the Creator who gave it. The spirit in man makes us different. There is still much to be learned and understood, but this much is clear, according to the Biblical record, our spirit, the spirit of man, doesn't end with death of the body as it does for creatures including Homo sapiens prior to Adam.

Mankind, and mankind alone, has the potential for immortality or life in the spirit. Even though mankind has a spirit, and it returns to God who gave it, there still is a second death[16] of the spirit just as there was a second creation according to the Biblical record.

It is this potential for life everlasting in the spirit that sets man apart from all physical creatures, including other Homo sapiens, no matter how closely they may have been genetically. It is this spirit imparted by God to Adam and his physical descendants, that's all of us, that creates this distinction. Man and creature may have one breath and bodies that return to dust, but they have two different spirits and two different destinies.

This distinction between man and creature is further in evidence in the Book of Daniel when God had the Babylonian King Nebuchadnezzar live as a creature for seven years. "Let his heart be changed from a man's and let a creature's heart be given unto him and he [Nebuchadnezzar] was driven from men, and he did eat grass as oxen...."[17]

It is the Creator who makes the distinction between man and creature. Both man and creature have the same breath, could even have 99.6% or more DNA in common, and at death their physical bodies both return to dust. Man's distinction is of the spirit.

All life comes from the Creator. The Creator gave man a spirit that sets man apart from creatures. This is evidenced by God's reference to those who are found written in the book of life. Any creature, no matter how close physically or genetically to man, who lacks the spirit that was given by God that came down through Adam, will not be found written in the book of life. Sorry, folks, there is no salvation for Fido. The spirit of man was given to Adam about 6000 years ago. This is when man was created. Man was created and geographically separated in Eden from other Homo sapiens on Earth.

Adam's physical predecessors and yes, contemporaries, Homo sapiens, outside Eden, regardless of fossil data indicating age and how close genetically they may have been, had the spirit of a creature. God set man apart through the spirit in him, not by his DNA. DNA accounts for man's similarities to other physical beings. "And the LORD God formed man of the dust of the ground..." Man's form, a head, two arms, two legs are from the dry dirt of the earth as are all other physical creatures with this form. Man is not formed from elements of heaven. Man's physical form and flesh are from the dirt. Both the body forms of men and creatures are all of the "dust" or the same A, T, G and C, which make up the DNA sequences for Homo sapiens. We shouldn't be surprised that physically our bodies are very close genetically to creatures whether they are chimps or vanished hominids. The earth is our common physical place of origin.

The fact that our physical bodies and trees may have some gene sequencing in common doesn't mean our family tree is literally our family tree! Just that the physical universe as we know it is made a certain way. The billions of potential combinations of

# Three Creations of Life: A Bridge To Understanding

DNA would lead one to believe that each species[18] would have the ability to change within its current format given certain influences affecting the biodiversity on planet Earth, which is part of the creation, our physical universe. From a creationist point of view, Adam and Eve in only 6000 years are progenitors of the 6 billion plus Homo sapiens on Earth today be they midgets or giants, Chinese, Indian, Middle Eastern, African or European including redheads, blondes, brunettes and people with jet black hair. Also we have folks with various shades of green eyes, blue eyes, and brown eyes not to mention violet, amber, gray and hazel colored eyes. Genetic variations are a form of evolution or change; the secondary causes that have come from Adam and Eve. The physical body's genetic variations occur within the parameters of creation. Our bodies, and the bodies of all physical creatures, are from planet Earth and therefore share common ingredients. It is a non-physical entity, not of planet Earth that makes mankind different.

There have been three creations of life: first, living creatures that have the spirit common to creatures; second, mankind with the spirit of man; and thirdly, those with the Spirit of God. Life differences are of a spiritual nature. The similarities of life among all creatures are physical in nature. The building blocks for physical life come from our physical Earth. We can understand why Adam can be the first man, but not the first hominid. We can understand that Adam was created 6000 years ago, separated in the Garden of Eden initially, then in Eden from the other Homo sapiens that lived outside Eden. We have documented scientific evidence of their existence in 4000 BC. We can understand why a common chromosome in man can be traced back about 150,000 years ago and that all this is no way diminishes Adam's stature as the first man; the first to be created in the shadow of the likeness of God due to the spirit that gives life to our mortal bodies and then returns to God at the death of the body.

There is no contradiction between scientific evidence and Christianity concerning evolution and the first man Adam. Adam quite likely was created about 6000 years ago. Nor is there any contradiction that hominids and Homo sapiens pre-dated Adam by tens of thousands of years or more. It makes absolutely no difference if scientists discover DNA in a fossil close to mankind's that dates from a million or more years BC. This is just the physical creation, the same "dust of the earth," common to all physical beings on Earth.

Adam, Eve and their descendants, you and me, have a different spirit that gives us a greater potential than just a physical life here on Earth, something much greater than even the noble qualities acknowledged by Darwin. We have the promise of something better, something creatures don't have access to…life beyond the flesh, a life not inherent in DNA. It is a promise of life in the spirit outside the limits of this speck of cosmic dust we call Earth, beyond our universe with its billions of galaxies and trillions upon trillions of stars.

Physically, there are no contradictions between the theory of evolution and it's secondary causes noted by Darwin and that of creation. In one sense, they are like base pairs bound together. The Creation base dealing with primary causes and the evolution base dealing with the secondary causes. Together, we have life as we know it today.

The first Homo sapiens to walk the Earth were of the first creation and had the spirit of creatures marking the animal kingdom. Adam and Eve marked the beginning of the second creation on Earth, the kingdom of man. They were the first Homo sapiens created in the image and likeness of God with the spirit of man who, no doubt, walked on the grass in Eden in their bare feet.

# Chapter Two: Did The Second Man Marry His Sister?

Did you go to Sunday school? I had to. My parents thought it would be good for me to get some religious training in addition to my secular public schooling. Of course, any protests on my part were dismissed with "You'll thank us someday." I guess I have to thank mom and dad because it gave me the ammunition for beginning this chapter.

When I went to Sunday school, it wasn't with the sweet young wife of the new assistant pastor of the church who actually liked little kids. Nope. This was hardcore, maximum security Catholic Sunday school. The classroom was spartan and cold. The rigid starchy habits the nuns wore with those black hoods instilled fear in elementary school age kids of people in 17th century regalia. I mean, mom never dressed that way. Well, at least not in front of the kids. [Thanks again mom] Our Sunday school teacher was Sister Mary the Severe of the Order of 18 Inch Hardwood Rulers. She had found her calling too. Sister Mary the Severe looked the part. I seem to recall that she even had a little dark moustache. She also had the uncanny ability to always keep one eye on everyone in class all the time. I don't know how she did it. It was a mystery.

We were given our catechisms and assigned a page or so of questions with the answers printed below for us to memorize for the following Sunday morning. If we missed a question when called upon by Sister Mary the Severe, no matter how creative an answer it was, well woe unto that little kid. The Order of the 18 Inch Hardwood Rulers was now in session. Many a palmed hand felt the sting of that ruler. Some kids more than others. I won't name names. However, when we asked Sister Mary the Severe a question that she didn't know the answer to, we got "It's a mystery." With my inherent childhood acumen for such things, I realized immediately the enormous potential of that answer. It was so cool of an answer, it could handle just about any question thrown at it. Having learned this most valuable lesson, I figured I didn't need Sunday school anymore. Sister Mary the Severe was a much better teacher than I first thought.

When next Sunday rolled around, I announced at breakfast that I didn't need to go to Sunday school anymore. So I was staying home to watch football instead. Dad was a bit more liberal with these things, but mom gave me a look that she must have learned from Sister Mary except for the moustache part. I explained that the catechism had all the answers in it that we knew. The other questions we didn't know the answers to could be quickly answered with "It's a mystery." I could read the catechism at my leisure, say during the football game's halftime. I challenged my mom, "Go ahead. Ask me any question you want." She continued giving me that look. She had dealt with my, shall we say, unique approach to childhood on many occasions prior to this. "Okay." I said sensing very thin ice, "you don't have to ask a question because I can tell you the answer in advance which is "It's a mystery!" Grinning ear to ear, I was delighted beyond delight with myself. Mom's look became even sterner. "It's not my fault," I said throwing my arms up in the air, "I learned it from Sister Mary the Severe!" So it was that I missed the first part of the football season.

Nevertheless, there were some questions whose answers seemed

# Did The Second Man Marry His Sister?

to remain a mystery to me over the years. Do you remember what you were told about what happened with Adam and Eve and Cain and Abel? Adam and Eve were created in the Garden of Eden. They ate the forbidden fruit, original sin I think Sister Mary called it, and they both got kicked out of the Garden of Eden. They had Cain and Abel. Cain got angry because God didn't respect his offering as he did Abel's. So Cain killed Abel in the field. When God asked Cain where his brother is, Cain answered, "I don't know. Am I my brother's keeper?" I always thought this was a rather smart aleck remark that would have gotten me a good whack upside the head if I said that to my dad. Cain was saying this to God!

Cain should have been thankful the proverbial lightning bolt didn't issue from the clouds with the resulting rather large smoky hole in the ground where Cain once stood. Instead, God placed a curse on Cain and kicked him out of Eden to be a vagabond and wanderer on the earth. Cain was afraid someone would kill him, so God marked Cain who left with his wife. That was about the last we heard of Cain in Sunday school.

Even as a child two things always bothered me about this account. One, if Adam and Eve were the only people on the planet, and they only had two sons, who possibly could be out there who would want to kill Cain?

The second point that bothered me was Cain marrying his sister. I was told as a little kid you couldn't marry anybody that close to you for fear of producing offspring grossly lacking in IQ points. Besides, sisters were worse than regular girls.

The image created in my young mind was that of a brand new Earth, no one on it yet except Adam, Eve and now Cain who is going to marry his sister and venture off, exploring a brand new planet. The thought of being the first person to discover the wonders of a new planet seemed like the opportunity of a lifetime to my adulatious mind. How could Cain complain? Of course, if the catch was you had to marry your sister, well that would do it for me.

As an adult, it's interesting how some of these ideas remain steadfast in our memory. They are almost unshakable. But their relevancy for us in everyday life is nearly non-existent. I think many folks just file the "Garden of Eden" saga away as another Santa Claus story. Finding out if this is what really happened isn't on any priority list. Day to day, does it really matter? Strangely, it does matter and in a profound manner.

Let's set out, then, to discover what's going on. Did Cain really marry his sister? Who was out there that Cain thought would want to kill him? Of course, if you've read chapter one you have some idea. Cain has a very fascinating story. Although it takes up about one page in the entire 1500 page Biblical record, the implications domino into our lives today in a most peculiar way.

Back to Sunday school for a moment. Adam, we are told was created about six thousand years ago. That means Adam, and Cain not too long thereafter, were first walking on this planet about 4000 BC. Cain said he was fearful that someone outside Eden would kill him if they found him. Who would that be? How could that be? No one else was supposed to be there. But was it an empty planet? It doesn't seem so.

What evidence do we have of other hominid life forms outside Eden by 4000 BC? Turns out there are plenty. And they were all over the place in Europe, Asia, North America, Pacific islands and Africa. How can it be like that?

The Biblical record is our earliest written record of mankind. To know anything other than what is written therein, we have to go digging for information, literally. Archeologists have made extensive studies all over the world. Before we dismiss what they tell us out of hand, let's look at what's been found.

For reference purposes, let's examine how ancient time periods are classified. Paleolithic is the Old Stone Age. Lithic is the word used for Stone Age because evidence of archeological finds from this time period shows hominids used stones for tools such as axes, arrowheads, etc. It's not much different than what I used to put tent stakes in the ground on camping trips though my "tools" were a bit more of the "Johnny, go get daddy a rock" variety. Paleo is the word for old. The Paleolithic extends from 10,000 BC and earlier. The Mesolithic period is from 10,000 to 8000 BC. Meso is middle. The New Stone Age, Neolithic extended from 8000 BC to 4000 BC, just about the time Cain would have made his way across the river with his bride. As copper was beginning to be formed into tools from 4000 to 3000 BC, it became known as the Chalcolithic or the Copper-Stone Age. I suppose with our ozone, UV and global warming issues, someday our age may be defined as the Coppertone Age. Sorry, but who can resist a rare opportunity for an archeological pun?

Let's start in Europe, Ireland to be exact, to see what was happening on Earth by 4000 BC. There are several well-known archeological sites in Ireland including Mount Sandel, Lough Boora, Offaly, and Ferriter's Cove. They show evidence of hominid activity dating back to 7000 BC. Offaly has evidence of a settlement of hide covered dome like huts complete with a fire pit for cooking in the middle of it.[19] However, no evidence of other built-in kitchen appliances have been found. Hominids are still considered hunter-gatherers in 7000 to 6500 BC.

By 4000 BC, Ireland has evidence of farming. Stone walls and houses indicated a less wandering lifestyle. There's evidence of domestic herds too, by this time.

In Scotland, by 4000 BC forest land had been cleared and mixed agriculture was taking place with wheat and barley being grown. Sheep and cattle had been domesticated as well.[20]

And one of the largest ever "digs" for archeological purposes in England is taking place adjacent to Heathrow airport. It is the site of Terminal 5.[21] It is about 100 hectares in size and bits of history dating from 6000 BC down to Roman times have been found there.

Moving across Europe, France has evidence of farming by 4000 BC including evidence of pottery, and bones from various sites.[22] Poland has a well-documented site at Oslonki. Teams of Polish and US archeologists have discovered a large village including "thirty trapezoidal longhouses" and graves with significant amounts of copper radiocarbon dated to 4300-4000 BC.[23]

In Lithuania, cultural relics date from 10,000 BC. In the Mesolithic, there is evidence of villages along rivers and by 4000 BC there are other villages further away from the river shorelines, closer to forest land where farming was in evidence. This would indicate there must have been some form of irrigation as well.[24]

In Asia, China has evidence of farming including growing barley, rice as well as domesticating chickens and pigs by 5000 BC. The growing of millet has been found to occur by 4500 BC along with various polished tools on the coastal areas of southern China. A Neolithic farming site has been unearthed near Shanghai dating back to this same period.[25]

In Borneo, according to the AAAS magazine Science, "Volcanic glass found at Bukit Tengkorak comes from sources on the Admiralty Islands and New Britain. It testifies to 3500 kilometer trade routes in 4000 B.C."[26]

In Mesoamerica, radiocarbon dating has placed the advent of domesticated maize to 5000 BC.[27] Just outside Chicago, on the grounds of Fermilab, the well-known site of the particle accelerator in Batavia, Illinois, they have on display a collection of arrowheads and other hominid artifacts dating as far back as 7000 BC.[28] In Canada, there are settlements in Labrador and along the St. Lawrence River down into New York State by 4000 BC.[29]

And in Egypt, King Menes is said to have built a canal for transport of water for irrigation purposes around 4000 BC.[30] Even as early as 4500 BC, there is some indication of copper smelting and casting in Mesopotamia.[31] And one of mankind's most important tools, the wheel was in use by 4000 BC.[32]

What we see worldwide is that by 4000 BC, farming at similar, but varying degrees of sophistication was in evidence. Scientists tracked the melting of glaciers from 15,000 to 4000 BC. It may have been that as the climate was warmer, it was more conducive to settling in one area to grow grain crops.

Whatever exactly was taking place, one thing is very evident, Cain didn't venture into an uninhabited planet when he crossed the river leaving Eden. There were some rather sophisticated uses of tools, including smelting copper, as well as advanced pottery and structured farming villages when Cain crossed the river and stepped into the world outside Eden. Farming was the "high tech" industry in 4000 BC. God told Cain that when he farmed, the soil would not yield to him anything but weak crops. This wouldn't be too different today if you were thrown into Silicon Valley, but God told you that anything you did related to computers wouldn't be successful. What do you do? The Genesis account tells us that Cain built a city. Perhaps it served as a fortress for Cain, the original fugitive. Interestingly, archeology shows us that the first cities appeared between 4000 and 3000 BC in Mesopotamia. Was Cain, then, the architect of the first city?

Where did we get this 4004 BC date as the commonly accepted time for the creation of Adam? That distinction goes to Mr. Ussher, a bishop who headed up the Anglo-Irish Church in Ireland in 1625. Bishop Ussher's exact date for creation was 4004 BC in the month of October. The significance of this date is that it created a fracture line between science and religion. How can you put all of creation into 6000 years say scientists when we have evidence of hominids 7000, 10,000 and more than 100,000 years ago? And as we all know, this fault line was cracked wide open by various interpretations of Charles Darwin's observations.

Bishop Ussher is said to have arrived at this 4004 BC date by adding up the chronologies in the Biblical record and adding in the years up to the death of Babylonian king, Nebuchadnezzar. While the 4000 BC date is still adhered to by creationists, scientists know that hominids existed more than 6000 years ago.

The underlying fundamental issue is one of fear and mistrust of science on the part of creationists. The world we live in has a duality to it. It is a physical-spiritual duality. Science cannot, by definition, quantify or measure the spiritual. It is outside the realm of their expertise. Likewise, most religious people have never made the effort to truly study science and/or the Biblical record for that matter. Over the past one hundred and fifty years or so, the two camps have drifted away from each other. And in our current political atmosphere, those on the right end of the religious spectrum have reacted negatively to "liberal" science often inventing their own version of science, based in large part on faulty assumptions, to suit their beliefs. This is just as ludicrous to serious scientists as scientists declaring, "God is dead" to serious theologians. The creationist's mindset is if the scientists are right, then the Biblical record has to be wrong. If the Biblical record is wrong, then what can be believed? This shakes down to questioning the very existence of God. If the creationists give in on this point, its downhill for everything they believe in. Their house collapses.

However, an objective look at the Biblical record reveals that science and God's creation are not at odds when it concerns the facts. Scientists' personal conclusions about the existence of

God should not figure into the equation because science, per se, cannot prove nor disprove the existence of God. It is a matter of faith although chapter five presents a very strong indirect scientific proof God does exist. It boils down to this. It is likely Adam was created in 4000 BC or thereabouts, but creation itself began about 13-15 billion Earth years ago with the "Big Bang" birth of our universe and light. We'll explore all this in Chapter Four, Creation in Six Days, But Who's Counting?

The universe, our planet and all the life on it were created. It just didn't happen the way creationists think it did. Sunday school, after all, is not a hotbed of critical thinking. Unfortunately, many religious people have not critically studied the Biblical record to move past the Sunday school stage as we witnessed in the Prologue. But when we look at the Biblical record, clear out the Sunday school stories, and then look at what science has discovered, we find out there are no contradictions. Creationists need to be a little less fearful and have a bit more holy curiosity and faith in the Biblical record. It's much more exciting too.

Cain was extremely fearful of leaving Eden and the presence of God, as it was different on the outside. Cain said, "My punishment is more than I can bear." What a whiner! Come on, being a wanderer on the earth can't be so bad. Scores of college students and adventurers do it every year. So what's the problem? According to Cain, "...you [God] have driven me out this day from the face of the earth [Eden wherein adam was first created] and from your face shall I be hid...every one that finds me shall slay me."[33] Okay, anyone who found him would kill him. That changes the scenario. But they wouldn't kill Cain because he was a murderer. They would kill him because he was an adam, a man.

Cain had a spirit that made him different from everyone else outside Eden. God marked Cain so that anyone outside Eden that considered killing him would be aware that vengeance would fall upon them sevenfold. Who was outside Eden that Cain knew was there? Hominids. And where did Cain get the idea that he would be killed once he was outside of Eden? We can only speculate, but how many times had Cain stood on the banks of the rivers Hiddekel or Pishon and gazed across water to see these hominids? How many times had they looked back? Had Cain seen one hominid slay another as he had later killed Abel? Had there been no reaction to this by other hominids nearby who witnessed it?

It's obvious, however, that Cain was shocked at the punishment handed down for his slaying of Abel. Henceforth, mankind's lineal descent in the Biblical record is passed from Adam to Seth now that Cain was cast out. The lineal descent passes through the oldest son. Seth not Cain was considered the legitimate heir.

Hominids existed more than 6000 years ago. The fossil record and DNA studies clearly show these hominids did exist. But hominids were creatures. They had a different spirit. Literally speaking, Cain was being thrown into the animal kingdom. The rules were different. Animals do kill. And normally it's for food or mating rights without knowledge of the morality that their actions are good or evil. Cain would be very sensitive to this.[34]

It is likely that these hominids were aware something was happening in Eden that was different from the world they lived in. Also, it's very probable that these hominids had developed a spoken language. As daunting as it was, Cain had no choice.

"Cain went out from the presence of the LORD, and dwelled in the land of Nod, on the east of Eden."[35] The Biblical record clearly does not mention any other human leaving Eden. It's just not there.

On this point, the account in Genesis is clear that no one else is said to have left the presence of the LORD except Cain. Cain was marked, left Eden to dwell in Nod apart from the presence of God and his parents, Adam and Eve. We can only speculate as to how traumatic it was leaving Eden. What thoughts were going through Cain's mind when he crossed the river taking his last step in Eden and his first tentative step into an alien world? Cain's initial "close encounter" with these hominid creatures must have been somewhat akin to Hominid 12.6 meets Hominid 2.1. Or was it something not quite so radical?

Now we come to perhaps the most shocking statement we will make in this book. It is a quantum point of understanding. No doubt there will be wailing and gnashing of teeth over this. Some will say that this crosses the line and slam shut the book not wanting to consider the implications. Quite possibly some will call for bringing back book burning because of it. Yet remember, God is the Creator of life, all life. Once we examine what we think may be totally bizarre to our current way of thinking, we can come to see it is the way God caused it to be. We should not fear the truth that makes us free. This is one incredible part of our adventure that leads to greater understanding of the word of God.

The Genesis account tells us Cain knew his wife. She conceived and bore Enoch. Here it comes. Cain's wife was not a woman or descendant of Adam and Eve. His wife was a female hominid who had the spirit of a creature, but was genetically close enough for him to have offspring.

Yes, you read that right. It's a quantum step, a magnitude ten in its implication for science and theology alike. It does upset the apple cart. It changes the scope of everything. But it does mesh perfectly with what science has discovered in the archeological record, with DNA studies and what is stated in the Biblical record. I can already feel the rumblings among evangelicals on this one. But, before you run and hide from this, read the entire chapter. We've all heard many times, God works in mysterious ways. And so it is with Cain.

The first point we need to examine is that according to the Biblical record, at the time of Cain's leaving Eden, no other siblings, male or female are mentioned to have existed. This is Biblical fact. It was just Cain and Abel. Abel was killed and Cain was banished from Eden for life. Adam and Eve had been kicked out of the garden of Eden into Eden to till the soil. Any farmer will tell you this is hard work. On top of this, one son murders the other. Then God casts the other son out of Eden. This is what the Biblical record states. For Adam and Eve, life sucks to put it in the vernacular.

Admittedly, Adam and Eve felt they were "snake bit" at this point which is the case figuratively speaking. They may have waited some time before trying for more children especially as God told Eve upon being kicked out the garden that "in sorrow you shall bring forth children."[36] Cain and Abel certainly had been a major source of sorrow. Did this just apply to Cain and Abel or to any children they would have? They both would be "gun shy" not knowing what would happen with other children they might have. It certainly would put a damper on intimate marital relations.

The Biblical record relates that Adam knew his wife again. This is the second time the Biblical record states that Eve got pregnant.[37] If you read the account concerning the birth of Cain and Abel, there is one conception but two births mentioned.[38] This would indicate Cain and Abel were twins, but identical looking or not we can't say for certain.  At the end of the second pregnancy, she gave birth to a son, and called his name Seth. Seth means appointed. For Eve said, "God has appointed me another seed instead of Abel whom Cain slew."[39]

The Biblical record tells us that Seth was the next one born to Adam and Eve. No other "sons or daughters" are mentioned yet. Seth was appointed to replace Abel as Adam and Eve's bearer of mankind's seed. Cain was banished and gone. The birth of Seth comes after the entire Biblical account of Cain being put out of Eden and after the Biblical record account of Cain knowing his "wife" and even after the Biblical record account of Cain's death. It is therefore possible that Seth wasn't born until after Cain's death as the Biblical record does not tell us how long he lived as it does with Adam, Seth and others in mankind's lineage.

Thus, it appears that the third child of Adam and Eve was not born until after Abel was killed and Cain left Eden at minimum. Plus Seth took the place of Abel being "another seed." This, too, indicates that Eve realized Cain's life on the outside would not be counted as "seed" for both her and Adam. This wouldn't be the case, it would appear, if Cain took a sister as his wife with him out of Eden.

Seed here in Hebrew is zera and it means literally a seed that when planted can produce further crops. Being farmers this would be an appropriate term for Eve to use. But zera also means to be progeny or one who will carry on the family line. Thus, the second pregnancy mentioned in the Biblical record produces a son who will carry on mankind's lineage and it's not Cain.

The Biblical record tells us Adam was one hundred and thirty years old when Seth was born. This, too, would appear to indicate that some time had elapsed between the events of Abel's death and Cain's leaving and life outside Eden before Adam and Eve had Seth.

The written evidence and the timing all points to the fact that Cain had no brothers or sisters at the time of his leaving Eden. When Adam and Eve did have a third child, it was a son. We aren't told when the first daughter was born to Adam and Eve except this occurs after the account of Seth's birth. Objectively, the Biblical record leaves us with one conclusion. The second man didn't marry his sister.

The argument that Cain married his sister doesn't hold for several reasons. One, no mention is made of anyone else leaving Eden with Cain. It is a non-Genesis assumption. The Biblical record states, "Cain went out from the presence of the LORD."[40] Nothing in the Biblical record states that Cain went out from the presence of the LORD with his wife. It is a subjective hypothesis that Cain took a sister as his wife. But there is a Biblical record of Cain having a "wife."

The translators of the King James Version [KJV] of the Bible were the most educated and scholarly men of their generation. They were motivated by a joy for the sacredness of God's word. "But among all our joys, there was no one that more filled our hearts, than the blessed continuance of the preaching of God's sacred Word among us; which is that inestimable treasure, which excels all the treasures of the earth; …that out of the Original Sacred Tongues, together with comparing the labours, both in our own, and other foreign Languages, of many worthy men who went before us, there should be one more exact Translation of the holy Scriptures in the English tongue;…."[41]

These scholars were intent on getting it right. They made the assumption that Cain must have taken someone with him because he had Enoch. What else could they possibly have thought at the time? There was no archeological evidence of other creatures. Even though the Biblical record didn't indicate Cain having a sister, what other explanation could there be in the days of King James? Adam and Eve were the first two people on earth at creation as the thinking went. While only Cain and Abel are mentioned by name, surely there must have been others too. There were others, but they weren't of adamkind.

We have the benefit of seeing into the past prior to man's first written record through archeology and DNA analysis. The translators of the KJV didn't have this information, yet in a sense they still got it right. The first real discovery that mankind had a physical predecessor was the Neanderthal man found in the Neander Valley in 1856 just a few years before Darwin's Origin of the Species was published. Between this book and his Descent of Man in 1871, Thomas Huxley put a point on creation theory in his "Evidence as to Man's Place in Nature" published in 1863. Today, the most well-known fossil discoverers are Louis Leakey and his son Richard. The third generation Leakeys are active in the field of paleontology today.

Collectively, their work and the work of many others have presented the rest of us with evidence that prior to Adam there were other hominids living on Earth. They just weren't dumb cave men, but were rather sophisticated in many ways by the time Adam was created in 4004 BC. As the translators of the KJV had no knowledge of this to guide them in deciding which meaning to give a word, Cain was said to have known his wife who gave birth to Enoch. A wife had to be as human as Cain. Therefore, it had to be his sister even though it raised many questions that have since been glossed over by many religious thinkers.

But, if Cain was fearful of leaving Eden, wouldn't a sister of Cain have the same fears of being killed, or worse, outside Eden as would Cain? Remember, Cain was fearful of being killed because he was mankind not creaturekind. He was an outsider. Hominids would not have had the knowledge of good and evil just as lions and tigers don't when it comes to killing their prey or one of their kind for mating rights.

Presumably a sister of Cain's would have had the additional burden of being the object of fierce competition on the part of male creatures to mate with her. Cain, as a husband, almost certainly would have been killed immediately in this case, being marked or not. But, there is no mention of God marking anyone else for protection outside Eden.

Cain does not raise the issue with God of not finding a mate on the outside. Maybe Cain had seen female creatures across the river as the Biblical record indicates he knew there were others outside Eden. Maybe he saw them bathe in the river. We aren't told that Cain had a sister during his time in Eden. Whatever the reason, Cain didn't seem to have any concern about having a female mate. His only concern was that he, and he alone, would be killed. The Biblical record has no mention of his asking God to take someone with him. And perhaps most importantly, why would God punish an innocent sister of Cain's and cast her out for his transgressions? Cain could live his life celibate. No mention is made of anyone, female or otherwise, leaving with Cain. We've just assumed it. And it's become accepted Sunday school tradition.

Chimps are 99.6% genetically identical to man. Neanderthals are estimated to be 99.5 to 99.9% genetically identical to man. As mankind today is 99.9% alike, how close genetically would these hominids have to be for Cain to have fertile offspring? Perhaps the second most startling point we can make is how ironic it is that while anthropologists have been scurrying around, digging in the dirt looking for the "missing link" connecting hominid creature to hominid man, it was right under our noses all this time in the pages of Genesis. Let's take it point by point.

First, to quickly recapitulate the findings in chapter one, our human container is not a sacred entity any more than the stones and timbers used for the temple built by Solomon were sacred. It is what is inside the physical container that makes the difference. This container, our body, has no preeminence over that of a creature according to the word of God. To put it in everyday language, our hardware makes us alike. It's the software package that makes us different.

Next, remember, the Genesis account very clearly says that at this time only Adam and Eve, who were created and Cain, who was born, were mankind. Cain voices his concern about being killed by every one that finds him well before Seth is born, much less other sons and daughters according to the record in Genesis. And it's only after Seth's birth that the Genesis account says Adam had other sons and daughters. Cain is not mentioned, nor his wife nor his progeny, in the generations of Adam or man.[42] Cain's line is mentioned separately and only up to his death.[43] Nothing is mentioned after the death of the man outside Eden.

Also, in the Genesis account of Cain's lineage, Lamech makes a specific point of slaying a man. If everyone outside Eden was mankind, what's the big deal of slaying a man?

Undoubtedly some will point out that Lamech says "...I have slain a man to my wounding and a young man to my hurt..." proves that Cain had a son of a woman. It is correct that the context is Cain and his offspring, either direct or a generation or more removed. But this does not mean that Cain's offspring was considered mankind or an offspring of a man and a woman. Closer inspection shows it means a man, an adam, fathered the offspring either directly or generations removed. This distinction is significant.

While the only hominid alive today by which a man can father offspring is a woman, this was not the case for Cain. The Hebrew phrase in Genesis, chapter four, verse twenty-three, "...young man..." [yeled adam] is used just once in the Biblical record. And it is a specific reference to Cain's offspring. It is never used in the Bible in reference to the child of a man and a woman. The Hebrew word, yeled, simply means something born. So the text should read, "I have slain a man...and something born of man." A male offspring fathered by Cain and a female hominid directly or descended from Cain clearly would be something born of man, but wouldn't be mankind. But it would be 100% Homo sapiens. Remember, life similarities are of the flesh. The differences are of the spirit.

The word yeled is translated as young only in four other examples in the Old Testament. In Kings and Chronicles it is used to describe those that King Rehoboam had grown up with who gave him bad advice that led to the division of Israel into the House of Israel and the House of Judah after the death of King Solomon. The use of yeled here appears to be a derogatory reference to these adult men as the term men is the less dignified Hebrew word, enowsh, as opposed to adam. Other uses of yeled describe the young born offspring of male and female animals, specifically lions, wild goats, cows and bears in Job and Isaiah.

If Cain killed a man and was avenged seven times over, Lamech boasted he should get avenged seventy and sevenfold for slaying a man. The only man [adam] on the outside was Cain. All Cain's descendents were mixed breeds but were not sterile hybrids like a mule bred from a horse and donkey, which have 64 and 62 chromosomes respectively. These hominids, therefore, must have been very close genetically to man if not virtually identical excepting the spirit, and therefore the Godly potential, within them.

Cain's female hominid is referred to as his wife in the English translation. So often we tend to impute our modern day meanings into words used in a different context with different meanings. The Hebrew word translated into the English word wife is ishshah. Ishshah is a word with a wide range of uses referring to the female gender. Among them is woman, adulteress, female, each, every, one, etc. So use of the word is context dependent. This explains the KJV translators translating it as wife for Cain's mate. They had no other context for comparison.

In other verses in Genesis, ishshah is translated as women. For example, in chapter fourteen, verse sixteen, "And he brought back all the goods, and also brought again his brother Lot, and his goods, and the women also, and the people."

In chapter seven, ishshah is also translated by its context. We see in verse two, ""Of every beast [creature] you shall take to you by sevens, the male and his female: and of beasts that are not clean by two, the male and his female."  Thus using the context of Cain being the only one of mankind outside Eden, when we read "Cain knew his ishshah, and she conceived…," the context would more accurately read "Cain knew his female…."

But now realizing that there is no record in Genesis of any woman having been born at this point much less leaving with Cain, and the fossil record shows there were other hominids out there, coupled with DNA studies that demonstrate our common genetic ancestor goes back 150,000 to perhaps 195,000 years ago, the evidence points to a female hominid by which Cain had offspring. However, it is still possible that Cain's relationship with his female hominid could be characterized by translating ishshah as wife.

Therefore, in context ishshah could be translated female or even wife, as the KJV translators did, but definitely not woman. We've just assumed the word wife meant woman or offspring of Adam and Eve.

It's clear God set mankind inside Eden for a reason. And one of those reasons appears to be to keep them separate because they were so close genetically. The physical containers of Homo sapiens creatures and Homo sapiens man, it appears, were compatible. Outside, east of Eden, only Cain had the spirit of man. We are not told what spirit the offspring of Cain had, but one would most likely assume it was not the spirit of man. The spirit of man would continue with Adam and Eve's seed, Seth.

Cain specifically was expelled from Eden for the murder of his brother Abel. You can't find in the Genesis account anyone else who was expelled from Eden. It's simply not there. There may be lots of gnashing of teeth over this point in churches everywhere. Religious folks may desperately want a woman leaving Eden with Cain. But it simply isn't there. Therefore, as we are told Cain knew his wife and she bore something born of a man, it pretty much leaves just one option. Cain's wife was a female hominid, a Homo sapiens genetically similar enough to mankind to produce fertile offspring, but not for "seed."

What we have here is a bridge in our understanding of creation. Rather than rent our clothes and put on sackcloth and ashes, let's remember God is the Creator of life, all life here on our planet Earth. This raises interesting philosophical questions. Why didn't God stop Cain from slaying Abel? Why didn't God just strike Cain down in Eden? Why was Cain sent out of Eden instead? Was the punishment suited to the crime in that Cain would live in fear of his life everyday? The list of questions is long. Rather than react hysterically in a knee-jerk fashion, perhaps we should start by asking one question first, how can it be like that?

Likely, one answer is that God wants us to realize that the spiritual side of life is what is important rather than the physical. After all, "flesh and blood cannot inherit the kingdom of God, neither does corruption inherit incorruption."[44] Mankind's potential lies in the spirit. Creatures have no such future potential. This life is all they get. Religions place so much emphasis on the flesh that they lose sight of the spiritual nature that is man's alone and not of hominids past. Why then is there such an uproar over evolution saying man and hominids are close, if not identical, physically? It makes no difference to God who created all forms of life on Earth. Society today places nearly all its emphasis on the carnal side of life. Christmas allegedly is about the birth of Christ, yet it is nothing more than a retail carnival embedded in pagan tradition. Its "season" starts in October and lingers into January. As this retail trend continues, perhaps in the near future Labor Day in the US will mark the end of the summer season and the beginning of the Christmas season. The Biblical record says we are "altogether stupid and foolish" for doing this.[45] The kingdom of God is not comprised of shopping malls. Yet one gets the distinct feeling that today's concept of heaven is a place no longer inhabited by harp playing angels, but rather by angel chauffeured SUV's that take you from mall to mall with unlimited credit on your plastic key to heaven.

The cover of the January 2000 Scientific American magazine shows two beings. One is a man, the other a creature. Yet an interesting question was posed. "Our species had at least 15 cousins. Only we remain. Why?" Scientific American continues, "Homo sapiens is the only hominid that still walks the earth. Yet over the past four million years, 20 or more types of creatures similar to us and our ancestors may have existed...."[46]

This is a bit different than what we learned in Sunday school. But as we learned in chapter one, it is the spirit in us that separates us from creatures and not our physical container, the fleshly body. Our bodies come from the earth, and they return to the earth after death. It is our spirit that returns to God who gave it. This potential sets man apart from every other hominid that has walked the Earth.

The fact that the Biblical record tells us Cain had a female hominid for his wife, and that she gave birth to fertile offspring is supported by scientific findings of DNA. Remember, God is the author of science as much as he is the Creator of life. Hominids and adamkind were both created on day six of creation according to the Biblical record.[47] There is no contradiction that Cain had physical offspring with a female hominid.

The great irony in all this is that science's "missing link" very likely is found in the Biblical record rather than in the dust of the earth. Science doesn't put much, if any credibility in the Biblical record. Christianity doesn't tend to give scientists any credit for hominid life prior to Adam 6000 years ago. Yet, the first man conceived, Cain just may be the missing link that brings science and religion together. It appears a bridge between science and religion exists. A mystery can be solved. Are any on either side of this bridge adventurous enough to cross it?

## Chapter Three: If Life Begins At 40, Where Does That Leave Conception?

Life and death seem to have a yin and yang relationship. And probably since man first realized his flesh wasn't immortal, the philosophical questions about life and death have consumed some of the best minds in history as well as the rest of us. But I can tell you exactly about life and death. I was The Only Kid in the family for the first five years of my life. The Only Kid died the day my younger brother was born. Granted, nothing lasts forever, but life as The Only Kid was pretty good. However, the change was so abrupt that it would have taken a B western movie audience by complete surprise; the hero taken down in his prime. When people came over to the house to visit, it wasn't me they were happy to see any more. It was that little no-good bundle of diaper filling, crybaby of an intruder that showed up at the house one day and wouldn't leave. It was worse than putting up barbwire on free range. If they would have ignored him, he might have gone someplace else. But no, there was a steady-stream of people that came just to see him. I'd never even seen some of these people before. Was there an ad in the local paper? And they brought him presents too.

To make matters worse, he was going to bunk with me and Hopalong Cassidy, or Hoppy as he was to his friends. I had a Hoppy bedspread and sheets, a Hoppy hat and six-shooters. I even had a Hoppy bike with saddlebags. Hoppy and The Only Kid had many a great adventure together. Now here was this interloper messing up a perfectly good thing just like a girl coming between a cowboy and his horse!

I realized one day that all that Hoppy stuff showed up when little brother was already on his way. Darn, I'd been sweet-talked by my own parents. They tried to reassure me everything would be just as it was before. They still loved me. In fact my new brother, they told me, would be like having a new friend, you know someone new to throw the football to. After this build up, I anxiously awaited my new "sidekick." The big day arrived. They brought him home, so I was looking around the house for The Other Kid [he needed a cowboy nickname after all]. I told my parents I wanted to play football, so I asked. "Where's The Other Kid?" They pointed to a little white basket. "That's him?!" I said, shocked. The Other Kid was just a peanut! He was hardly bigger than the football. He didn't have any teeth. He couldn't even walk much less ride a horse. Yeah, that was the day my life as The Only Kid died. That afternoon I waved good-bye to Hoppy as he rode off into the sunset...alone. I was no longer a sidekick. I was a brother now.

I've grown up, mostly anyway. The Other Kid is doing fine. I found out there are all sorts of "life begins" moments always accompanied by those "petite mort" moments too. Aside from the obvious birth one, there was the puberty one. Then graduation from high school. Then college. Then marriage. Then divorce. You've probably heard the expression that life begins at forty. Some claim that sixty is the new forty. And I suppose someday, eighty might be the new sixty. They keep pushing it up on us baby-boomers. I can hardly wait to hear that one hundred is the new eighty. Yippee!

But the heated question in society today concerning when life begins doesn't directly concern us baby boomers but rather our

# If Life Begins At 40, Where Does That Leave Conception?

children and grandchildren. Of course, all this goes to the heart and core of the abortion issue. Does life begin at conception? Or does life begin at some other point? If so, what is it? And who says so?

Very strong points have been raised that abortion is murder mostly among the conservative religious community. Legally, murder is a capital offense in the United States, as it is in various other countries of the world. Yet, abortion is legal in most states although a Supreme Court decision in 2007 has struck down the "partial birth" method of abortion. Legally, however, abortion itself is not considered murder. This has to be considered an oxymoron of sorts by religious groups that oppose abortion as murder. This wouldn't be the first time behavior condoned by a government would be considered to run contrary to the word of God.

The basis for those proponents in the religious community that abortion is murder is derived from alleged Biblical sources. For those not versed in the written or verbal arguments, pro-lifers are very happy to provide photos of bloody aborted fetuses to drive home their point. Yet as gruesome as these photos are, they are no more gruesome than photos of babies crushed and torn as car crash victims of drunk drivers, or of those children dismembered by bombs dropped from military jets. They do evoke powerful emotions. Any normal human being would be repulsed by any of these photos. But photos and emotions do not get to the root of the dilemma.

The root is simply to determine the answer to the simple question, "When does life begin?" By definition, it is impossible to murder something that does not have life. As the religious community declares, "abortion is murder," we should examine the Biblical record to see if this is so.

The Catholic Church is probably the leading religious organization condemning abortion as murder. Recent verbal attacks by Pope Benedict and other high-ranking church officials described abortion as "terrorism with a human face" equating this act with terrorists who kill defenseless human beings. This goes to the heart and core of the issue. Is a fetus a human being? When does life begin? The Catholic Church and other religious "pro-life" groups say life begins at conception. Are they right? And by what authority do they make their claim? According to the on-line New Advent Catholic Encyclopedia under the section, Life, it states, "The enigma of life is still one of the two or three most difficult problems that face both scientist and philosopher...."[48]

God, the Creator of life, nonetheless, makes it a whole lot simpler for the rest of us. In Genesis chapter two, verse seven we read, "For the LORD God formed man of the dust of the ground and breathed into his nostrils the breath of life and man became a living soul."

This straightforward statement is, well, pretty straightforward. It is the quantum point concerning the beginning of life in the flesh. Let's examine this statement, without prejudice, to see what it is telling us. After all, according to the word of God this is the very first human being we're talking about. It is discussing the very crux of the matter before us, when life begins. The Creator gives us a clear and unequivocal answer.

First, who is creating the life here? It is the LORD God. I believe most religious people and organizations would consider this a credible source. And the life the LORD God is forming is the very first man or as it reads in Hebrew, adam. Okay, so far so good. Next what happened? Breath is put into the nostrils of man by the LORD God. Which breath is put into adam's nostrils? It is the breath of...life. This is the critical portion of our question as to when life begins. We have the breath of life put into man's nostrils by the LORD God who formed him. Okay. What happens once the breath of life enters man's nostrils? Man becomes a living soul [Hebrew, nephesh a breathing creature, not a soul as in spirit]. Adam received the breath of life and became a living breathing creature.

It appears that the answer to when life begins is rather simple and straightforward. We breathe in the breath of life into our nostrils and we become living flesh. Therefore, life for mankind in the flesh begins when we take that first breath of life into our nostrils at birth. Can we seriously think God got this wrong?

Failure to take a breath at birth and you are stillborn...dead. This in itself raises a question. If conception equals life, how can you be considered alive one instant without breath inside the womb, and dead the next instant without breath outside the womb? Isn't the fetus still conceived? It is. But it lacks breath, the breath of life to be precise.

Every argument that life begins at conception starts and stops with this clear and definitive verse in Genesis, "For the LORD God formed man of the dust of the ground and breathed into his nostrils the breath of life and man became a living [i.e., breathing] soul." Three times in one sentence in Genesis concerning the first man, the beginning of life is associated with breath! Yet some still stubbornly insist it is at conception.

For life to have any credible chance of beginning at conception, you have to disprove this plain and simple statement that life begins with breath. The question goes begging, where is the plainly stated Biblical record reference that life begins at conception? Some claim that vague inferences referring to a person in the Biblical record prior to birth equates to independent viable life of the fetus which somehow proves life begins at conception. For example, in the beginning of the book of Jeremiah God states, "I formed you in the belly, I knew you and before you came forth out of the womb I sanctified you, and I ordained you a prophet unto the nations." Yes the fetus that was born and took his first breath and became Jeremiah was formed, sanctified and ordained in the womb. First, we are all formed in the womb. Secondly, the sanctification and ordaining didn't take effect, obviously, until birth or are we to believe Jeremiah was prophesying in the womb? Our only record of his prophesies are written Biblical records all taking place after his birth. He did not have independent life in the womb! All these actions referring to Jeremiah are on the part of the living God. Jeremiah at that point in time was a dependent life form, a fetus. Remember, however, it is our spirit that sets man apart from physical creatures, not our bodies. Jeremiah's sanctification and ordaining were spiritual in nature conferred by God who is a spirit being on a fetus that at first breath became Jeremiah. There are no statements in the Biblical record that physical life begins at conception.

In the Catholic Encyclopedia under the section Abortion, the

Catholic Church references "Aristotle and St. Gregory of Nyssa."[49] However, there is not one mention about the LORD God, who created life at first breath, stating abortion is murder because life begins at conception. There are only man-made conclusions.

Before we go any further, it is very important to understand one thing. Just because life starts at birth or first breath, it does not automatically imply a pro-abortion position. It doesn't. It just means life begins at first breath at birth as the Creator has clearly stated. The issue at hand is the beginning of life. Please keep this distinction clearly in mind. Otherwise emotions will cloud the clarity of what the Biblical record and science says.

The Catholic Encyclopedia continues, "Now it is at the very time of conception, or fecundation, that the embryo begins to live a distinct individual life."[50] No scriptural source is provided for this catechistic conclusion. Motives aside, we know, of course, that this statement is directly contrary to the word of God as just examined in the Biblical record.

But what does the Biblical record say about life beginning at conception? Upon reading every example in the Old Testament where conception, conceive, conceived is mentioned, a pattern in the text becomes very clear. We read about Samson, "And the angel of the LORD appeared to the woman, and said to her, Behold, now you are barren, and bear not: but you shall conceive, and bear a son."[51] Bear simply means to give birth. When was Samson a son? At birth.

In 1 Chronicles we read, "And when he went in to his wife, she conceived, and bare a son...."[52] In Hosea, we read, "So he went and took Gomer the daughter of Diblaim, which conceived, and bare him a son."[53] The pattern is the same over and over again: conception, birth [breath], life, conception, birth [breath], life. It is never conception, life and birth. The Old Testament record consistently shows life begins at birth when we take our first breath in exact accordance with the creation of Adam in Genesis.

In the New Testament, we read in Luke's gospel, "...and the angel answered and said to her, 'The Holy Spirit shall come upon you, and the power of the Highest shall overshadow you; therefore also that holy thing which shall be born of you shall be called the Son of God.'"[54] This, of course, is a reference to the birth of Christ. If life begins at conception according to the Biblical record, then why are we not told in reference to Christ himself "that which shall be conceived in you shall be called" especially as this is popularly referred to as the "Immaculate Conception" rather than the "Immaculate Birth?"

The order of events culminating in life is made clear by Isaiah regarding this same event, "...a virgin shall conceive, and bear a son, and shall call his name Immanuel."[55] Luke's account is in complete agreement with Isaiah, which is in complete agreement with Genesis. For it is at birth that we take the breath of life into our nostrils not at conception. Conception merely denotes the beginning of cyesis or pregnancy, not life itself.

For the sake of those who still insist on conception as the beginning of life, logically and Biblically, who is the first man? You have a bit of a conundrum here. You can't answer Adam. He didn't have a belly button. That's because Adam wasn't conceived, but he definitely had life. Who does that leave you with as the first man then? The first man with a belly button would be Cain, the first murderer. This isn't exactly great PR for the life begins at conception folks. The Biblical record is consistent. "And so it is written, The first man Adam was made a living soul"[56] ...which in Genesis reads "was made a living breathing creature." Adam was made a living soul by the breath of life in his nostrils.

A conceived Cain as the first man line of reasoning doesn't work too well for many obvious reasons. This has led to the claim by some that Adam and Eve were "special cases" when it comes to the beginning of life because neither was conceived. According to one theologian, God doesn't need special cases. It's only when man mistakenly decided to use conception as the benchmark for the beginning of life that they become special cases. The beginning of life is consistent for all mankind including Adam and Eve, Cain and Abel, you and me. We have life at first breath and we die after our last breath. As we read in the epistle of James, chapter two, the body without breath [the movement of air] is dead. In essence, our first inhale is life. Our last exhale is death. Simple.

Rather interestingly, Pope John Paul II, prior to his death, frequently insisted, according to Vatican sources, that he intended to carry on "while there is breath in my body."[57] So, at least, the pope agreed that life and breath do have a direct relationship as the Apostle James stated.

For those who are perhaps more comfortable with analogies, let's say your church was having a baked goods bazaar to raise money for the church school to purchase two more computer study stations for the students. You are asked to make a cake to sell at the bazaar. So you get out your best mixing bowl and put in the flour, the eggs, the sugar, the salt, yeast, and all the other required ingredients and mix them up perfectly. You arrive at the bazaar. The other parents greet you and ask you to put your cake on the table with the others. You walk over and put down on the table your mixing bowl with all the perfectly mixed ingredients. However, one of the parents asks you what that is. You tell them it's your cake. But, they reply, it's all the ingredients mixed up in a bowl. It's not baked. It's not a cake.

Would they be right? Of course. Just because all the ingredients are mixed in a bowl, it doesn't make it a cake. It has the potential to be a cake. The ingredients have to be baked in an oven for a prescribed amount of time. Then, at the right time, when it comes out of the oven, you have a cake. The same is true for life. Just because the ingredients are mixed perfectly as they should be at conception in the womb, it's not a distinct, individual life. The "ingredients" normally gestate for approximately nine months, and then at birth, we have our "cake." It's only life after it's out of the oven. Life begins at birth when we can take the breath of life into our nostrils.

The Biblical account relates that there are three spirits that interface with mortal bodies as we read in the Chapter One. One is the spirit of creatures. The other is the spirit of man. And the other is the Spirit of God found in the sons of God. In a manner of speaking, there have been three creations. At the creation of life, the spirit common to beasts or creatures, too, was created. Later, with Adam in Eden, came the spirit of man. Later, with Christ, came the Spirit of God.

Paul further explains this when he says, "And so it is written, The first man Adam was made a living soul; the last Adam was made a quickening spirit. How is it that was not first which is spiritual, but that which is natural; and afterward that which is spiritual. The first man is of the earth, earthy: the second man is the Lord from heaven...And as we have borne the image of the earthy, we shall also bear the image of the heavenly."[58]

This is why Christ said to Nicodemus, "except a man be born again...." [or born from above].[59] Only Christ had the Spirit of God during the time of his mortal ministry. And continually we see Christ referred to as the only begotten son of God. Begotten means born. At that time, the only one "born from above" was Christ. It wasn't until Pentecost, fifty days after the resurrection of Christ, when the disciples were filled with the Holy Spirit.

The key is that a Christian's new life in the confines of a mortal body starts with a birth, albeit from God above, and not exiting from the womb when mankind's initial mortal life starts at birth [or first breath] rather than at conception. The context of the first twelve verses of John chapter three is life beginning with a birth whether it is physical or spiritual. What is very interesting is that many religious people, who claim life begins at conception, who oppose abortion as murder, call themselves Born Again Christians. One wonders that they don't refer to themselves as "Conceived Again" Christians.

Those who support life beginning at conception have scarcely a Biblical verse to stand on. There is one that is universally used to peg their point to the Biblical record and therefore God. The key verse quoted by Catholics and other religious groups is found in the Old Testament Book of Exodus.

"If men strive, and hurt a woman with child, so that her fruit depart from her, and yet no mischief follow: he shall be surely punished, according as the woman's husband will lay upon him; and he shall pay as the judges determine. And if mischief follow, then you shall give life for life...."[60]

Those who claim life begins at conception, and thus abortion is murder use this Biblical verse to make their case. So let's examine it from that point of view first. If men strive, which means to struggle, and a pregnant woman is injured so that "her fruit departs" yet no mischief or no harm results from the premature birth, then the man who caused it to happen shall be financially responsible. But if harm results, then it shall be life for life. Life for life is a correct understanding here.

This seems to indicate that if the woman aborted, then the man would forfeit his life for the conceived, yet dead fetus. Life for life. This would prove that life does indeed begin at conception and that God considers it so. In English, this could be the case. But when we keep in mind that life begins with a breath, would this still hold?

If men struggle and a woman is injured so that her fruit depart from her and harm results, then the man causing the injury must give up his life too. In Hebrew fruit departs is yeled yatsa. Yeled means something born. Yatsa means to go out. Even at this point, either life begins at conception or at first breath holds as a correct interpretation if yeled could include a stillborn fetus.

# If Life Begins At 40, Where Does That Leave Conception? 117

The key to this verse is the life for life penalty. Reading it in English, we can see quite readily how one could take this to mean that if a woman were caused to abort under these circumstances, the person causing this would have to forfeit his life. This would mean a conceived fetus is considered to have an independent life. It would follow in some people's minds then that abortionist doctors are fair game. Life for life.

However, we need to look at the meaning of the original Hebrew word to make sure we correctly understand what is being said here. The Hebrew word life used in this verse means "that which breathes" or a "breathing creature." It is the same word in Genesis used for the creation of Adam, nephesh.

Thus the "life for life" penalty when harm follows correctly reads, "breathing creature for breathing creature." Once again, breathing equates to life not conception. If the miscarriage results in a non-breathing birth, then only a financial amount is due.

If the child takes a breath, has life, then dies, the perpetrator must also die. This verse is incorrectly used to show that life begins at conception and a stillborn fetus requires the death of the man causing it, quid pro quo, life for life. But as we see, this verse actually negates the intent put forth by those claiming life begins at conception and abortion is murder. Rather the verse here in Exodus reinforces what the Biblical record has shown us elsewhere, namely that life in the flesh begins at first breath when we are born.

The fact that life begins with breath and not at conception is consistent throughout the Biblical record. Let's take a look at the

"Valley of the Bones" prophesy in Ezekiel. The dead dry bones are made to come to life. When are these bones considered to come to life? "Thus says the LORD God to these bones; Behold, I will cause breath to enter into you, and you shall live." There it is again, breath and life. No conception. Then we drop down a bit further in the prophesy, "...the breath came into them, and they lived...."[61]

The Biblical record is abundantly clear and consistent. Life of the physical body begins at first breath, which occurs at birth. No doubt somebody will devise an argument to show the fetus is a breathing creature. But God made the distinction of life beginning with the breath of life entering into man's nostrils rather than oxygen into a fetus's blood stream via the mother's nostrils. Let's look at the biological side of the coin. As God is the author of the Biblical record and science as the Creator, what does the science say about this?

Science is in perfect agreement with God's point about life beginning at birth. You correctly may point out that some people in science claim that brain wave activity marks the point for the beginning of life or when the fetus has its own first heartbeat or reacts to certain stimuli at some other point as initiating life. But these are man-made determinations based on scientific measurement by some extremely sophisticated medical equipment. God has made it very easy for anyone to make the determination of when life begins. No scans or tests are necessary. When a child is born and takes its first breath, life begins. It's no more complicated than this.

In 1977, English physiologist Douglas Wilkie discovered that prior to birth, the fetus metabolically, which includes all the biochemical reactions that take place in an organism, behaves just like one of its mother's organs, rather than as a separate life form, relying on her breathing for its oxygen needs."[62] The fetus shares its mother's metabolic rate for the entire gestational period. However, a decisive change takes place once the umbilical cord is severed and the dependent fetus becomes an independent neonate at first breath. The most dramatic changes occur in heart rate and respiration involving the lungs.

According to Professor of Neonatal Pediatrics, John Wyatt, University College London, "At birth the lungs have to undergo a rapid and dramatic transformation to enable them to become the organs of gas exchange. [The air we breathe is a gas.] During fetal life they are filled with liquid and receive only 10% of the cardiac output yet within seconds of birth they must take over from the placenta the function of external respiration [breathing]. In addition a regular breathing rhythm is quickly established."[63]

There are significant cardiovascular, immune, pulmonary, as well as other changes taking place between mother and offspring all at birth or first breath as well as changes in heart rate, respiration and other metabolism rate differences.

Metabolism rates are singular to the organism. That is, an independent life will have its own metabolism rate that is dependent on its size.[64] An adult elephant will never have the metabolism rate of a man, a dog or a mouse for example.

If the fetus has a wholly separate life of its own beginning at conception, its metabolism rate would never be the same as the mother's and would not significantly change at birth. Yet, just the opposite occurs. From the moment of birth or first breath to within the first 24-36 hours of life, the metabolic rate about doubles for the newborn baby. This places the newborn baby in line with mammals of similar size rather than with the larger size of the mother whose much slower metabolism rate the fetus shared during gestation.

This is provable, observable scientific fact. As we saw above, medical science shows that a fetus behaves exactly as one of the mother's organs and not as a distinct individual life. All its biochemical processes for growth and energy, its metabolism, and its respiration needs are that of the mother's until birth. It only takes a "breath of life" into its nostrils at birth.

Nowhere in the Biblical record is man said to become a living, breathing creature at conception. As we read above, however, the Catholic Encyclopedia claims, "Now it is at the very time of conception, or fecundation, that the embryo begins to live a distinct individual life." If the Catholic Encyclopedia used the words "individual life" describing the embryo the same way life is used to describe Adam or any other living individual, then the terms are contradictory both scientifically and theologically. It is neither an individual nor does it have its own life. The word life in Hebrew is nephesh and means a breathing creature. As we have scientifically noted, a fetus is not a breathing creature. Breath does not pass through its nostrils until birth. The mother does the breathing for the fetus's oxygen needs during gestation. The mother and conceived embryo are one life, one flesh prior to birth and first breath.

Man becomes a living, breathing creature when? When does God say man becomes a living soul, a living physical entity? When do we start life? The answer is all the same. Life starts with a breath according to Genesis and the Biblical record. And scientifically, at birth the neonate no longer relies on its mother for metabolism or breath.

Thus, when the fetus is in the womb, it is a part of the mother. The mother through the placenta nourishes it. The fetus's metabolism rate is the same as the mother's. No air is taken into its nostrils. Its own life begins when the placenta's umbilical cord is severed and the newborn takes its first breath using its own lungs. Its metabolism rate dramatically changes from that of the mother's to the metabolism rate of a living mammal equal in size. This is proven, commonly acknowledged, pediatric science and it is in complete agreement with the Biblical record.

For those of you who have accepted the idea that life begins at conception, whether on personal religious beliefs or based on the fact that your church says so, it may not be easy to come to accept this overwhelming evidence. You may be repulsed by the very idea of abortion. How can anyone condone such cruelty you might ask? How could anyone who cherishes life have an abortion? These are fair questions if asked on moral or ethical grounds. But, the issue that divides us is the one of abortion. Is it murder or not? Murder is a legal term. Legally then what are we dealing with here? As life begins at first breath, prior to this first breath, the fetus does not have its own individual life. Legally, abortion is no more murder than surgically removing a mother's arm. This is what the Biblical record tells us whether, on a gut level, we like it or not, whether we fully understand it or not.

Remember at the beginning, you were asked to keep emotions distinct from what we are examining. There is a reason for this. While the subject of abortion is very emotional, legal decisions must be based on fact. You may wish to continue to protest abortion on moral or ethical grounds. But legally, you cannot call it murder. You cannot murder that which does not have an independent individual life.

You may be sorely tempted to remain in the familiar darkness rather than bask in the light of new understanding. This is normal. After all, you have invested time and energy establishing this belief. You may have attended rallies. You may have been a speaker. You may have written a blog claiming life begins at conception for a religious audience. As we mentioned earlier, just because life begins at first breath, it doesn't necessarily mean abortion is fine and dandy. It merely means legally, according to the Biblical record, abortion is not murder. It has nothing to say about personal or societal morals or ethics.

But we must not fear the truth of God's word. We need to give God credit for knowing what he was doing when he created the universe, our planet and life. At the time of new discovery, old falsehoods cling to us like swamp leeches. It has been my experience, however, that when one proves that which God establishes in the Biblical record, accepts it, growth and greater understanding will result. A look back in history at one such example will help us to analyze our current situation and put it in perspective.

It may be difficult to realize that not so long ago historically speaking, there were issues that were as contentious as abortion, perhaps even more so. People lost their lives over them. Today, no one blinks an eye at them. They'd ridicule you for being daft if you seriously espoused the opinion. Back in the seventeenth century, religious doctrine, supposedly based on the Biblical record, did not agree with Galileo's telescopic observations of the planets and their relative motions that showed we lived in a heliocentric system, not a geocentric system. Galileo's observations matched the Copernican theory put forth in 1543 by Nicolaus Copernicus, the Polish astronomer in his "De Revolutionibus Orbium Coelestium," or "The Revolutions of Celestial Orbs." Today, we take for granted that the planets orbit the Sun. Well most of us anyway. Incredibly, a 2007 science survey found that upwards of 20% of those surveyed said the Sun orbits the Earth! The church authorities more than 450 years ago chose not to believe Copernicus either, allegedly based on assumptions found in the "Holy Scripture" that the Earth had to be the center of creation. Hipparchus, the Greek mathematician who measured the distance from the Earth to the moon using a solar eclipse, put the Earth in the center of the universe as well as the solar system about 150 BC. Aristachus of Samos put forth the idea of the stars apparent motion through our sky as the Earth rotated on its axis as it traveled around the Sun in the third century BC. Galileo's direct observations proved Aristachus and Copernicus to be right.

In the official papal condemnation and sentencing of Galileo in 1633 by the church, it states in part: "Whereas you, Galileo, son of the late Vincenzo Galilei, Florentine, aged seventy years, were in the year 1615 denounced to this Holy Office for holding as true the false doctrine taught by some that the Sun is the center of the world and immovable and that the Earth moves, and also with a diurnal motion... This Holy Tribunal being therefore of intention to proceed against the disorder and mischief thence resulting, which went on increasing to the prejudice of the Holy Faith, by command of His Holiness and of the Most Eminent Lords Cardinals of this supreme and universal Inquisition, ...The proposition that the Sun is the center of the world and does not move from its place is absurd and false philosophically and formally heretical, because it is expressly contrary to Holy Scripture."[65]

Well, put that way, there was no arguing with these guys. Galileo was a potential two-legged shish waiting to be kebobbed. He never stood a chance, all scientific observations aside. The papal condemnation of Galileo, that the Sun is the center of our solar system is "absurd, false philosophically, and formally heretical because it is expressly contrary to Holy Scripture," however, was an amazingly grand, shall we say "faux pas" on the part of the church.

How is it the Creator set the Sun, the Earth and the moon in their places and then when it came time to jot it down in the Biblical record, he forgot where he put them? "Let's see, I put the Sun here, or was it the Earth and moon? No, wait, the Sun goes around...nope...." Given the circumstances of alleged heretics being burned at the stake during the supreme and universal inquisition, and presumably sent on to hell for eternal scorching, we can only wonder then what the fate must be of the pope and the cardinals who, as it turns out not only were "false philosophically, and formally heretical" but were also guilty of murdering these poor souls which is expressly contrary to the Holy Scriptures. Thus it is not difficult to appreciate why Galileo probably didn't want to make an issue by pointing out the flawed reasoning of the Most Eminent Lords Cardinals Gessi, Bentivoglio, Verospi, Ginetti, as well as the Cardinals of Ascoli, Cremona and Onofrio. He was too smart to be that stupid. But, this tragedy illustrates exactly why it takes science and theology working together to see both sides of the coin.

Allegedly the Most Eminent Lords Cardinals refused to even look through Galileo's telescope to see if what Galileo said was correct. Galileo's first simple telescopes made in 1609 and 1610 were of wood, leather and some copper to form the tube with the lenses at the ends of the 98 and 136 cm [38.5 and 53.5 inch] scopes. They were able to magnify 20 to 30 times. Looking at these telescopes of Galileo, on display in the Istituto e Museo Storia Della Scienza in Florence, it is amazing that something so simple as these elementary devices were able to open the heavens to mankind's observations, but they were unable to open the minds of those steeped in dogma and tradition.

However, while the original condemnation of Galileo was inexcusable, what is more amazing, and a faux pas on a grander scale is that it took the church from 1633 until 1992 to officially recognize that Galileo was right about God's creation! Scientists and engineers knew enough about celestial mechanics to have Armstrong's Eagle land on the moon and take pictures documenting the Earth's diurnal motion nearly fifteen years before the church absolved Galileo of his "false doctrine," his scientific absurdity "expressly contrary to the Holy Scriptures" that the Earth orbits the Sun with a diurnal motion.

While the official admission of error was a tad late in coming, John Paul II was more than kind to his predecessors in his understatement "... Galileo, a sincere believer, showed himself to be more perceptive in this regard [scientific and Biblical truths] than the theologians who opposed him."[66] No bold mention of "His Holiness and the Most Eminent Lords Cardinals" as there was in the official papal condemnation. And it only took the church about 360 years to come clean. Not bad. So, how are they doing today with scientific evidence, the Biblical record and the law established by the Creator concerning the beginning of life? What's Latin for "Déjà vu?"

We see that the Biblical record is in perfect agreement with science or vice versa depending on your point of view. It is crystal clear that life begins at birth or first breath. Ironically, at the October 1992 meeting of the Pontifical Academy of Science when Pope John Paul II "exonerated" Galileo for being correct, he made the following statement, "The underlying problems of this case concern both the nature of science and the message of faith. One day we may find ourselves in a similar situation, which will require both sides to have an informed awareness of the field and of the limits of their own competencies."[67] The underlying nature of science and faith is the same. It is the nature of God as the author of both.

John Paul's "one day we may find ourselves in a similar situation" may have arrived. For Pope Benedict XVI made what appears to have been an unwittingly profound comment in an address to the Pontificia Universita Lateranense posted on the Vatican website in early February 2007, in a reference to life beginning at conception, "No law made by man can overturn that of the Creator without dramatically affecting society in its very foundation." Clearly the Creator made Adam's, and all of our lives since, begin with a breath at birth. Thus, according to the pope, any man made law opposing this truth, life beginning at birth, will dramatically affect society. And of course, these laws of the church have done just that. What does the Catholic Church do now that those opposing this truth, of life beginning at birth as made by the Creator, certainly have affected society in dramatically divisive ways? Pope Benedict's comment underscores the error of the life beginning at conception hypothesis.

Abortion, regardless of the strident ethical and moral issues associated with it, cannot be labeled murder based on theological truth. Abortion is a foundationally divisive issue in societies. People who are anti-abortion have bombed clinics. They still attempt this. Doctors have been murdered by those claiming to oppose murder. Placards decrying that "Abortion Is Homicide" are paraded at anti-abortion demonstrations. Most of this is done in the name of God according to those who misguidedly believe life begins at conception. Pregnancy begins at conception. Life begins at birth. Both scientific and Biblical truths bear this out.

The question we need to ask is how open-minded are we to new understandings that challenge our accepted set of beliefs? Are we willing to consider new concepts that challenge tradition like the fact that the Earth does indeed revolve around the Sun? Are we willing to accept scientific and theological truth or do we stubbornly, clinging to a falsehood, retreat into doctrinal caves shunning the light no different than our ancestors in the Dark Ages?

If the only thing at stake here was a difference of opinion, then so be it. If you believe abortion is wrong for any reason, refuse to have one. If you believe they are horrible and abhorrent, shun abortion. If any organization, be they religious, political or philosophical wishes to ban abortions for their membership, then so be it. And it's okay to accept that life begins at birth and still be against abortion on moral or ethical grounds. It just takes away the flawed, slam-dunk legalistic logic that abortion is murder. It isn't.

Societies may well wish to establish ethical guidelines that are tempered with understanding of the truth, reason and compassion rather than misperceptions based on fear of erroneous religious doctrine. However, by hanging on to the belief that life begins at conception, great strides forward in medical research are being held back. If we still believed the Sun orbits the Earth today, or that angels flapped their wings to push the planets in their orbits, Neil Armstrong probably wouldn't be a household name at least not for his walk on the moon.

What major medical breakthroughs are waiting to be discovered, but might not be due to ignorance of the fact that life begins at first breath and not conception? Ignorance of the fact that the Earth orbits the Sun caused people to be put to unjust deaths by others who were indeed wrong. Can we consider ourselves any more enlightened today?

Stem cell research holds promise for victims of injury and disease with major positive social and economic impacts. Which loving parent would hold back the gift of being able to walk again to their nine-year-old paraplegic daughter who was injured in an accident caused by a drunk driver? Yet, do we deny this possibility to another human being simply because we refuse to have a curiosity regarding theological and scientific truth that life begins at birth or first breath?

While there are heated arguments about stem cell research due to the destruction of the embryo or fetus, there are other viable options available for scientific research. There are organ donor programs in place. If a woman organ donor five months pregnant were killed in an automobile crash, could not the fetal stem cells be used for the betterment of society? Of course, continuing strides in medical research to develop stem cells from other cells, such as skin cells by using gene controlling proteins, or techniques such as preimplantation genetic diagnosis may make the case for the use of embryonic stem cells moot or much less of an issue.

The point here is that while abortion should not be taken cavalierly, it is not murder either. A dignified balance, respectful of individual and societal needs can be achieved, but only in an atmosphere devoid of ignorance, fear and self-righteousness. As Supreme Court Justice Antonin Scalia said, "Take the abortion issue. Whichever side wins, in the courts, the other side feels cheated. I mean, you know, there's something to be said for both sides."[68]

When theological and scientific truths are in agreement, we need to realize that God is the author of both. Rather than fear the implications of what it means that the Earth orbits the Sun, and life begins with our first breath at birth, we need to rejoice and embrace the fact that we are closer to our knowledge of the Creator. As Albert Einstein put it, "The important thing is not to stop questioning. Curiosity has its own reason for existing. One cannot help but be in awe when one contemplates the mysteries of eternity. Never lose a holy curiosity."[69]

Which path do we choose then? Do we choose the path that which leads to fearful ignorance or do we choose the one that leads us to the understanding that life, on our planet that orbits the Sun as the LORD God created it, also begins with a breath?

# Chapter Four: Creation In Six Days, But Who's Counting?

Science fiction was really big in the '50s. Cars were sprouting fins just like rocket ships. Cadillac always had the best fins I thought although Chevy gave them a run for their money with their '57 Bel-Air. While the sci-fi movies look a bit hokey by our standards today, they were really cool back then. And what made them even cooler to an eleven year old was a trip to the Planetarium. It had to be one of the coolest places for a kid to go. It was a portal to a young mind's fantasies. We didn't have game consoles back then in the "old days." I could hardly believe it the first time I was touching a real meteorite that came from outer space just like the Blob!

Another highlight at the Planetarium was the Tesla Coil demonstration. Huge spidery electric bolts of a million volts would shoot out in a bizarre and scary display of power. The loud crackling, popping sound made it even more impressive and menacing. Eventually one of the Planetarium's employees, probably the science geek from the local college, would be forced to go into the electrically veined pit to demonstrate that he wouldn't get electrocuted. That's a lot of faith in science right there. Disappointingly, the volunteer never once looked like Boris Karloff, the original 1931 movie Frankenstein monster. I used to watch in wide-eyed anticipation, as the guy in the white lab coat just like the ones they wore in the movie laboratories, would step inside with snakes of electricity darting towards him. I was certain one of these times he'd get cooked. He never did. After several trips to the Planetarium, I finally thought it would be cool to do that and brag to the kids in school. But they said it wouldn't be good PR for the place if they fried a little kid, accidentally or not.

My favorite exhibit was much more mundane to look at, but to me even more astounding. It was a big shiny brass ball weighing over 200 pounds slowly swinging on the end of a strong steel cable hung from high above in the ceiling. Attached to the underside the big brass ball was a metal pointer that skimmed just a couple inches above the floor. On the floor was a giant compass rose showing north, south, east and west as well as points in between. In a large circle on the floor were small, dark rods about the size of a piece of chalk but not quite as long. They had them set up side-by-side around the circle. Every few minutes or so, the big brass ball appeared to move just enough to knock one of them over. This was the Foucault Pendulum. Leon Foucault, the French scientist, first demonstrated it publicly in 1851 in Paris.

As a little kid, I was nearly mesmerized by the methodical swinging of that big brass ball moving ever so slightly with each swing. What was the neatest part was that the brass ball wasn't changing its angle of swing. It wasn't changing direction. What I was seeing was the entire planet Earth literally rotating beneath my feet! The whole Earth mind you! The floor of the Planetarium was moving around the arc of the pendulum's swing due to the Earth revolving on its axis. I could hardly believe it when I read the explanation. And had I stayed there all day, I could tell when the whole day had taken place because the floor of the Planetarium would have revolved back to the same place it was twenty-four hours earlier.

It was really neat that Leon and the other scientists figured out a way to show us things even though we couldn't detect them normally with our five senses. We had to use our brains too. I sort of had a newfound respect for my brain after that. What this helped me understand at such a young age was that everything was not as it appeared to be. Scientists discovered that our universe wasn't a static entity but it was growing. It was actually expanding and at the speed of light no less. But what was it expanding into? Little by little we've discovered a universe that was a lot different than what we thought it was just by looking.

We've discovered as human beings that our four dimensional, carbon based physical existence is woven into the fabric of the universe the same as galaxies, distant pulsars and black holes. This is also referred to as the space-time continuum. We have three dimensions of space...length, width and height. And we have one dimension of time. We are keenly aware of our 3-D spatial surroundings on the Newtonian level and how we interact with them in our normal everyday lives. Possibly, never before in the history of mankind have we been so acutely aware of time. Most folk's lives are governed around time. We wake up at this time. We eat breakfast and get the kids to school by that time. Arrive at the office by such and such time. We eat lunch at this time. And if we google the subject "time," it tells us it took their computers only 0.12 seconds to return just under 2.5 billion results. On and on it goes, day after day, 24/7.

Time means different things to different people in different circumstances. Time is money for business. In sports, an announcer tells us the losing team doesn't have time on its side. If we're retired, we may have time on our hands. When up against deadlines, time flies. On a long flight when we're anxious to get to where it is we're going, time may drag on, but it certainly doesn't fly.

In our modern day, we have time most of us didn't even know existed. By now, just about everyone familiar with computers knows about nanoseconds, those bunyanesque one-billionths of a second compared to picoseconds, femtoseconds as well as attoseconds, one-quintillionth of a second or $10^{-18}$ second? But even these are huge amounts of time compared to Planck Time, which is considered the smallest amount of time possible at $10^{-43}$ or $10^{-44}$ second.[70] This is the time it would take a photon traveling at the speed of light to zap across a Planck Length,[71] which is very, very, very small indeed.

While these amounts of time and space may appear insignificant to us at the Newtonian scale in which we live our normal daily lives, they are critically important as they are an integral part of the quantum fabric of the Creator's universe in which we live. In fact, it is this seeming contradiction of scale between the microscopic universe and the macroscopic universe that physicists are wrestling with in their quest for a grand unified theory that accounts for the apparently weird differences between the two, perhaps best popularized by Nobel Prize winning physicist Erwin Schrödinger's Cat thought-experiment.[72]

Thankfully, most of us don't have to deal with units of time smaller than minutes in our daily lives unless you happen to live in New York City where minutes are said to move much faster. As we're all scurrying around on the surface of planet Earth, an hour for us is the same as an hour for everyone else. This is the classical reference of time used in Newtonian physics. Alas, it is not so simple.

Until 1905, no one realized this except an office clerk who had flunked his entrance exams in physics to the local polytechnic. Let's see. What was that 26-year-old kid's name again? Oh, yeah. Einstein. Anyway, this Einstein kid managed to get his paper on special relativity published [On the Electrodynamics of Moving Bodies][73] that sort of pushed Sir Isaac Newton's concept of absolute time off the edge of the expanding universe. Even then only a few people knew time was relative and not absolute. Fewer really understood it. Gradually, the rest of us heard about time's relativity, but most probably still don't understand it much less see any significance for us in our daily lives. While we may not be aware of the significance of various aspects of time, it is important for us to understand the basic concepts of the nature of time. The nature of time is a part of creation as much as we are.

A minute will continue to pass slower and slower to a person accelerating closer and closer to the speed of light compared to an observer of a minute on Earth. If we could travel at the speed of light, then time would actually stand still. However, the minutes for the observers looking at their watches, whether on Earth or whizzing around in a spaceship, will appear to pass normally, not slower or faster for either of them.

This is what Princeton professor-to-be Einstein discovered and called his special theory of relativity. Time passes at different rates relative to where the observer is in the universe and what the observer's velocity is as well. What can take place in a "twenty-four hour" period at one location in the universe can take "billions of years" at another and vice versa. It is completely in the eye of the beholder according to the findings of Einstein.

Let's take an example. If a star in the Virgo Supercluster that contains our own Milky Way galaxy, 100 million light years from Earth [again from our perspective of the normal rate of passage for time] exploded sending its energy in the form of light waves racing out in every direction, how long would it take for us to observe its light reaching Earth? Yes, it would take 100 million "Earth" years to reach us. Obviously, no human or creature has been able to live anywhere near this long to witness this journey of light reaching Earth.

But what if you were on that star when it exploded, and you were able to travel with that light until it reached the Earth [even though you'd have to be a massless being], how much time would have passed for you? Well, no time whatsoever. Zero. Nada. None. Traveling at the speed of light, time would have stood still for you. You would have reached the Earth "in no time at all" from your point of view. "Beam me up, Scotty."

But let's say that you traveled just a tad slower than the speed of light and reached the Earth just about an hour after the light from the exploding star arrived. You traveled the 100 million "Earth" light years in an hour from your perspective. Now in terms of Earth's perspective observing your arrival, one hour of your time would equal 100 million years on Earth. Twenty-four hours of your time, therefore, would equal about 2.5 billion years in Earth time. Six of your days are about the amount of time the universe has been in existence according to earthbound scientists.

Now reverse the points of view. Six days of Earth time could equal nearly 15 billion years of time in the universe depending from whose point of view it is seen. As God was the only observer present, the Creator, who created time, could certainly measure time in this way. It is scientifically accurate that the six days of creation in Genesis, from God's point of view as the only credible observer, could have taken 15 billion years from our current Earth based perspective of time.

Some of you are probably thinking this is some kind of scientific hocus-pocus to get around God creating the universe in six literal Earth days. It's a fair concern. Therefore, let's take an example of just how time can stand still if you were traveling at the speed of light. We'll use the example of a film projector. Film projectors on Earth have 24 still frames per second rolling through them to create the illusion of motion we see in movies. The still frames move through the projector to produce real time looking motion as perceived with our eyes and brain.

Let's say you have a twin, and your twin is seated in a theater next to our film projector, which is relatively speaking, our stationary observation point. Watching the screen, it appears as though the still frames running through the projector produce images in motion through time. Individually, each frame is like a packet, or quantum, of light. Run through a projector, the film produces a smooth continuous image much like a wave. So, the nature of a film is dependent upon how we view it. This is analogous to the wave-particle duality of light we see in our universe.

What would happen if we changed our observation point of time from that of your twin sitting in the theater next to the projector to that of you moving with the film through the projector? Let's say you could travel at the unheard of "speed of film!" And the world's scientists have measured the speed of film from your planet's perspective to be 24 frames per second. And let's say the film coming out of the projector, instead of being taken up by another reel, just goes out in a line from the projector. As you are able to travel at the absurdly fast rate of the speed of film, you decide to accompany the film on its journey from your planet Alpha as it comes out of the projector. But let's say the film is pointed at a nearby planet, planet Omega. Thus, the film will leave the theater's projector next to your twin and end up on this other planet. As the first frame of the film rolls out of the projector, you are there with it traveling at the speed of film! Wow.

Traveling at the speed of film, both you and the first frame of film travel together from Alpha on the way to Omega. The frame you see remains a still photo to you. Bummer. You don't get to watch the in-flight movie! Then you arrive at Omega. When you get there, the scientists tell you they determined that this film left your planet 100 million frames ago. Maybe it was the director's cut of "Gone With the Wind." They ask you how many frames you took to get from Alpha to Omega. You reply, "Why none really. I traveled with the first frame all the way here." "No frames passed while you were on your way here?" they ask incredulously, unable to comprehend that, as they measure it, no time had passed for you. You answer them quite honestly, "No."

Which is true? Both are if you use the speed of film as your measurement of time. How can it be like that? Remember, time passes at the rate of the observer. For you, no frames had passed.

For your twin, one hundred million frames had passed through the projector the same number as counted by the relatively stationary scientists on Alpha. And if our biology of life was tied into the speed of film so that the average life expectancy was seventy-five frames, then more than 1.3 million lifetimes would have passed while time would have stood still for you being from Alpha and traveling at the speed of film. Sorry, but your twin has long since passed away while you wouldn't have aged at all. This is the nature of time as it was created.

What if you altered your travel plans from the speed of film to just a tad slower? And you decided to change course, take the intergalactic scenic Route 66 and take six of your normal days to travel from Alpha to Earth. As you arrived on Earth, scientists here would ask you how long it took you to reach them from Alpha. You could honestly reply it took you six frame days. But they tell you that's impossible! We've measured the frames with all our latest hi-tech equipment. It had to take you fifteen billion frame years to get here! Who is correct? Both. It just depends on whose time frame the passage of film frames is measured.

What we realize is that time in the universe, as created by God, is relative. The passage of time is dependent on the observer of time. This is the nature of time. Technically there are three time references mentioned in the Biblical record.[74] However, only the first two concern us here. Up until the creation on day six in Genesis, who was the observer of time according to the Biblical record? The time frame or observer status is that of our Creator's. Once man is created, and the primary creation is completed, the measurement of time switches. Man becomes the observer of the passage of time. It is quite clear in the Biblical record.

This is just the same as you being the time-traveler in the example above. As you traveled massless through space at the speed of light, time references, vis-à-vis the Earth, were on a completely different scale. But as soon as you reached the Earth and set foot here, your time clock would change to Earth time. Time here would pass at the same rate for you as for all of us living on Earth. Suddenly, your six-day trip would have become a fifteen billion year odyssey. Welcome to Earth, Dorian Gray.

Time is relative for us humans in this physical universe. God is light.[75] At the speed of light, time stands still or, in essence, ceases to exist. Time does not apply to God. It is a dimension of our physical universe. Our universe is a space-time continuum. That is space and time are connected to each other and don't exist separately. God created and connected space with time.

Einstein and other scientists have discovered the space-time continuum within the past one hundred years. Perhaps startlingly, the space-time continuum was mentioned in the Biblical record about 3000 years ago. While this may seem a bit astounding, let's read what the Biblical record states, "That which has been is now; and that which is to be has already been; and God requires that which is past."[76]

The Biblical record is discussing an aspect of the nature of time as created by God. We are told that which has been, the past, is now or the present. And that which is to be, the future, has already been or is the past. This is saying, the past is the present and the future is the past. The past, present and future are all one when it comes to the nature of time as God created it. What this verse in the Biblical record is describing is a singularity. It

## Creation In Six Days, But Who's Counting? 141

is the same point made by Stephen Hawking, the Cambridge University cosmologist, when he says, "The beginning of real time, would have been a singularity....."[77]

Time at the quantum level remains a singularity. That is, the past, the present and the future exist simultaneously as do our three dimensions of space in our everyday macroscopic world. In quantum theory, we can move in any direction in 3-D time, just as we can move in our 3-D space. There are no psychological or other arrows of time to restrict us. How can it be like that? We don't know. But this is the way it works as God created it. At our level of experience in daily life, time appears in a linear fashion going in a direction from the past to that we call the future. In other words, tomorrow never gets here.

The concept of time being a singularity is a relatively new scientific discovery of an aspect of the universe as created by God and written down in the Biblical record three millennia ago. It may be a bit difficult to understand how the fundamental nature of time is that the past, present and future all exist at once on the quantum level, but this is the basic fabric construction of our universe. Space and time are interwoven. At the beginning of universe, at the last instant just preceding the Big Bang, time was a singularity.

Think of a balloon that isn't inflated. You take a felt tip marking pen and put a dot on it. The dot represents time as a singularity. Now stretch the balloon out to one side. What happens to the dot? It stretches to become a line. Time as we experience it at the macroscopic level in our universe is like that dot stretched on the balloon. Time is linear. It goes in one direction for us. In our case, time moves in the direction of the expansion of the universe just like the dot moves to become a line in the direction of the stretching balloon. We aren't told why it's this way; just that this is the way it was created. It has created a reality unique to our experience of physical life in the universe.

If time, the past, the present and the future are a singularity, why is it we can only remember the past and not the future? Again, how can it be like that? That's the way our universe was created. Or as we read in Ecclesiastes, "God requires that which is past." The word requires here is baqash [baw-kash'] a primitive root meaning to search out but can also be translated as requires. The word past is radaph [raw-daf'] a primitive root meaning to run after, figuratively, of time gone by. So the Creator, by implication, "requires" us to run after and search out the past, but we aren't allowed to do the same with the future even though, according to the laws of quantum physics, time is equally accessible in both directions. Maybe it's another way to tell us we should learn from the past.[78]

Richard Feynman, the Nobel Prize winning physicist, said in regards to only knowing the past while attempting to understand time as a singularity, "It may prove useful in physics to consider events in all of time at once, and to imagine that we at each instant are only aware of those that lie behind us."[79] This is not unlike watching a movie for the first time. While the entire movie is a singularity, that is, it's on a single disk, our dot, yet at each instant of the movie we are only aware of the events in the movie that we have already seen or that lie behind us. The movie, by comparison as it exists on the disk, is in its microscopic state. We can move from any point on the disk into the movie's future or into the movie's past with equal ease using our remote control. When we watch it on a screen, it expands into its macroscopic state. In both cases it is bound by the speed of light. The entire movie may be burned onto the single disk within seconds, yet it may take us two hours to watch it relative to our "normal" frame of time. So how long is the movie, two hours or just a few seconds? It depends on the observer. If we could watch the movie there in the disk in its microscopic state, then we'd have to answer in seconds not hours. In our normal experience here with time, we'd have to answer two hours.

When we look at time's relativity and it being a singularity, Einstein, Feynman, Hawking and our Biblical non-physicist 3000 years ago have reached the same conclusion about the construction of our universe, but from two different, though, complementary routes.

Now what gets a bit more interesting is the Hebrew word used for the "past is the present," "the future is the past" is kbar [keb-awr'] and can be defined as an extent of time. It is derived from the primitive root Hebrew word, as found in easily accessible Hebrew lexicons, kabar [kaw-bar']. Kabar means to bind together; or to be great, to be long and continual or length of space, continuance of time. Hmmm, does this sound anything like our English phrase space-time continuum? Bind together an extent of time. Bind it with what? Time and space are bound together!? How can it be that in the pages of the Biblical record we find the concept of the space-time continuum and that time is a singularity written thousands of Earth years ago when physicists have only recently discovered these same principles? Hmmm, just maybe, God did create the universe. But just maybe it wasn't created the way we thought it was. He created the Earth. It just isn't flat. God created time. It just isn't absolute.

We can explore the universe through the eyes of orbital telescopes or through experimentation, but physical beings have a boundary that we can't get past. That boundary is the speed of light. The speed of light, and apparently the speed of gravity, is 299,792,458 meters per second in a vacuum [in a laboratory or in space] as measured on Earth. Space and time contract as they get closer to this speed. To attain the speed of light, mass increases in such a way that it would require an infinite amount of energy. It just won't happen. The speed of light is an absolute, even though physicists are searching for possible exceptions. While the speed of light is a boundary for our physical universe, it has no hold over the non-physical or matters of the spirit. The potential for a full understanding of life, therefore, comes not from the flesh in our four dimensional universe, but rather from mankind's fifth dimension, the spirit. Until we focus on the spiritual, our understanding of life remains incomplete.

Let's read two rather interesting quotes. "In our endeavor to understand reality we are somewhat like a man trying to understand the mechanism of a closed watch. He sees the face and the moving hands, even hears its ticking, but he has no way of opening the case. If he is ingenious he may form some picture of a mechanism which could be responsible for all the things he observes, but he may never be quite sure his picture is the only one which could explain his observations. He will never be able to compare his picture with the real mechanism and he cannot even imagine the possibility of the meaning of such a comparison."[80]

And secondly, "He has made everything beautiful in his time: also he has set the world in their heart, so that no man can find out the work that God makes from the beginning to the end."[81]

The two quotes make the same point. The second quote is from the Biblical record in the Book of Ecclesiastes. The first quote is from Albert Einstein. In other words, man will never be able to discover through observation, or the scientific method, the ultimate mystery of our universe and our life in it. We have to be told. And the Biblical record contains one of the keys to understanding. By using our brains and combining the knowledge we can glean from scientific observation coupled with an understanding of the non-physical or spiritual, we have the opportunity to have a fuller and more complete understanding of the world around us.

What makes the points in the above quotes all the more fascinating is the meaning of the Hebrew word translated into English as world in the Ecclesiastes verse. The word in Hebrew is 'owlam. It means concealed, i.e., the vanishing point, generally time out of mind, past or future.

The world is a vanishing point of time, both past and future. That vanishing point is our boundary of our expanding physical universe, the speed of light. We can't open Einstein's watch nor can we peek past the vanishing point of time in the universe. Knowledge of what's on the "other side" of our expanding universe, or what was on the other side prior to its inception, is concealed from mankind at least by direct physical observation. Scientists will never be able to "stare God in the face" as it were. They can, however, certainly know his work.

God has set the vanishing point of time [singularity] in man's heart [feelings, will, intellect] so that no man can find out the work that God makes from the beginning to the end. Physicists have shown that we can't know what takes place on the other side of time's vanishing point prior to the Big Bang or into our future. The universe, the space-time continuum had a beginning and will have an end according to the author of Ecclesiastes. Thus, neither space nor time is absolute, but it's relative to the observer and his or her motion through the fabric of our four-dimensional space-time continuum that is our God created universe.

You might ask, "Okay, time is relative, yada, yada, yada, but the Biblical record in Genesis one states that creation took place over six days. Verse five states very plainly, 'And the evening and morning were the first day.'" There are six of these virtually identical phrases in Genesis describing creation. We don't need to know about the ends of space and time, just a twenty-four hour period, an evening and a morning. And you are absolutely correct. But the big picture helps us to properly understand the details. The details in this case are that there is an evening and there is a morning, then Genesis says it was the first day. Did creation take place in six days or not? According to one popular evangelical organization, Answers In Genesis, it "stands firmly on the authority of Scripture, which entails that Creation occurred in six normal-length days about 6000 years ago." But is this what the Biblical record in Genesis is literally saying? Well, let's examine it because like the example of the Foucault pendulum, we need to use our brains because we can't always see everything with just our eyes.

First let's consider what constitutes an evening and a morning that makes up a "normal-length day" on Earth. Evening is the time just after sunset, or dusk and turns into nighttime when it is dark. Morning is the time just after dawn and sunrise and turns into daytime when it is light. This was the way the Hebrews and early man kept track of the days. When the sun set, one day ended and the other began. You could see the sunset from any vantage point on Earth. You didn't need an atomic timepiece to determine when the clock struck twelve at midnight to know the day was ended. The point here is that the events describe a nychthemeron, that is, a night followed by the daylight of a twenty-four hour day. If you agree that this is correct understanding of the Genesis phrasing "And the evening and morning were the first day," then we have a conundrum.

What is a normal-length day? Simply, a day is the time it normally takes our planet to make one full rotation on its axis in relation to the Sun in our solar system.[82] Seen from Earth, this would constitute "the evening and the morning were the first day." Remember, though, time is relative. On Venus, where the day is actually longer than the year [one rotation on it axis in relation to the Sun versus one orbit around the Sun], creation of the universe in "six days" there would translate to 1458 Earth days. Looking at it from the opposite point of view, the events of creation of the universe in six normal-length Earth days would have taken just over thirty-five normal minutes on Venus. There is no absolute time frame for what constitutes a day, normal or otherwise, in our own solar system. We see that time is indeed relative depending on the location and velocity of the observer.

Another way to understand this relativity is the concept of gravity and our weight on a planet. A 150-pound person on Earth would weigh only 25 pounds on the Moon where gravity is just one sixth of what it is here on Earth. A "normal" six-pound weight, therefore, will weigh only one pound on the Moon. Gravity [weight], like light [time], both move at nearly 300,000,000 m/sec and are relative to where the observer is located. Every location in the universe has its own gravity and its own velocity. Thus every location has its own rate at which "local" time passes as Einstein noted in 1915 whether we are standing on the Moon or Venus or the Earth. If we change our gravity and our velocity, we also change our rate of the passage of time.

Even with an observer located on Earth and assuming our gravity and velocity has not changed dramatically in the past 6000 or so years, the Biblical record in Genesis chapter one would appear to have a contradiction in terms. Our normal creation that we experience every day defines a day as the time of one full rotation of the Earth on its axis in relation to the Sun as created by God. Yet, we read in Genesis that our Earth wasn't created until "day three." [Scientists estimate the age of the Earth at 4.5 billion years]. And the Sun wasn't created until "day four," along with the Moon, [Scientists estimate the age of the moon at 3.9 billion years] when "the day" was divided from the night. How can the day be divided from the night on day four when the very repetitive phrase "the evening and the morning was the … day" means this division existed from day one?! Something is not kosher here. Either there was an evening and a morning, a night and day from day one or not until day four. Which is it? From the vantage of our normal experience on Earth, day four is the correct answer in Genesis.

# Creation In Six Days, But Who's Counting?

Taking it a step further, there wasn't a man as an observer to witness any of this until sometime on "day six." Thus for all three verifiable ingredients [Earth, Sun and observer] of a normal-length day to come into play, according to the literal account in Genesis, the earliest this could have occurred would have been "day six." This is hardly a confirmation that creation took place in six normal-length days as currently viewed on Earth.

Our quantum point is that the universe being created in six literal 24-hour normal Earth days is completely contradicted by what the Biblical record in Genesis literally says. Earth wasn't created until the "third day." Where was this evening and morning taking place for day one and two when no Earth and no Sun were yet created? The validity of literally determining a day needs both the Earth and the Sun. And, from whose point of view was it being observed? Man didn't show up as an observer until the six days of creation were completed. There are no absolute time frames given. We just have the repetitive phrase "And the evening and the morning" constituted a day. We have assumed this to be twenty-four current Earth hours because that is our perspective of time now that mankind is measuring time on Earth.

There is another possibility. Moses is generally considered to have penned the book of Genesis. Is it not possible, perhaps quite plausible, that the precisely repetitive phrase, "And the evening and the morning were the ...day," was used as a marker or dividing line as an example to the Hebrews as they counted their days in this same manner? After all, the phrase does literally contradict the account of "day four" with the creation of the Sun to rule over the day and to divide the light from the darkness. Moses, then, must have had something else in mind as he certainly would have been aware of the obvious contradiction involved.

It's probable that Moses used this repetitive literary device to help separate the timelines, whatever they may have been relatively, of the six key events of creation seen from the point of view of the Creator prior to man's creation. In the Jewish Publication Society Bible the first five verses of Genesis read, "In the beginning G-d created the heaven and the earth. Now the earth was unformed and void, and darkness was upon the face of the deep; and the spirit of G-d hovered over the face of the waters. And G-d said: 'Let there be light.' And there was light. And G-d saw the light, that it was good; and G-d divided the light from the darkness. And G-d called the light Day, and the darkness He called Night. And there was evening and there was morning, one day."

There was evening and there was morning, one day. There are two possibilities with this wording. One is reference to an occurrence or event. The event in this case would be an evening and a morning taking place which is considered a day. If this is the correct understanding that this was a day, then one other point is very clear as well. As there was no Earth formed at this point, these were not Earth days. Remember, every location in the universe has its own gravity and its own velocity. The passage of time is relative. Therefore, this could not be a reference to a normal-length day on Earth. It merely references that there was an evening and a morning, thus a day. But it is a day of undetermined length. No location is given, no gravity or velocity can be determined thus we have no way of telling, from our current observation of time, how long these days were relative to our days here on Earth. Of course, some religious groups will speculate that they had to be equivalent to our normal-length days on Earth. But, no matter the reasoning, it is purely conjecture.

The other possibility with this wording is that it is a reference to location, "There was evening, there was morning." Therefore we have to ask "Where is there?" The primary definition of there is in reference to location such as in a place other than here or in that place rather than this place. The first few verses in Genesis make clear that the Earth was unformed and void. It didn't exist at this point. The only there mentioned is the face of the deep and the face of the waters. Consequently, the possibility of Moses repetitive phrasing then is that the evenings and mornings are not a reference to Earth days at all. It is extremely unlikely Moses would have used the repetitive phrase if it contradicted the events of day three and four with the creation of the Earth and Sun. It would call all of the creation account into question. But if the evening and the morning were taking place elsewhere, then it could describe the key events of the Genesis creation account without contradicting the order or length of time of events. It would also mean that the second day or the fourth day or the sixth day was from the Creator's perspective and not from the perspective of Earth time. This would explain why the repetitive wording is not used for day seven. Creation is completed and mankind, adam, has been created. The keys, if you will, to the kingdom of man have been turned over to Adam where the point of view for determining days is from Earth and not elsewhere any longer. The time calculation for days, therefore, was now here not there.

The Jewish Publication Society's Genesis account of day seven reads, "And the heaven and the earth were finished, and all the host of them. And on the seventh day G-d finished His work which He had made; and He rested on the seventh day from all His work which He had made. And G-d blessed the seventh day, and hallowed it; because that in it He rested from all His work which G-d in creating had made."

So no matter which interpretation we use, the repetitive phrase, the evening and the morning were a day, they were not days on Earth as we normally experience them. The universe is a large place. The order of creation events in Genesis start large and end with the creation of adam. There are no absolute time frames, no "normal-length days" in Genesis one. There is a sequence of events. Somewhere, near the Creator there is evening and there is morning well before the Earth and the Sun are created.

So where is there? It doesn't say exactly except it's not on Earth. How long is evening and morning? It doesn't say. How long is the interval between one day and a second day? It doesn't say. But it does tell us it couldn't have been here on Earth without the account creating a contradiction. Thus if we are to stand "firmly on the authority of Scripture," we'd have to say Creation did not occur in six normal-length days as we know them to be on Earth. These were six Creator days of unmentioned length.

Therefore, which is the most plausible explanation for the six days of creation in Genesis? Literally, that the "evening and the morning were the first day" when there was no Earth, no Sun, no place to set or rise and no earthly observer to witness it according to the account in Genesis? Or that Moses used this phrase to delineate the six different primary phases of creation as God created them in succession over "six days" from the Creator's observation of time ending with the creation of mankind?

Time is relative as God created it. Is it not possible, then, for the Creator, a massless being who is not bound by the physical laws of the universe, to have created the universe in six "Creator days?" And is it not possible that the six "Creator days" corresponds to thirteen to fifteen billion "Earth years?" Yes, of course. The location and velocity of the observer determines the rate of the passage of time. With creation completed, both God's watch and Adam's watch would be Earth-based. Time would pass at the same for both on day seven but not before.

Remember our previous example of traveling through space near the speed of light? Time on your watch for the passage of an hour or a day traveling near the speed of light would appear as normal as it did on Earth. Your watch would not appear to run any faster or slower. But the actual passage of time would be different relative to each location. This is the same example as we mentioned earlier to explain the relativity of time with you being the time-traveler. As you traveled, massless through space at just a bit slower than the speed of light, time references, vis-à-vis the Earth, were on a completely different scale. But as soon as you reached the Earth and set foot here, your time clock would change to Earth time. Time here would pass at the same rate for you as for all of us living on Earth. Suddenly, your six normal-length day trip would have become a fifteen billion year odyssey.

We have come to understand that the nature of the universe as God created it is not as simple-minded as we humans may think it is or think it may have been. We must be careful not to make

God in our own image in our attempt to understand the workings of the universe and the Biblical record. The Creator is vastly superior to mankind, who, lacking understanding, attribute our shortcomings to God. God can't exist because I've never seen Him. The Earth has to be flat because if it were round, we'd fall off. The Sun revolves around the Earth because it moves and we don't.

We can't possibly know, let alone understand the mind of the Creator. All we can do is assess the evidence left for us in our physical universe. Little by little, we have come to realize the Earth is not flat. We have come to understand the Sun doesn't revolve around the Earth. We have come to see that time is relative, not absolute, in our universe. Time's measurement is in the eye of the beholder. Six days for the Creator can be fifteen billion years for mankind. This is the nature of time as created.

We are not detached physical entities from the Earth and the space-time continuum. We, our human bodies, are part of the fabric of the universe as God created it. We are subject to the laws that govern the space-time continuum that is our universe. But we're also subject to the laws that govern the spirit of man. Perhaps the universe, including Earth is one large box just like Schrödinger's, and we are the cats. We are in a state of being both dead [unto sin] and alive [unto God],[83] but also in a simultaneous state of the physical and the spiritual through the spirit in man.

Our bodies, and the bodies of all the creatures on Earth return at death to the dust of the Earth. The Earth is part of the solar system, which is part of the Milky Way galaxy, which is part of the universe. The mass and energy that comprise our bodies were created at the instant of the Big Bang [Let there be light...] and very shortly thereafter. The mass and energy that exists in the universe today was created then. Our physical bodies on planet Earth are a result, not necessarily direct, of the cascading processes God put into motion then as demonstrated with the formation of quarks, which gave way to protons and neutrons eventually leading to the formation of elements. These include carbon and oxygen as well as all those found on our Periodic Table.[84] However, God created Adam from the patch of dirt in Eden separately from creatures. God gave mankind a different spirit.

It is our spirit, the spirit of man that sets us apart from other creatures, past and present, on Earth. Our spirit is separate from the woven texture of space-time to which our bodies are entwined. Whether or not creation took place in six days from the Creator's point of view or that it took about fifteen billion years from man's current perspective of time, really makes no difference. God created it this way. There is no contradiction that if the universe is fifteen billion years old then the Biblical record in Genesis is wrong. Both are correct. It just presents a different observer's point of view of the passage of time as God created it.

As the Apostle Paul told the Romans, "For the invisible things of him from the creation of the world [kosmos] are clearly seen, being understood by the things that are made, [even] his eternal power and Godhead; so that they are without excuse: ...Professing themselves to be wise, they became fools...."[85]

Let us not profess to be wise in limiting God's eternal power by claiming he could only do something the way we think he did. Let us not become fools by making God in our own image. Instead let us rejoice that God has given us a spirit that separates us from other creatures in our universe that we may know both the Creator and the creation.

# Chapter Five: I'd Like An Ottoman To Go With That!

I was sitting on my four-piece sectional the other day reading Stephen Hawking's book, "A Brief History of Time," and I just couldn't get completely comfortable. At first I wasn't sure what it was. As I waited for the psychological arrow of time that pointed into the future where my answer was moving towards me, eventually making it to the present, I realized my four-piece sectional was missing the defining piece, an ottoman! I immediately rushed down to the local furniture store where I had purchased the sectional, found the floor model, grabbed a salesman, pointed to the sectional and said, "I'd like an ottoman to go with that!" A few days later I was happily ensconced on my four-piece sectional with the missing fifth piece, my ottoman, comfortably in place under my feet with all ten toes free to wiggle as they please.

Now that I was comfortable, I was back to reading about Hawking's arrows of time. Arrows of time, for those of you not familiar with them, are simply those things that point out to us the asymmetry of time in our daily lives. Simply stated, it's how we can tell the past from the future. Of course this seems very obvious almost to the point it doesn't need mentioning. However, in quantum physics time works differently. How can it be that in everyday life, we can move toward the future but not back into the past while in quantum physics we know that there is no such barrier? Time can move equally in both directions. Hawking calls this "imaginary" time to distinguish it from our observation of "real" time that we experience in our macroscopic existence. There are many arrows of time labeled by scientists including:

thermodynamic, cosmological, psychological, kaon, subjective, memory, electromagnetic, quantum, black hole, entropy, radiative, casual, weak, etc. For our purposes, however, we'll keep it relatively simple.

As we read in Chapter Four, it wasn't but a hundred years ago or so that man thought of time as being absolute. A minute was a minute, an hour an hour and so on. We've discovered that time's passage is in the eyes of the beholder according to Einstein's special theory of relativity. That is, a clock on Earth will tick, second by second as we see it, and will appear normal to us in every way. Yet, it will move much faster relative to a person rocketing through space closer to the speed of light than the speed at which we are moving on Earth. The clock in the spaceship will appear normal to the person riding along with it. A minute will be a minute and an hour an hour, a day a day. Time will appear to pass no differently for that person than it did before blasting off from Earth. We know that time here is recorded more quickly than in the spaceship traveling closer to the speed of light. Thus we have the story of the two twins, one in the spaceship, the other remaining here on Earth. They will age at different rates relative to each other. The twin left on Earth after seventy years may greet his identical birth twin on his return from space to see him just half his age. Time passes at a different rate in relation to each observer. The fountain of youth has more to do with Einstein's relativity than Ponce de Leon's fabled quest for the magic elixir in Florida.

Hawking discusses three arrows of time in his book. The first, the thermodynamic arrow involves the Second Law of Thermodynamics. Essentially, this means the universe is moving from a state of higher order into a state of lesser order, or higher entropy, over time. We always move through time in one direction, forward as we perceive it in our universe. We've all probably read about the example of the fine bone china cup, or any other cup for that matter, falling off the table breaking into a thousand pieces. We've never seen, however, a thousand pieces of a cup reassemble and hop back up on the table whole once again. Time is asymmetrical in this regard. This is an arrow of time, the thermodynamic one.

Another arrow of time is the cosmological arrow. This refers to the cosmos or the universe. The universe is expanding. The direction in time in which it is expanding is the cosmological arrow of time. The arrow that concerns us here is the psychological arrow of time. This is the one that allows us to remember the past but not the future. It is a proven tenet of time. It is the way we perceive the universe through our human eyes in our macroscopic experience we call life.

The psychological arrow of time says the universe is constructed in a specific way that lets us only remember the past. This is not news as it is the way we experience time all our lives. What is news, however, is that in quantum physics there are no restrictions to moving either forward or backwards in time. The past, the present, and the future are really all one.[86] It's just that we're made a certain way in relation to our universe. We can remember the past but not the future. Time stretches out in a linear manner for us rather than being a singularity. Remember our analogy of putting a dot on a balloon from Chapter Four? Stretch the balloon side to side and the dot will appear as a line with a beginning and an end. Return the balloon to its original shape and the line will appear as a dot once again. Our day-to-day experience sees the "time dot" stretched out side to side. In quantum physics, it remains a dot, a singularity.

It's probably a good thing we can't remember the future. We'd probably be running around like crazy, at least at first, trying to avoid anything unpleasant. We couldn't of course. Just imagine that you want to get into a prestigious law school only to remember your LSAT scores will be too low. You would study and study and study, but nevertheless, your score doesn't change. Life would be very frustrating indeed.

Then again, we'd also remember the fun times to come. High school juniors would remember with whom they were going to the senior prom next year, who would win the football games, who would get the scholarships and on and on it would go. This would certainly remove the entire concept of spontaneity from our lives. Life would become a series of wonderful highs tempered by knowing about all those lows that follow. It would be like watching re-runs over and over again. This could either be very boring or absolutely terrifying. When you pause to give the idea of knowing the future some thought, it really doesn't seem appealing. So the psychological arrow of time makes us live our lives looking into a dark void called the future.

There is an exception to this immutable law of quantum physics however. I call it the theological arrow of time. In some very specific cases, we can know the future. In the Book of Daniel, written down in Aramaic,[87] there is a prophecy that mentions successive world empires over a rather long period of time that history shows us to be valid. How can that be? The future according to our current understanding of quantum mechanics is not deterministic but comprised of probabilities. If there is no way for us to know the specific location and momentum of a single particle, how would it be possible for us to know the explicit future of human history? Thus, there is no way man can determine the future according to the laws of the universe discovered thus far by physicists. The theological arrow of time says we can know the future that the Creator has shown us. The laws of this universe and the laws that govern our carbon-based life in the flesh do not bind the Creator.

Physicists have proven that it is impossible for man in this universe to discern the future. As we can know the past, we can prove, from records of the past, that the future was made known to us back then. Using historical records as our "map to the future," we can go back to the time of Daniel to look forward to know that what is history for us was the future for Daniel. And this being the case, then we know that our Creator knows the future because he brings it to pass,[88] even though mankind's inherent ability to know cannot extend into the future.

Daniel was a man, so how could he know what was going to take place over the next couple thousand years with back-to-back world empires? He couldn't and he didn't. God revealed the theological arrow of time to Daniel who then wrote it down. We can't prove by direct physical observation using the scientific method that God exists,[89] at least at this point in time. But wouldn't a "map of the future" telling us what would be taking place over the next 2000 plus years into Daniel's future be a very solid indirect scientific proof of God's existence especially if we invoke the principle of Ockham's Razor?[90] It would. And it is a quantum point of understanding.

Let's examine the theological arrow of time shown to Daniel. In the Book of Revelation, there is a statement, "five are fallen." This quote comes from the Book of Revelation, chapter seventeen, verse ten. It refers to five world empires raised up by God, and then brought down by God according to His word. You may ask what do these allegedly God induced five empires have to do with me today? "It's ancient history, man." It wasn't always history. It was the future at one time. Plus, the last of the five empires is a bit more recent than you may think. And these five have a direct bearing on the immediate future because they point us to number six. But that's the next chapter.

The five empires can be found in any history textbook that concerns itself with "Western Civilization." These five world empires are primarily described, however, in two books of the Bible, the Book of Daniel in the Old Testament and the Book of Revelation in the New Testament. There is a specific order and time frame given in which these five empires appear on the world scene and then disappear in the wind like the "chaff on the threshing room floor" never to be seen again according to the theological arrow of time in Daniel.

This is an important point. These five will not reappear in some historical reprise as many erroneously assume. Although, a sixth empire is rising with some notable common characteristics shared by the previous five empires.[91] Most current day historians indicate a reprise of the Roman Empire as the most likely scenario for empire number six. But we do get ahead of ourselves here. Let's take a look at who these five empires are and their descriptions.

These empires comprise the great image mentioned in the Book of Daniel in the Biblical record. For the present, we will examine Daniel's account for evidence of five world empires. All in all, six kingdoms or empires are mentioned in Daniel, to varying levels of detail, while three are mentioned in the Book of Revelation. As we've stated, the first five mentioned in Daniel's now historical account have already come and gone. Although the first five are fallen from the world's stage, it is important for us to realize that they were not just some empires that appeared on the world scene and later went the way of all earthly empires by disappearing into the pages of history books entombed until some eager student opens them to the light of day.

The important thing to know and understand here is that God did indeed raise each one in succession and then, at the appointed time, brought them to an end. The reason for this is that mankind needs to realize that God is still in control of events here on Earth.[92] God also established the rulers of these empires. It may be for the edification of the people or for their punishment despite any so-called "sophisticated, God doesn't exist" mentality on the part of some contemporary thinkers.

The reason why it is important for us to know this about the first five empires is that there is a sixth empire that God is raising up, before destroying, in order for mankind to again realize the validity of Daniel.[93] There are other purposes as well, but we will concern ourselves with this for the present time. Although we may harbor some doubts, it would be foolish to discount the preponderance of historical evidence and the sequence and timing of these events.

Before we begin with Daniel chapter two, it might be useful to have a world history text nearby to reference or at least access on-line for purposes of verification. Daniel's account says Nebuchadnezzar, king of Babylon, had a dream concerning an image. Daniel, who was an Israelite captive, came from the family of Judah. Daniel was called in to interpret the dream for Nebuchadnezzar. Daniel says, "But there is a God in heaven that reveals secrets, and makes known to the King Nebuchadnezzar what shall be in the latter days. [As we'll see, his dream foresaw the future to less than one hundred years ago] Your dream, and the visions of your head upon your bed are these; as for you, O king, your thoughts came into your mind upon your bed, what should come to pass hereafter: and he that reveals secrets makes known to you what shall come to pass. But as for me, this secret is not revealed to me for wisdom that I might have more than any living, but for the intent that the interpretation may be made known to the king, and that you might know the thought of your heart."[94]

Daniel was up front with Nebuchadnezzar as to the source of this vision and interpretation. Daniel wasn't looking for a following nor looking to make a bundle on a book with Oprah's book club. Besides as we know now, Daniel, as a man, would be prevented from knowing the future, as the psychological arrow of time makes clear to us. This message was from God to Nebuchadnezzar for his edification. Daniel goes on to explain the dream to the king.

"You, O king, saw, and behold a great image. This great image, whose brightness was excellent, stood before you; and the form thereof was terrible.[95] This image's head was of fine gold, his breast and his arms of silver, his belly and his thighs of brass, his legs of iron, his feet part of iron and part of clay."

"You saw until a stone was cut out without hands, which struck hard the image upon his feet that were of iron and clay, and broke them into pieces. Then was the iron, the clay, the brass, the silver, and the gold, broken into pieces together, and became like the chaff of the summer threshing floors; and the wind carried them away, that no place was found for them: and the stone that struck hard the image became a great mountain, and filled the whole Earth. This is the dream; and we will tell the interpretation thereof before the king."[96]

It should be noted that the five empires mentioned here in Daniel are the same "five are fallen" of the Book of Revelation. If one reads through the notable Christian Bible commentaries today, there is major agreement that the gold, silver, brass and iron represent four empires...the Babylonian, Persian, Greek and Roman empires.

There is no scholarly consensus however on whether or not Daniel's description mentions four or five empires. Nelson's Dictionary Articles comments on five metals, but he relates them to the four mentioned kingdoms. Matthew Henry, too, mentions four empires. Adam Clarke's commentary says there are five, but the fifth is mixed with barbaric nations and is then divided into ten kingdoms. Jamieson, Fausset and Brown's commentary mentions four metals but the fifth kingdom is that of Christ with the ten toes being part of the Roman Empire.

What this all means is that none of these highly regarded scholars knew for certain if there were only four or there were five empires.

Or if there was a fifth, where is or was it exactly? Strange that the first four empires are so clear and readily identifiable but the fifth empire is so enigmatic. Or to paraphrase Winston Churchill, this fifth empire appears to be "a riddle wrapped in a mystery inside an enigma." Why, especially as the first four are so readily discerned? Perhaps it's just as God told Daniel in chapter 12, verse nine, "Go your way, Daniel: for the words [are] closed up and sealed until the time of the end." Even though Daniel was told the future, he didn't know the future.

The question is, then, are there five empires or are there four distinctive empires and some shadowy fifth kingdom that is there but we really don't know where? It wouldn't appear that the fifth empire is Christ's for the Book of Revelation says, "five are fallen." It's hardly the case that Christ's kingdom would be considered "fallen," never to be seen again.

Plus the commentaries agree that as you go from the head of gold to the feet of iron and miry clay, we are getting baser and baser. One would hardly consider the Kingdom of God being base or basest in any case especially when compared to these other four.

Daniel continues his interpretation of the dream for King Nebuchadnezzar. "You, O king, are a king of kings: for the God of heaven has given you a kingdom, power, and strength and glory. And wheresoever the children of men dwell, the beasts of the field and the fowls of the heaven has he given into your hand, and has made you ruler over them all. You are this head of gold."

"And after you shall arise another [second] kingdom inferior to you...."

"...and another third kingdom of brass, which shall bear rule over all the earth."

"And the fourth kingdom shall be strong as iron: for as much as iron breaks in pieces and subdues all: and as iron that breaks all these, shall it break in pieces and bruise."

"And whereas you saw the feet and toes, part of potters' clay, and part of iron, the kingdom shall be divided; but there shall be in it of the strength of iron, for as much as you saw the iron mixed with miry clay. And as the toes of the feet were part of iron and part of clay, so the kingdom shall be partly strong, and partly brittle. And whereas you saw iron mixed with miry clay, they shall mingle themselves with the seed of men: but they shall not cleave one to another, even as iron is not mixed with clay."[97]

It is clear from this description that there are five separate kingdoms described by Daniel, not four as many have assumed. Some of this confusion, no doubt, is brought about by the fact that Daniel didn't use a number with the word kingdom as he did with the third kingdom, the fourth kingdom.

Nevertheless, we have five empires occurring in a specific sequence with characteristics and traits of each mentioned as well. Of course, the most important kingdom, which is not of these five, was to be established within the time frame of these five.

Daniel continued, "And in the days of these kings shall the God of heaven set up a kingdom, which shall never be destroyed: and the kingdom shall not be left to other people, but it shall break in pieces and consume all these kingdoms and it shall stand for ever."[98]

This, of course, is the Kingdom of God established by Jesus Christ in the early days of the Roman Empire. Perhaps more accurately, the death and resurrection of Christ and the gift of the Holy Spirit to those who are called and chosen and faithful established the seeds of the Kingdom of God. It was marked on that Pentecost day when Christ's apostles gathered together and received the Holy Spirit. The seedling of the sixth kingdom took root about sixty-six years before this event.

The return of Christ at his second coming will mark the end of the sixth kingdom. We should also note that both the kingdom of God and the sixth empire are established by God and are real. They are not some imaginary, fairy tale kingdoms. They are not quaint Bible stories for Sunday school. They have real meaning for us today as we'll see in Chapter Six. The kingdom of God established at Christ's first coming will never be destroyed and it will stand forever. This is important to remember when the "10 kings" and the beast of the sixth empire "makes war against the Lamb, and the Lamb shall overcome them: for he is Lord of lords, and King of kings: and they that are with him are called, and chosen, and faithful."[99] However, God will raise the sixth kingdom for His purpose and he will destroy it according to His will as He has the previous five.

Daniel continues about the first five empires, "For as much as you saw that the stone was cut out of the mountain without hands, and that it broke in pieces the iron, the brass, the clay, the silver, and the gold; the great God has made known to the king what shall come to pass hereafter: and the dream is certain, and the interpretation thereof sure."[100]

This is the heart and core of the theological arrow of time concerning the kingdoms mentioned to Nebuchadnezzar by Daniel. As we noted above, there is pretty much total agreement about the first four, but where in the world was this fifth empire if indeed there really was a fifth empire? How can you hide a world empire in plain sight? As Daniel was told, it was to remain hidden until it was time for it to be seen. Now, it's time.

Part of the misinterpretation to date is due to the word "iron" mentioned in the description of the fourth kingdom, Rome, which has legs of iron. The fact that the fifth kingdom, the feet, has some iron in them, therefore suggests to some, that this kingdom has something to do with the Roman Empire. This is especially true as Daniel chapter seven, verse seven[101] mentions the fourth beast with feet. However, Daniel chapter seven, verses one through eight are descriptive characteristics of the first four beasts and are not concerned with identifying individual parts of the total image as we have in Daniel chapter two. Plus, historically, the fourth beast, the Roman Empire, is "one-legged" for nearly a millennium after the fall of the Western Empire in 476 AD.

Let's look at the image of Daniel chapter two a bit more closely to see. Definitely there are five empires or five descriptions given. Without biblically and historically identifying this mystery fifth kingdom, speculation by scholars have pulled this fifth kingdom all over time and place like some piece of prophetic taffy.

Traditionally, the problem has been that scholars agree who are the four kingdoms. The difficulty arises when some try to take the description of the fifth and squeeze it into four or take a guess that the fifth kingdom is a version of the Roman Empire or some agglomerated, though vague phantom empire. The fifth empire, however, is not some elusive mystical apparition technically fulfilling the future from Daniel's perspective.

In fact, the fifth kingdom is quite well known and distinct. And you can read about it, and you probably have at some point in your life, in just about any encyclopedia, various history books and, of course, on the Internet. By not positively identifying this fifth empire, it has placed a major roadblock to discovering the sixth and the relevant events taking place around us today.

In Daniel chapter two, verses 32 and 33 we read, "The image's head was of fine gold, his breast and his arms of silver, his belly and his thighs of brass...." If we note that the head is separate from the arms and breast that in turn is separate from the belly and thighs, and we maintain this logic we will see five distinct entities described. "His legs of iron, his feet part of iron and part of clay." Notice there is no word "and" connecting the legs to the feet as is the case with arms and breast or belly and thighs.

Lest we think that this might be an oversight by scribes, read Daniel's inspired order in chapter two, verse 45, "...it broke in pieces the iron [that's one], the brass [that's two], the clay [not connected to the word iron, that's three], the silver [that's four] and the gold [that's five]." Also Daniel describes the fourth kingdom as having the strength of iron whereas the fifth is described as being partly strong and partly brittle. There are five empires. The question is, who is behind door number five?

"And whereas you saw the feet and the toes, part of potters' clay, and part of iron, the kingdom shall be divided; but there shall be in it the strength of iron, for as much as you saw the iron mixed with miry clay. And as the toes of the feet were part of iron and part of clay, so the kingdom shall be partly strong and partly brittle. And whereas you saw iron mixed with miry clay, they shall mingle themselves with the seed of men: but they shall not cleave [or stick] one to another, even as iron is not mixed with clay."[102]

Remember, all this was told to Nebuchadnezzar by Daniel in the second year of his reign as king of Babylon. Okay, you may think, I understand what you're saying up to this point. But where do we find this missing fifth empire?

One, we know that it is a part of this total image of world empires. Therefore the head bone is connected to the arms and breastbones. The arms and breast bones are connected the belly bone...leg bones are connected to the feet bones. You get the point. Even though they are separate, they are connected. As there is a historical connection from the Babylonians to the Persians to the Greeks to the Romans, there is a connection to the fifth empire. Common historical atlases will give us a big hint.

Also, from historical documents we know that the first four shared some common characteristics. Their underlying principles would be considered anti-Christian despite words to the contrary. Their common form of government was dictatorial. They were all militaristic in nature. Perhaps their most telling and interesting feature, which you can plainly see in any historical atlas, was that all five empires, at least during their zenith, controlled territory that included both Babylon and Jerusalem! Both these cities figure heavily in Biblical prophecy.

All we have to do to bring this phantom fifth kingdom or empire out into the light of day is to look at a historical atlas. Which empire followed Rome, was not Christian, was dictatorial and militaristic and at its zenith controlled territory that included both Babylon [or its ancient site] and Jerusalem? There is only one empire that fits this description. It is the Ottoman Empire!

The Ottomans? Wow, that's rather anti-climatic! How can we possibly rate these guys with Rome, or even with Alexander's empire? And how do we know that they are the ones God intended? These are all valid questions. So we have to ask, does the Ottoman Empire fulfill God's description...partly iron and partly clay...what about ten toes that don't stick to one another, who are they?...and how is this kingdom divided? The most important key to the entire image and theological arrow is a timing element that this fifth kingdom must fulfill. We'll save the most incredible revelation for last just like the movies.

For now, let's check the description of Daniel two. First, it should be noted that the Roman Empire had legs of iron, plural meaning at least two. The Roman Empire is commonly thought to have come to an end in 476 AD. That, however, was only one leg, the Western Empire we mentioned earlier. The other leg, the Eastern Empire, continued until the year 1453. The last emperor of the Roman Empire was Constantinus XI, 1449-1453, when Ottoman Sultan Mahomet II put an end to the Roman Empire at Constantinople where people there still referred to themselves as Roman citizens until that year.[103] Roman Emperor Constantine had officially created his new power center, the "New Rome," by

## I'd Like An Ottoman To Go With That!

330 AD in Byzantium along the Bosphorus calling the new city Constantinople. Leg bone connected to the foot bone….

Secondly, as Rome had two legs, the Ottoman's had two feet. They, too, had a Western and an Eastern empire. Their territory reached in Europe to Vienna on the west and nearly into Poland on the north, to Algiers in Africa, to the Gulf of Aden in Arabia, to the Caucasus's in Russia and to Persia and the Persian Gulf, all of which encompassed Babylon and Jerusalem.

Okay, but what's the deal with the ten toes? This has everyone confused. At this point, let's turn to an apparently objective third party who seems to have no known interest in Daniel two. This is British Lord G.J.S. Eversley who wrote an extremely thorough treatise on the history of the Ottoman Empire, "The Turkish Empire 1288-1914." Lord Eversley had his work first published in 1917. From an objective point of view, this date is important.

Lord Eversley states. "Solyman was the last of the first ten [his word] Ottoman sultans who, succeeding one another from father to son, in rather less than 300 years, raised their Empire from nothing to one of the most extended in the world." I would only beg to differ to whom he gives the credit for their unmatched rise in history's annals.

He continues, "With one exception [out of the ten, Bayezid II], they were all able generals and habitually led their armies in the field. They were all statesmen, persistent in pursuing their ambitious aims. Many of them were addicted to literary pursuits, were students of history and even had reputations as poets. In spite of all these softening traits [miry clay], there was in nearly all of them a fund of cruelty [iron]. It may be doubted whether, in the world's history, any other dynasty has produced so long a succession of [ten] men of such eminent and persistent qualities."

These ten toes have mystified historians. Yet, plainly we see ten remarkable sultans. But are they the ten toes? Let's take a look at the three key points about the fifth kingdom as mentioned in the book of Daniel. In chapter two, verse 41 Daniel says, "the kingdom shall be divided...." Just as the toes are divided from the rest of the foot, was there a division between these ten toes [the sultans Othman, Orchan, Murad, Bayezid, Mahomet, Murad II, Mahomet II, Bayezid II, Selim, Solyman] and the succession of rulers of the kingdom?

Again, Lord Eversley states in his brilliant account, "If the persistency of type and of high qualities of the first ten sultans was remarkable, no less so was the break ["the kingdom shall be divided"][104] which occurred in their successors down to the present time [1914]. One is tempted to question whether the true blood of the Ottoman race flowed in the veins of these 25 degenerates."

And though the kingdom was divided by the rule of the first ten [toes] from the next twenty-five [that comprised the feet], "there shall be in it the strength of iron." There were times in the 15th and 16th centuries that certainly looked as if the Ottoman Empire would fall to pieces. Yet, the Ottoman Empire did not fail in spite of these 25 degenerates because God said it would not fail…until its appointed time.

In verse forty-two of Daniel two, it says, "As the toes of the feet were part of iron, and part of clay, so the kingdom shall be partly strong, and partly brittle." Notice that the description of the kingdom here occurs in context with the ten toes and not the feet.

Again, let Lord Eversley make his observation about the Ottoman Empire. "On the death of Bayezid [fourth toe] in captivity, it seemed as though the Ottoman Empire was doomed to extinction. Asia Minor had passed out of its hands...the Christian populations of Bulgaria, Bosnia, Wallachia would soon reassert their independence, and the Greek Empire might be expected to recover some of its lost provinces. The Turkish Empire, however, showed a most unexpected vitality. It survived not only invasion by Timurlane, but also civil war [1403-13] by four sons of Bayezid after his death. The Empire emerged under the able rule of Mahomet as strong as ever and without the loss of a single province!" The hand of God guided this remarkable turn of events. The theological arrow of time delivered to Daniel was true despite the psychological arrow of time saying it can't be so.

All this seems like it makes sense, but what about the ten toes or ten sultans as Eversley says there are? How do we know that it's not just his opinion about these ten guys? Maybe another historian feels that 14 of these Ottoman guys were pretty good. It's certainly possible. Daniel says, in chapter two, verse 43, "They [toes] shall mingle themselves with the seed of men: but they shall not cleave [stick] one to another, even as iron is not mixed with clay." Was Daniel correct about something this detailed more than 2000 years into his future?

As we all know, each toe is anatomically separate from the next. Some could say that these sultans had many heirs to the throne [Bayezid for example had four sons]. Just maybe, one of these other sons could have taken over for their brother making eleven, or twelve or fourteen. As this was possible, wouldn't it nullify the Ottoman's from fulfilling the Daniel two prophecy? Well, yes it would. However, the word of God is true. Exactly as the theological arrow of time laid out the future to Daniel, God brought it to be. How?

All ten sultans practiced fratricide. That is, each sultan in turn killed all his brothers so that only he [his toe, if you will] alone remained to carry on the empire. This occurred toe after toe after toe after toe until the last of the ten toes, Sultan Solyman.

Then a rather remarkable thing happened. Just as God said there would be ten toes and not eleven, Solyman even killed his own sons! No legitimate heir to the throne of the first ten sultans of the Ottoman Empire remained after Solyman's death. The Y chromosome bloodline of these ten remarkable men ceased.

God said there would be ten toes and no more. There were just these ten. As Eversley remarked, one questioned whether the true blood of the Ottomans flowed in the veins of their successors because their seed line stopped at ten. How could Daniel possibly have known this?

Now we come to the most compelling aspect of the prophecy of the image of Daniel as it relates to the ending or completion of the image that Nebuchadnezzar saw in his dreams and to the scientific fact man cannot know the future. Obviously, the image would have an end because we were told that Nebuchadnezzar saw the image until it was struck upon its feet [not toes] by a stone and broke into pieces and disappeared in the wind. The fifth empire, the Ottomans would mark the end of the great image of the five empires in the vision of Nebuchadnezzar as written down in the Book of Daniel. How long were these empires in the image to exist from beginning to end?

We have our answer in an unexpected place. Time is money as we've heard on numerous occasions. In fact, a quick search on Google™ brings up more than half a billion results for "time is money." In many ways, this relationship of time and money identifies man's daily struggle. Nearly every person I've worked with when asked, "What do you want?" almost universally answered, "more time off and more money." Ask most people and they'd probably say they'd like to have more money. And folks who, at least for 99% of the world's population, appear to have more than enough money, often are time poor because they are busy tending to their source of wealth, they don't have time for much else. It's our way of life as probably it has been throughout mankind's history.

Ironically, perhaps, God has placed the definitive key to understanding this theological arrow of time within two examples in Daniel's account, one of time and the other of money. While we are all caught up using our time on Earth pursuing money in our daily lives, God is in control of what happens here on Earth. God is not dead. God is not absent from our worldly affairs. It's just that most are looking in the wrong places or aren't looking at all. So what better way to drive home a point to us than not only to tell us what five empires he raised up and brought down in succession, but also leaving two clues for us to know exactly how long these five world empires would last from head to foot. Those two clues are there for us to see. One is hidden in time, the other in money.

According to the psychological arrow of time, man can't know the future. The universe isn't made this way. How then did Daniel come up with this? Man can't look down the road to see what happens in our future. We can't prove God exists through direct observation using the scientific method. However we can know God exists and rules in the empires of man. We just need to read a little history.

Interestingly, God caused the head of gold, Nebuchadnezzar, to live in the image of a beast for seven years. "Let his heart be changed from man's, and let a beast's heart be given unto him; and let seven times pass over him…seven times shall pass over you, till you know that the Most High rules in the kingdom of men, and gives it to whomsoever He will."[105]

This is the point God is making to us today. God rules the empires of men, and He chooses to whom will go the empires on Earth. God raises up and God tears down. God controls the kingdoms or empires of men as He wills.

A time, biblically speaking, is a year. Nebuchadnezzar lived as a beast for seven times or years. The Babylonian base unit of a year is a day. The Babylonian numbering system was not a base ten as ours is today, but a base sixty.[106] Their years had 360 days in them or six times sixty.[107] Thus, seven years in days is 2520 days. As Nebuchadnezzar was a beast for seven years in type, the image in Daniel of these five empires would last for seven "times" as well so "you know that the most High rules in the kingdom of men, and gives it to whomsoever he will." According to our theological arrow of time, then, this great image of five world empires would last for 2520 years into Daniel's and Nebuchadnezzar's future.

Our second clue is found in Daniel chapter five concerning the existence of this image. This one is given to us in the form of a monetary clue. It is the well-known MENE, MENE, TEKEL, UPHARSIN prophecy given on the last night of the head of gold, the Babylonian empire.

"And this is the writing that was written, MENE, MENE, TEKEL, UPHARSIN. This is the interpretation of the thing: MENE; God has numbered the kingdom and finished it."[108]

For in that same night Belshazzar was slain, and Darius the Median, [the arms and breast of silver of the great image] the second kingdom of the great image, took the empire. The head of gold of the great image was finished. The head was just the first part of the image of five kingdoms or empires.

The key to the length of the entire great image's tenure in Daniel is contained in the units of monetary weight: mene, tekel and upharsin. Mene is fifty shekals. Tekel is one shekal, and upharsin is twenty-five shekals. Therefore, two mene are one hundred shekals, one tekal is one shekal, and one upharsin is twenty-five shekals for a total of one hundred twenty-six shekals. What's so significant about this? Well, the Babylonian base unit of monetary weight was not the shekal, but the gerah. It takes twenty gerahs to make one shekal. So the base unit gerah times the one hundred twenty-six shekels equals, you guessed it, 2520!

Both Babylonian base units of time and monetary weight give us the same exact number. It numbers this great image from the head of gold at the beginning to the feet partly of iron and partly of clay at its end. Now that's detail. There's nothing vague here. There's no mysterious missing phantom empire.

Daniel says the dream came to Nebuchadnezzar in the second year of his reign. This makes it 603/602 BCE[109] We are told 2520 years later the image would come to an end. Remember that Daniel told Nebuchadnezzar, "But there is a God in heaven that reveals secrets, and makes known to the King Nebuchadnezzar what shall be in the latter days."[110]

Recall that Daniel said the five empires of this great image lasted until Nebuchadnezzar saw a stone which struck the image upon its feet [not the toes which was the first part of the Ottoman Empire] that were of iron and clay, and broke them into pieces, and this is what shall be in the last days.[111]

Counting forward 2520 years will bring us to the end of this great image of the five world empires. The last empire is the Ottoman Empire. Counting then 2520 years forward, it brings us to …1918! This is the year WW I ended.

Remember, for 2520 years these five world empires controlled territory containing both Babylon and Jerusalem. Who controlled the territory of Jerusalem and Babylon until 1918? "The feet partly of iron and partly of clay," the Ottoman Empire!

# I'd Like An Ottoman To Go With That!

Now we were told a stone[112] would smite the image upon its feet and destroy it according to the prophecy in Daniel. So what happened to the Turkish or Ottoman Empire at the end of WW1 in 1918?

"Turkey's military strength was broken ["Stone smote the image on the feet and broke them into pieces"]. Turkey was compelled to sue for an armistice, which became effective October 31, 1918."[113] The defeated Ottoman Empire surrendered and the armistice was officially accepted on November 11, 1918. The geographical area containing both Babylon's ancient site and Jerusalem ceased to be part of the Ottoman Empire.

The Ottoman Empire, the fifth empire, came to an end exactly 2520 years after the king of Babylon, Nebuchadnezzar had his dream as foretold in the Book of Daniel in absolute violation of the psychological arrow of time thus proving the validity of the theological arrow of time.

All five empires have been swept away completely just as the chaff was blown away from the summer threshing room floor never to be seen again exactly as God said it would be in Daniel's written record! There was no Rome II or some vague phantom empire hiding mysteriously in some dusty history book. The fifth and final empire of Daniel's prophecy in chapter two very plainly was the Ottoman Empire.

The psychological arrow of time has been proven to show by leading and respected physicists that man cannot know, or remember as the case may be, the future. How do we explain, then, a man, Daniel, penning a look into the future in which five world empires are described in key detail, succeeding one to another, and then ending precisely 2520 years later as predicted? How can it be like that?

The answer is clear. "I am God-- I only-- and there is no other like me who can tell you what is going to happen. All I say will come to pass, for I do whatever I wish."[114]

Many, perhaps most people, believe that the Biblical record is an archaic, even prosaic collection of stories written by some men a long time ago whose "static scripture scribbling" is completely out of touch with the dilemmas facing modern man. Nothing could be further from the truth. Not only is the Biblical record up-to-date, it is ahead of current events found daily in newspapers or on blogs. Its examples are extremely relevant for us today in our increasingly tumultuous world, from the pages of Genesis to the events in Revelation. While they were written in the past, we can read them in the present, they are yet to take place in our future. And despite the psychological arrow of time allowing man to only know the past, God has made known to us our path into the future. And it would be well for all those who are wise to heed what we are being told.

Herein is the lesson for modern, sophisticated man. God exists. He controls the empires of men. He raises them up and he brings them down according to His will. He knows the future. Man can't know the future except as God tells us what shall happen. This is the theological arrow of time.

Next time you relax and prop up your two feet on an ottoman, look at your ten toes. Remember the empires in Daniel, remember the

Ottoman Empire's ten toes, and remember that God knows the future. He raised up and brought down five successive empires of men from Babylon, to the Persians, to Alexander's Greek empire to Rome and the Caesars down to modern times with the Ottomans over a precise period of 2520 years. Then remember the other theological arrow of time in the Book of Revelation, chapter seventeen, "Five are fallen, one is…."

# Chapter Six: The Genesis Birthright

One is.

It's just two words. Five letters.
Never have two little words held such ominous implications for our age. For they lie, today, at the heart of the Genesis Birthright.

As a kid, I would sit in a corner, just out of sight, and listen. My dad and his friend, Fred would talk about religion, including the apocalypse, whenever Fred and his wife came over to visit. After some initial howdy-dos, mom and Fred's wife would sit on the sofa in our very '50s grey and pink modern living room, in our very new '50s tract house and talk about womanly things important in the '50s. Those were the days when milk was delivered every morning to your door in glass bottles, brushes were sold door-to-door by the friendly folks from Fuller, and your insurance man always paid the family visits in person at least twice a year. Our insurance guy, I swear to this day, was Fred MacMurray. He was the dad in the 1959 Disney movie "The Shaggy Dog" and the professor in "The Absent-Minded Professor" of flubber fame. I figured he made it to the big time only after selling us insurance.

Dad and Fred, the friend not the actor, however would go sit at the dining room table lighted by a very cool '50s ceiling lamp with a conical shade that could be raised or lowered on a cable. When pulled closer to the table, its light gave these talks the feel of a backroom used for secret meetings. Dad and Fred would have a sociable scotch whiskey and talk religion, their unfiltered cigarette smoke wafting through the light. It was kind of a sharing between friends of what they had heard or read that was new since their last meeting. Sometimes, they would continue where they left off the time before. Sometimes they would share their take on a new radio program they'd heard.

It was fascinating for me eavesdropping on the adult conversation. I would sit on the kitchen floor on the other side of the built-in four-foot counter that divided the dining room from the kitchen. I'm sure Dad and Fred realized I was there, although I don't think they knew how interested I was in their conversations. Looking back, it was sort of weird for a kid being more interested in what the adults were talking about than watching TV. I certainly got an apprentice's education in layman's religion. They would talk for hours about all sorts of subjects. Frequently, they talked about the apocalypse. This always puzzled them. The descriptions found in the Book of Revelation were quite vivid; enough to keep me from falling asleep a few times after listening to them talk about it.

The apocalypse sounded more like science fiction half a century ago. Perhaps that what's made these evening talks so much more interesting than usual. Science fiction was big back then. This apocalypse stuff fit right in as far as I was concerned. In fact, it sounded rather incredible in a fantasy sort of way. Although I remember one time my father started to talk about events in the Book of Revelation with another friend who was Lutheran and he really got nervous. In fact, he made my dad promise to never talk about it again. That sort of shocked me that an adult would be so scared about a subject especially as he had been a Marine making beach landings in the Pacific during WW2. Fear is different for all of us I suppose.

# The Genesis Birthright

187

Now half a century later, I wonder if we aren't fearful enough in the right sort of way.

What exactly are we talking about here? One is is a specific reference to the sixth empire described in the Biblical record mostly in the Book of Revelation. The sixth empire is the initiator of the apocalypse, as it is popularly known. The Genesis Birthright is the prize sought after by those heading up this sixth empire. This chapter traces the rise of this sixth empire into the current events of our world today. Sequentially, it follows the first five about whom you just finished reading. And it is just as real as the preceding five. It's just that this empire is current events not history. However, while there is considerable discussion currently about the advent of the apocalypse, it's doubtful many know who are the players involved. There is no shortfall of guessing however. And they aren't the ones most commonly named at least according to what the Biblical record tells us. In fact, throughout recent modern history, the identity of the anti-Christ has changed to suit the times depending on who was the antagonist of the day. One can look recently to Iraq and Saddam Hussein or go back to WW2 and Mussolini not to mention other candidates in between including the person at the moment occupying the title of Pope. And there is the generic inclusion of Arabs, Jews, homosexuals, and just about any other group not in favor among evangelical Christians at the moment. While all the "anti-Christ of the day" sentiment has raged on over the millennia, the real identity, according to the Biblical record, has remained steadfast and unchanged. The events of the apocalypse were set in motion at least four thousand years ago by the very characters involved today. So any finger pointing in the direction of the candidate of the moment is merely a Chicken Little exercise. As we'll read, we are in for some big surprises.

Let's look at this sixth empire of the apocalypse. The Biblical record describes it for us, "And I stood upon the sand of the sea, and saw a beast rise up out of the sea, having seven heads...."[115] Five heads have fallen and are gone. Head six is figuratively emerging out of the sea or out of a multitude of people, tongues and nations.

"And I saw one of the heads [the sixth] as it were wounded to death; and his deadly wound was healed: and all the world wondered after the beast."[116] The reason it refers to a deadly wound being healed is that the first five empires have long since fallen and disappeared without a trace of them left in our modern world. While we think of ourselves as sophisticated, beyond the arcane concept of "world dominating empires" in our day and age, head number six will have all the trappings of these past empires especially the first empire, the Babylonian empire.

"And I beheld another beast [the sixth] coming up out of the earth; and he had two horns like a lamb, and he spoke as a dragon. And he exercised all the power of the first beast before him [Babylon], and caused the earth and them which dwell therein to worship the first beast, whose deadly wound was healed. And he does great wonders, so that he makes fire come down from heaven on the earth in sight of men. And deceives them that dwell on the earth by those miracles which he had power to do in the sight of the beast; saying to them that dwell on the earth, that they should make an image to the beast, which had the wound by a sword, and did live. And he had power to give life unto the image of the beast, that the image of the beast should both speak and cause that as many as would not worship the beast should be killed."

"And he causes all, both small and great, rich and poor, free and bond, to receive a mark in their right hand or in their foreheads: and that no man might buy or sell, save he that had the mark, or the name of the beast, or the number of his name. Here is wisdom. Let him that has understanding count the number of the beast: for it is the number of a man; and his number is six hundred threescore and six."[117]

This description, however, would appear to present a conflict between proven science, that man cannot know the future, and the future being laid out for us to read about. We've seen that the theological arrow of time in Daniel described five successive world empires very exactly and precisely. But these five were in our past, a part of history. Now this theological arrow of time tells us about the sixth empire, an empire expressly in our future; its subterfuge exists in our present. God raised up the first five empires and he brought them down. God is raising up this sixth empire too. It is true the universe is constructed such that mankind cannot know the future. It is proven scientific fact. Thus we are left with the inescapable conclusion: The theological arrow of time shows us it is God who has told us what shall come to pass whether or not we choose to acknowledge the source.

This is what this chapter is all about. It is a singularity. It is the past, present and the future all rolled up into one empire. Remember we read in Ecclesiastes in Chapter Four, the past is now, and the future has already been. Knowing the future, however, means knowing the past. And this is exactly where we begin our linear look at this most pertinent of singularities. This chapter is a quantum step up in our adventure. It is our final ascent to the summit.

The Da Vinci Code written by Dan Brown shook up the Christian community with supporters and detractors of the book's controversial fictitious plot. As of 2006, the Da Vinci Code had sold more than forty million copies worldwide. Plainly, this shows an interest in stories based on Biblical premises.

Our story is non-fiction. While the names have changed, no one is innocent. And it is far more intriguing and meaningful in our every day lives than any fiction. Close to a hundred million[118] copies of this story are sold every year. Because this story is scattered in the pages of the Biblical record in bits and pieces like a puzzle, we are oblivious to its film noir essence not unlike a person who is shocked to find out that their quiet next-door neighbor has a cellar full of buried bodies. We are about to put those bits and pieces together. We will form a very clear picture that is of great importance for us today. And we will discover that everything is not as it appears.

The story is the metamorphosis of brothers into families, then into nations and ultimately into one world empire, a military-corporate complex invading all of us economically, politically, and most importantly, spiritually. It is a saga worthy of a Harold Robbins novel perfectly suited for the big screen. But when the complete story is known, the saga becomes a Shakespearean tragedy from one point of view and a psycho horror drama on the other. It is a story of devastation, humility and ultimately triumph. It is a classic battle of evil versus good, self-righteousness versus blatant rebellion, determinism versus ignorance. Its climax is one of death and annihilation when victory seems assured and victory when all appears lost but at an appalling cost. And what makes this so intriguing on the one hand, and utterly terrifying on the other, is the fact that this is real. It is not a movie. It isn't Shakespearean theater. It isn't a best selling novel. It is 24/7 news. It is a front-page story and it is shouted from satellite to satellite across the Internet.

The story erupts with a struggle, thousands of years ago, while the brothers are yet unborn in their mother's womb. Let's take a look at these two brothers, who they are and follow their story, which is our story today, throughout the pages of the Biblical record from Genesis to Obadiah to Romans to Revelation and places in-between.

We begin our journey in Genesis chapter twenty-five. Isaac's wife, Rebekah, became pregnant with non-identical twins. In what was a portent of events to come, the Biblical record tells us, "...the children struggled within her."

She inquired of the LORD, that after finally conceiving, why all the ruckus inside her womb? "And the LORD said to her, 'Two nations are in your womb, and two manner of people....'"[119] We are referring, of course, to Esau and Jacob. Today, these two remain at the crux of the apocalypse events.

From the very beginning, these two struggled within Rebekah's womb. This struggle continues today, unnoticed in our current events, although these individuals have grown into nations. One nation has hidden itself within the vital framework of the other brother's inheritance ever so slowly gaining control until the opportune moment arrives to ensnare his brother who, to this point in time, has been squandering the inheritance in a rather stupid and foolish manner. Nearly everyone today descended from Jacob has no idea that they are involved in a struggle to the death. Though evidence of this deception by our brother Esau surrounds us daily, we are blinded by our own ignorance. What exactly is this birthright that the struggle to regain it and that Esau should to seek to slay his brother continues through millennia with events moving closer to their conclusion? First let's look at what led up to the loss of the birthright in the first place.

While this struggle took place in Rebekah's womb, we aren't told exactly what the nature of it was all about in Genesis. We learn what God told Rebekah. "...and two manner of people shall be separated from your bowels; and the one people shall be stronger than the other people; and the elder shall serve the younger."

This is the theological arrow of time concerning these two nations that God told Rebekah. Events in the world today are directly tied into these two brothers, these two different manner of people. One of them is stronger. The oldest one shall serve the younger until a key point is met. Once this happens, the tables will be turned. Keep in mind as you read through this and your mind wanders off occasionally about current national and world events, there are two peoples here who are of a very different nature.

Esau the firstborn is described as "the first to come out, red, all over like an hairy garment." Then "after that came his brother out, and his hand took hold on Esau's heel; and his name was called Jacob."[120]

Our story takes us to the time when Esau and Jacob are adults. Esau has become a man of the field, a cunning hunter as he's described. He is his father Isaac's favorite son because he liked to eat of Esau's venison. Jacob has grown to become a "plain" man. However the Hebrew word here is tam and means perfect, complete as a person who lacks nothing in physical strength or appearance, but also one who is sound and wholesome, who has moral integrity. Jacob was also a smooth man not being hairy like his older brother. We are told that Rebekah loved Jacob.

One day, Esau is out hunting, and obviously something has gone wrong. Esau, the cunning hunter, showed up on Jacob's doorstep close to death. Again, we aren't given many details, but it may have been that Esau was dehydrated and exhausted. It must have been somewhat serious. Whatever the case, all we know is that he thought he was about to die as he said to Jacob, "Behold, I am going to die."

Esau did not ask for medical help, but he pleaded with Jacob to feed him. Jacob had some boiled food that was red. We are told this was lentils or food that is very basic, probably what we would call ground provisions today. When Jacob saw Esau he uttered five words that lie at the bedrock of today's current events. He said to Esau, "Sell me today your birthright."

The answer given by Esau was the tipping point that set in motion the apocalyptic events occurring and about to occur in our age. Esau had two options obviously in answering the question, yes or no. But what it boiled down to, pun intended, was that Esau didn't appeal to his brother's integrity to help him. In life, we often see others through our own eyes. That is, we tend to see other people's motives as we are motivated. If we are a liar and deceitful, we tend to see others as liars rather than truthful and honest.

Whatever else went through Esau's mind, he answered Jacob that as I am about to die, "what profit shall this birthright do to me?" He didn't exactly fight for the birthright or put the ball back into Jacob's court by asking Jacob, "Would you let your brother die for some food that you would gladly give to a passing stranger!?"

Instead Esau likely had something else on his mind. That is being a perceptive hunter, it is better that you live today to fight another battle tomorrow. Getting back his health, he just wouldn't tell anyone of his deal with Jacob. Who would believe he sold his birthright for some boiled food? Certainly not his father Isaac who loved him and his venison. And Isaac was the one to pass along the birthright blessings. Esau possibly saw it as a win-win situation. Apparently, Esau was not of the same moral character as his brother Jacob.

When Jacob said to Esau, "Swear to me this day,"[121] Esau made the biggest mistake of his life. He swore to Jacob and sold his birthright. That decision, to sell the Genesis Birthright, is at the heart and core of the events of the apocalypse. Then Jacob gave bread and red boiled lentils to Esau. He ate and drank, gaining strength and his health, got up and went his way. We are told Esau despised his birthright. Seller's remorse no doubt.

Years passed and Isaac was old. His eyesight was to the point he could no longer see. He called for Esau one day. He told him to go out into the field with his bow and arrows and bring him back some venison cooked the way he liked it. He told Esau that he didn't know when he would die, but that it was time to "bless you before I die."

At this point, the Biblical record does not tell us what Esau's verbal response was to this. But he took his bow and arrows and off he went in pursuit of deer. Apparently, Esau had no intention of mentioning that small detail that he swore an oath to Jacob and sold his birthright to him. His deceitful ways follow Esau even today.

Rebekah was aware of Esau's selling of the birthright. And she heard Isaac tell Esau to go and fetch venison. So Rebekah made a decision to right this wrong. Now mothers, regardless of men's ages, always are our mothers. It was the same for Jacob. Esau was married at this point in time. Rebekah and Isaac did not approve of Esau's two wives. In fact, the Biblical record says they were a "grief of mind unto Isaac and Rebekah."[122]

Being aware of the circumstances, Rebekah was not about to let her favorite son, Jacob, lose the birthright because Esau was not dealing honestly with Isaac especially when it would go to benefit these two wives who caused them mental grief.

Yet if they went to Isaac about this, Esau, Isaac's favorite, would more than likely deny this and the blessings would go to him anyway. So Rebekah came up with a plan. Esau sold the birthright for food. Rebekah would keep the birthright with food. Rebekah said to Jacob, "Now therefore, my son, obey my voice according to that which I command you. Go now to the flock, and bring to me two good kids of the goats: and I will make them savory meat for your father, such as he loves: and you shall bring it to your father, that he may eat, and that he may bless you before his death."

Jacob thought about it and saw mom's plan had one major flaw. He and Esau were about as different as night and day. Dad might be old and blind, but not so old and blind that he couldn't tell the difference. As Jacob said, "my brother is a hairy man, and I am a smooth man." He said to mom, "Dad will touch me and know that I am not Esau. I shall be seen as a deceiver and I will bring a curse upon me rather than a blessing." Good point. But mom thought of that as well.

Rabekah was very determined and strong. She told Jacob, "Upon me be your curse, my son: only obey my voice and go and bring to me [two goats]." So Rebekah made the savory meat that Isaac loved. She also took some nice clothes in her house that belonged to Esau and put them on Jacob. Then she took the skins of the goats and put them on Jacob's hands and the smooth of his neck. Esau had to be very hairy if the skin of goats could pass for his hands and neck.

When all was set, Rebekah sent Jacob off to get the blessing and the birthright. When Jacob reached Isaac, Isaac asked who was there. Jacob said, "I am Esau your first born: …" Then Isaac asked how it was that he could have gotten the venison so quickly? Jacob answered, "Because the LORD your God brought it to me." Okay his moral integrity didn't prevent him from doing what he had to do to get what was, now, rightfully his.

Now Isaac was old, but he wasn't so sure that this was Esau. So he said to Jacob, "Come here, I pray you, that I may feel you, my son, whether you be my very son Esau or not." Isaac said the voice is Jacob's, but the hands are Esau's. But Isaac didn't discern that this was not Esau because his hands were hairy, so he blessed him. Then Isaac asked him, "Are you my very son Esau?" Jacob answered, "I am."

So they sat and ate a meal together. At the end of the meal, Isaac said to his son, come near and kiss me. So Jacob did as he was told. And when he came near to Isaac, Isaac smelled the clothes Jacob was wearing and blessed him. Isaac said, "See, the smell of my son is as the smell of a field which the LORD has blessed."

At this point Jacob received the blessing and the birthright promises sold to him by Esau. This is by no means is the end of the story. It's just the beginning. It sets in motion events that domino into our lives even as you read this ultimately resulting in the apocalypse. Soon after Jacob left Isaac, guess who shows up for dinner? Esau comes in to see his father Isaac. "Come on dad, let's go sit down and have that venison you wanted so I can receive my blessing." Isaac answered him by asking, "Who are you?" Esau, being none the wiser except he was there for the purpose of receiving the birthright blessing, said "I am your son, your firstborn, Esau."

Upon hearing this Isaac "trembled with a great trembling greatly." He was all shook up. At this moment, the sudden realization that he gave away the birthright blessings given by God to Abraham to an unknown person hit Isaac. The magnitude of the consequences was beyond comprehension. Who could have known that he was about to pass along the blessing and birthright? It could have been someone in his own household, perhaps a servant? Isaac's thoughts rocked him to his core.

Isaac said, probably faintly with near disbelief, "Who?" "Where is he that brought me the venison that I ate before you came that I have blessed him?" Isaac's blessing was irrevocable regardless of who had received it. The greatness of the blessings, those passed by God to Abraham to Isaac were not only world encompassing, but have significance for an age yet to come. Isaac was staggered that he had given them, at this point, to an unknown person. A weaker man might have died of a heart attack on the spot.

When Esau heard these words, the reality of selling the birthright crashed down on him "...he cried with a great and exceeding bitter cry, and said to his father, Bless me, me also, O my father." Isaac said, now realizing what had happened, "Your brother came with subtlety, and has taken away your blessing."[123]

Esau replied, "Is he not rightly named Jacob? For he has supplanted me these two times: he took away my birthright; and now he has taken away my blessing." In Hebrew, Jacob means supplanter.

While Esau blamed Jacob for the current turn of events, the Biblical record has a different take on Esau's reaction. "Lest there be any fornicator, or profane person, as Esau, who for one morsel of meat sold his birthright. For you know how that afterward, when he would have inherited the blessing, he was rejected: for he found no place of repentance, though he sought it carefully with tears."[124]

Esau is referred to as a profane person for having sold his birthright. "Profane person" here in Greek is bebelos meaning lawful to be trodden and ungodly. Thus it seems that Esau was considered ungodly in his action and the fact he sold the birthright meant legally the blessing was his to lose. The word fornicator is pornos as in a man who sells his body or a male prostitute. The implication is that Esau prostituted himself by selling out the birthright given by God to Abraham and then to Isaac. If he sold it for a meal, he wasn't worthy of God's blessing. Once it was gone, he had no way to repent to get it back. Except, it appears, for one statement in the blessing Isaac did give to Esau. There is, in modern day vernacular, what seems to be a loophole.

This loophole is a quantum theological point. There is what seems to be an escape clause for Esau. And it is this clause, a prophecy actually, that has kept Esau's descendants of firm and unwavering resolution for thousands of years. It is this one point that has set in motion the struggle of two brothers for a birthright and blessing given millennia ago to one brother but sought after by the other brother down to our present day. The events affecting us, as we'll see, are the result of the struggle between these two brothers. And it is the prophetic promise by Esau that was set in motion since Christ's day. As Esau said in Genesis, "I will slay my brother Jacob."

Before we go further, let's take a look at what the birthright and blessing involved that Isaac gave to Jacob. Then we'll look at what

Isaac said in blessing Esau. Isaac said to Jacob, "Therefore God give you of the dew of heaven, and the fatness of the earth, and plenty of corn and wine: Let people serve you, and nations bow down to you: be lord over your brothers, and let your mother's sons bow down to you: cursed [be] every one that curses you, and blessed be he that blesses you."[125]

Essentially, the dew of the heaven and the fatness of the earth are agricultural in nature, which should not be a surprise as land and agriculture are the fundamental basis of wealth. All life and sustenance come from the earth. So when you look at what Jacob was given, it is staggering in scope especially when you consider that the fatness of the earth is the good farmland of the whole earth as well as the mineral and oil wealth it contains. When we get to our modern day, we'll see that this is what has been Jacob's descendants birthright blessing.

In addition to this specific blessing, we have the promises given to Abraham passed on to Isaac. Perhaps the most noteworthy for our discussion is the promise that out of Abraham shall come many nations and kings. Indeed, Abraham had two sons. His first son, by his wife's Egyptian handmaid Hagar, is Ishmael, father of the Arab nations and their kings. At this time Abraham was still called Abram. Hagar conceived. Hagar despised Sarai, or Sarah, who had dealt harshly with her. So Hagar fled into the wilderness. An angel of the LORD appeared to her directing her to return to Sarai and submit to her. For the angel of the LORD said to her, "I will multiply your seed exceedingly, that it shall not be numbered for multitude... Behold, you are with child, and shall give birth to a son, and shall call his name Ishmael [God shall hear]: because the LORD has heard your affliction. And he will be a wild man; his hand will be against every man, and every man's hand shall be against him: and he shall dwell in the presence of all his brothers."[126]

Abram's son by his wife Sarai, who was barren, but became fertile by the hand of the LORD, gave birth to Isaac. Upon Abram's faith in God, willing to sacrifice his own son, God changed his name to Abraham. And of course we know about Isaac's two sons. Thus we have the three main characters in our story, all descendants of Abraham: Ishmael, Esau and Jacob. Esau became Edom, meaning red, after selling his birthright to Jacob.[127] Upon wrestling with God, and enduring even when his hip was put out of joint, Jacob was blessed and became Israel.[128]

These three are our key characters today in world events. Yet, while we may be familiar with the descendants of Ishmael and Israel, it is the descendants of Edom that, for the most part, remain unknown. The stories of all three flow though history. We will see them back in confluence later on in the chapter. But we have a couple millennia to cover first. From this point forward, we will use the names Edom and Israel in place of Esau and Jacob.

We now return to Edom and his anguish at selling off his birthright in Genesis chapter twenty-five. Desperately, Edom asked his father Isaac, "Have you not reserved a blessing for me?" Isaac tells him, "Behold I have made him your lord, and all his brothers have I given to him for servants; and with corn and wine have I sustained him: and what shall I do now to you my son?" Having given Israel the wealth of the land of the whole earth, his brothers as servants and the nations of the world would be subservient to him, there wasn't much left that really mattered.

Edom said, "Don't you have one blessing, my father? Bless me even also, O my father." Esau raised his voice and wept. Yet no amount of weeping would bring about any change in his circumstances. That was a lot to lose over some food.

But Isaac then said to Edom, "Behold, your dwelling shall be the fatness of the earth, and of the dew of heaven above; And by the sword shall you live, and you shall serve your brother; and it shall come to pass when you shall have the dominion, that you shall break his yoke off your neck."[129]

This point, this loophole drives our story. It's revenge. Edom was given a way out. While this is a blessing for Edom, it is also a prophecy that reaches its climax in the apocalypse. Where you find Israel, you will find Edom. One note here to readers. For the sake of understanding, the nation-state of modern day Israel is not the Israel of the old covenant. This will become apparent as you continue reading. However, ask yourself, is the geography of this area in the Middle East occupied by the state of Israel the "fatness of the whole earth?" Please keep this piece of the puzzle in mind. The significance of the modern nation-state Israel is Jerusalem, not any agricultural largess. It will become quite clear later on where our three key characters are. But do keep in mind, where you find Israel dwelling, there will be his brother Edom.

As we mentioned above, because Edom hated Israel, he vowed to kill his brother Israel. When Edom breaks Israel's yoke off their neck, then they will have the dominion. This is the story of the sixth empire. Edom will wrest control over the blessings given to Israel. They will have thought to gain back the birthright in the process. But it is a prophecy, one that began to be fulfilled in the days of the Roman Empire, the fourth head of the beast, less than two centuries before Christ's first coming.

In their physical lifetimes, Edom and Israel made their peace. Edom was given a land to live in. It was called Mt. Seir and the general area was referred to as Idumea located south and to the east of the Dead Sea extending down towards the Red Sea. But as these two sons families grew in size, there was some animosity as Isaac's blessing had given Israel to be lord over Edom. When Israel left Egypt after more than four hundred years living there as strangers in the land, Moses led Israel towards the land promised to them. However God made it clear they were not to pass through their brother's land in Seir.

Israel settled into the land promised by God. By 1000 BC or thereabouts, David was king of Israel. He had brought the Ark of the Covenant by this time into the city of David, which is Jerusalem. David subdued the nations around Israel including Syria, Moab, Ammon, the Philistines and those of Edom. "And he put garrisons in Edom: throughout all Edom put he garrisons, and all they of Edom became David's servants."[130]

However, it was not that Israel just defeated Edom here. Joab, David's chief of the army, remained in Edom for six months and killed every male of Edom in the land. However, Hadad, who was but a little child and son of the king of Edom, fled to Egypt with some of his father's servants. No doubt many other men of Edom fled as well.

We are told that Hadad found favor in the sight of the Pharaoh. Hadad grew up in Egypt. Pharaoh gave his wife's sister to Hadad to be his wife. They had a son who was weaned in the Pharoah's household. And the son of Edom was considered as one of Pharoah's sons. If we recall an earlier time in Egypt, Joseph, of the popular "Joseph and the Technicolor Dream Coat" and the eleventh son of Israel, took the high priest's daughter as his wife.

We read in 1 Kings chapter eleven that when Hadad heard that David had died in Israel, he requested of the Pharoah to take leave of his hospitality he had known since a child to "depart, that I may go into my own country." Meanwhile Solomon had become king over Israel after the death of David. While Israel was blessed during the reign of David as he was faithful to the word of God, the same could not be said for Solomon.

Solomon had a soft spot for women we're told in 1 Kings chapter one. And as God had blessed Israel abundantly during the reign of David and during Solomon's early years, he had access to unimaginable wealth as king. We are told that Solomon "...loved many strange women." Not that these women were freaks, but rather they were strange as in strangers or those not of Israel. They included "the daughter of Pharaoh, women of the Moabites, Ammonites, Edomites, Zidonians and Hittites, of the nations which the LORD said to the children of Israel, 'You shall not go in to them, neither shall they come in to you: surely they will turn away your heart after their gods..." However, Solomon ignored this and was joined together with these women in love as we are told.

# The Genesis Birthright

All together, Solomon had seven hundred wives and princesses plus three hundred concubines. It would be fair to say that Solomon's time was diverted into keeping 1000 women as happy as one guy, king or not, could manage. Solomon definitely had to be the inspiration for the "Make love, not war" bumper sticker. The problem with all these strange women was not of the flesh, but of the spirit, the heart. "...surely they will turn away your heart after their gods." This has been Israel's downfall for millennia. They never manage to remain faithful to God. They always stray from that narrow path that leads to life. In place of blessings, their actions choose curses. It is the same today.

In the Book of 1 Kings chapter eleven we read, "For it came to pass when Solomon was old, his wives turned away his heart after other gods: and his heart was not perfect with the LORD his God as was the heart of his father David. For Solomon went after Ashtoreth the goddess of the Zidonians and Milcom the abomination of the Ammonites." Now Ashtoreth was known as Ishtar to the Assyrians and Babylonians and as Astarte in both the Greek and Roman empires. Ishtar was the Babylonian goddess of fertility associated with such fertility symbols as colored eggs and bunny rabbits. While some claim there may not be any direct etymological link, we are more familiar with Ishtar's anglicized name of Easter. Milcom is also known as Molech. Ahaz, king of Judah, centuries later sacrificed live children of Israel in the fire to honor Molech. Little deceits and errors, uncorrected, lead to big consequences.

It is no wonder then that we are told "Solomon did evil in the sight of the LORD and went not fully after the LORD as David his father." Solomon built "an high place to Chemosh, the abomination of Moab in the hill that is before Jerusalem, and for Molech the abomination of the children of Ammon. And likewise did he for all his strange wives which burnt incense and sacrificed to their gods."

All this leads us to another quantum theological point. Solomon was king over all Israel. There were twelve sons, now tribes of Israel. It was not unlike the thirteen original colonies. As the thirteen colonies formed the nation of the United States, the twelve tribes formed the nation of Israel. The twelve are Reuben, Simeon, Levi, Judah [the Jews], Zebulon, Issachar, Dan, Gad, Asher, Naphtali, Joseph and Benjamin from whom the apostle Paul was descended.

"The LORD was angry with Solomon, because his heart was turned from the LORD God of Israel, which had appeared unto him [Solomon] twice, and had commanded him concerning this thing, that he should not go after other gods." God told Solomon that the kingdom would be taken from his hand, but only after his death for David's sake. But here is a critical point of understanding for us today. "Howbeit, I will not rend away all the kingdom: but will give one tribe to your son for David my servant's sake, which I have chosen."[131] Israel was to be divided. And we are still divided to this day.

As this is such an important point to understand, let's read it in its entirety. "And the man Jeroboam was a mighty man of valour: and Solomon seeing the young man that he was industrious, he made him ruler over all the charge of the house of Joseph. And it came to pass at that time when Jeroboam went out of Jerusalem, that the prophet Ahijah the Shilonite found him in the way; and he had clad himself with a new garment; and they two were alone in the field: And Ahijah caught the new garment that was on him, and tore it into twelve pieces: And he said to Jeroboam, Take you ten pieces: for thus says the LORD, the God of Israel, Behold, I will rend the kingdom out of the hand of Solomon, and will give ten tribes to you: [But he shall have one tribe for my servant David's sake, and for Jerusalem's sake, the city which I have chosen out of all the tribes of Israel]: Because that they have forsaken me, and have worshipped Ashtoreth the goddess of the Zidonians, Chemosh the god of the Moabites, and Milcom the god of the children of Ammon, and have not walked in my ways, to do right in mine eyes, and to keep my statutes and my judgments, as did David his father.

"Howbeit I will not take the whole kingdom out of his hand: but I will make him prince all the days of his life for David my servant's sake, whom I chose, because he kept my commandments and my statutes: But I will take the kingdom out of his son's hand, and will give it to you, even ten tribes. And unto his son will I give one tribe, that David my servant may have a light always before me in Jerusalem, the city which I have chosen me to put my name there.

"And I will take you, and you shall reign according to all that your soul desires, and shall be king over Israel. And it shall be, if you will listen unto all that I command you, and will walk in my ways, and do right in my sight, to keep my statutes and my commandments, as David my servant did; that I will be with you, and build you a sure house, as I built for David, and will give Israel unto you. And I will for this afflict the seed of David, but not forever.

"Solomon sought therefore to kill Jeroboam. And Jeroboam arose, and fled into Egypt, unto Shishak king of Egypt, and was in Egypt until the death of Solomon."[132]

The twelve tribes of Israel were divided into two nations, the House of Israel with ten tribes and the House of Judah with one tribe, Judah. You probably realize that ten plus one equals eleven not twelve. The tribe of Levi was the priesthood. They were to serve God and were not counted either as part of the Houses of Israel or Judah, but were separated to God. From the time of the death of Solomon about 930 BC until the House of Israel was divorced from God for idolatry and taken captive by the Assyrians about 732 BC, the birthright promises given to Abraham and passed on to Isaac then passed on to Jacob, who became Israel, belonged to both the House of Israel and the House of Judah.

Let's recap here for a moment to keep track of our key characters, who, by now, had grown into nations. Israel's twelve sons were divided 10:1:1. Ten tribes formed the nations of the House of Israel or Israel. One nation formed the House of Judah, or Judah, and one nation was the priesthood. Hadad came back from Egypt into his own country to become an adversary of Solomon. Edom remained a single nation. Israel's sons had been split into two nations. This is how it remained for these three until 732 BC.

During the 200 years after the Solomon's death, the House of Israel went from good to bad. Real bad. In 732 BC, the House of Israel, all ten nations were taken captive by the Assyrian king Tiglath-pileser as part of his emerging Assyrian Empire that was the precursor to the Babylonian empire. "In the days of Pekah king of Israel came Tiglath-pileser king of Assyria, and took Ijon,

# The Genesis Birthright

and Abel-beth-maachah, and Janoah, and Kedesh, and Hazor, and Gilead, and Galilee, all the land of Naphtali [where Christ began his ministry], and carried them captive to Assyria."[133] The important fact is that the House of Israel was divorced from God and ceased to be an heir according to the Genesis Birthright given to Israel. They were disinherited. And their national identity was gone.

The ten divorced nations were scattered among the strangers of the Assyrian Empire. They no longer had any claim to the birthright Isaac passed to Israel. We come to another quantum point. The Genesis Birthright, the blessings passed down by Isaac therefore remained solely with the House of Judah. Edom made a prophetic vow to slay his brother Israel and get back the birthright. Edom's task was now made much easier. With the ten nations of the House of Israel out of the way, written out of the will as it were, only the House of Judah, the Jews, stood between Edom and his prophetic desire.

Were it not for the promises given by God to Israel and David, Edom could have walked right back into the birthright. For the House of Judah was just as idolatrous, if not more so, as her sister the House of Israel. Let's take a moment to read about what the House of Judah was doing. God told the prophet Jeremiah to go stand in the gate of the LORD's house, to tell all the people of Judah that have come there to worship,

"Thus says the LORD of hosts, the God of Israel, amend your ways and your doings and I will cause you to dwell in this place. Trust you not in lying words...for if you thoroughly amend your ways and your doings, if you thoroughly execute judgment between a man and his neighbor; if you oppress not the stranger, the fatherless, and the widow, and shed not innocent blood in this place, neither walk after other gods to your hurt: then I will cause you to dwell in this place, in the land that I gave to your fathers, for ever and ever. Behold, you trust in lying words, that cannot profit. Will you steal, murder, and commit adultery, and swear falsely, [sounds like today's headlines] and burn incense to Baal, and walk after other gods whom you know not; and come and stand before me in this house, which is called by my name, saying 'We are delivered to do all these abominations? Is this house…become a den of robbers…?"

"And now because you have done all these works…but you heard not; and I called you, but you answered not; therefore will I do unto this house, which is called by my name, wherein you trust, and unto the place I gave to you and your fathers, as I have done in Shiloh. And I will cast you out of my sight, as I have cast out all your brothers, even the whole seed of Ephraim." Ephraim was a son of Joseph whose descendant, Jeroboam initially, was made king over the House of Israel as David was a descendant of Judah and made king over Israel.

God tells Jeremiah, "Therefore, don't pray for these people, neither lift up, cry nor pray for them, neither make intercession to me: for I will not hear you. Don't you see what they do in the cities of Judah and in the streets of Jerusalem? The children gather wood, and the fathers kindle the fire, and the women knead the dough, to make cakes to the queen of heaven [Ishtar], and to pour out drink offerings to other gods that they may provoke me to anger. Do they provoke me to anger says the LORD: do they not provoke themselves to the confusion of their own faces?"

"For I spoke not to your fathers, nor commanded them in the day that I brought them out of the land of Egypt, concerning burnt offerings or sacrifices: but this thing I commanded them saying, 'Obey my voice, and I will be your God, and you shall be my people: and walk you in all the ways that I have commanded you that it may be well to you. But they listened not, nor inclined their ear, but walked in the counsels and in the imagination of their evil heart and went backward and not forward. This is a nation that obeys not the voice of the LORD their God, nor receives correction: truth is perished and is cut off from their mouth."

"For the children of Judah have done evil in my sight says the LORD: they have set their abominations in the house which is called by my name to pollute it. They have built the high places of Tophet, which is in the son of the valley of Hinnom, to burn their sons and daughters in the fire. And the carcasses of this people shall be meat for the fowls of the heaven, and for beasts of the earth. Then I will cease to cause from the cities of Judah and from the streets of Jerusalem, the voice of mirth and the voice of gladness, the voice of the bridegroom and the voice of the bride: for this land shall become desolate."

"Why then is this people of Jerusalem slid back by a perpetual backsliding? They hold fast deceit, they refuse to return. I listened and heard, but they spoke not right: no man repented of his wickedness saying, 'What have I done?'"[134]

Interesting that Judah would ignorantly almost in innocence ask, "What!? What did I do?" When we get off the narrow path and the straight way, we lose sight of where we need to be. While a little matter at first seems so insignificant, it leads to the broad way of destruction as the House of Israel experienced and as we've just read with the House of Judah as well. When we practice deceit in the little matters, we are deceived in the larger matters. In this case, Judah was making human sacrifices of their children to a pagan god. But when confronted with it, they were so blind at this point that they couldn't even comprehend it, hence their asking, "What did I do?" While we like to think we are more sophisticated than our ancestors, we would never do anything like that. Then why are we so far off on the answers to those five simple questions in the Prologue?

Reality is that both the House of Israel and the House of Judah today are far off the path that leads to life. In part, the sixth empire will exist to punish all Israel, both Israel and Judah, again. We have gone backwards. Will we listen and change or will we refuse to hear? And when the time comes, will we be so stupid and foolish as to ask, "What did I do?" According to the Biblical record, unless we thoroughly amend our ways and our doings, if we thoroughly execute judgment between a man and his neighbor, if we oppress not the stranger, the fatherless, and the widow, and shed not innocent blood, neither walk after other gods to our hurt: we, too, shall suffer a terrible fate as described in the pages of Revelation. The question before us is, can we learn from the example of our fathers? The most likely answer is, no. The history of Israel and Judah is they have to learn the hard way. We do have foreheads of brass.[135]

God fulfilled his word to the House of Judah. They were taken captive by Nebuchadnezzar, the Babylonian head of gold, the first empire of Chapter Five. For seventy years they were put into slavery before being allowed to return to their land, which

# The Genesis Birthright

had been settled by others in their absence. The temple was destroyed and all that was within it. The Ark of the Covenant has not been in any temple in Jerusalem since that time. Were it not for the promises of God to Israel and David, the House of Judah would have been divorced too.

Even so, Edom rejoiced at Judah's demise no doubt thinking that their quest to regain the birthright was one step closer to being accomplished. Edom had sworn to kill his brother Israel, but from all appearances, it looked as if Israel, both the House of Israel and the House of Judah, had committed suicide.

In the day when the Babylonians came to take captive the House of Judah during the reign of king Zedikiah about 586 BC, those of Edom wanted Jerusalem utterly destroyed. "Remember O LORD, the children of Edom in the day of Jerusalem: who said, Raze it, raze it, even to the foundation thereof."[136] "You [Edom] should not have entered into the gate of my people in the day of their calamity; yes, you should not have looked on their affliction in the day of their calamity, nor have laid hands on their substance in the day of their calamity; Neither should you have stood in the crossway, to cut off those of his that did escape; neither should you have delivered up those of his that did remain in the day of distress."[137]

The history of Israel and Edom since Israel's return from captivity in Egypt has been that of animosity and bloodshed between the two, especially the House of Judah once the House of Israel was divorced and dispersed. Edom did not want to recognize the terms of the birthright and blessings given to Israel. Edom did not want to acknowledge Israel's lordship over them. In the ninth century

BC, when Jehoshaphat was king over Judah, Edom revolted and established their own kings to rule over them. Edom, we are simply told, "remembered not their brotherly covenant."[138]

Thus, by 585 BC, Edom must have thought they were finally rid of their brother Israel. They felt they were the true heirs to the birthright. We read an interesting "conversation" that Edom has with God recorded in Isaiah basically explaining to God that Edom really are the children of the birthright not Israel. God needs to reconsider Edom's situation.

In Isaiah sixty-three, it begins, "Who is this that comes from Edom with dyed garments from Bozrah?" Bozrah was a fortress city established by an early Edom king, Jobab, before the days when Israel had kings. Who is this that is "glorious in his apparel, traveling in the greatness of his strength?" We have a picture here of Edom sort of strutting his stuff. Edom is asked, "Why are your garments red like someone who treads the winefat?"

Edom boastfully answers, "I have trodden the winepress alone; and of the people there was none to help me: ...For I will tread them [Israel] in mine anger, and trample them in my fury; and their blood will be splattered upon my garments, and I will stain all my clothing. For the day of vengeance is in my heart, and the year of my redeemed [Genesis Birthright] is come." This final day and year has yet to be fulfilled for Edom, but it appears it is on the horizon. Edom still looks to regain the birthright and slay their brother Israel in the process. Remember too, Edom "shall live by the sword." The sword not only draws blood, but wealth as well. Edom's wealth is derived from the sword of war, which today exists in the form of modern technological weapons and the financial support to develop them and to wage wars.

Edom continues in an arrogant manner, "There was none to help; and I wondered that there was none to uphold: therefore my own arm brought salvation to me; and my fury upheld me. And I will tread down the people in my anger, and make them drunk in my fury, and I will bring down their strength to the earth." Edom is boasting that what they have they got on their own. God didn't help them like he did Israel. Remember when the twins were struggling within Rebekah's womb? One was said to be stronger than the other? But Edom says he will bring Israel's strength to the earth. He has passionately vowed to bring all Israel to their knees. This has been and is today the intent of Edom's quest to get Israel's yoke off their neck to gain the dominion. The sons of Israel today are playing right into Edom's hands.

Then with a somewhat sarcastic sour grapes attitude Edom continues, "I will mention the loving kindnesses of the LORD, and the praises of the LORD, according to all the LORD has bestowed on us, and the great goodness toward the house of Israel, which he has bestowed on them according to his mercies, and according to the multitude of his loving kindnesses. For he said, 'Surely they are my people, children that will not lie: so he [Christ] was their Savior.'" [This last point is addressed in John, chapter eight below] Edom makes a point that they just get "loving kindnesses" while Israel gets the multitude of loving kindnesses.

Edom continues his rant with a "remember that time when" example. "In all their affliction [Israel], he [Christ] was afflicted, and the angel of his presence saved them: in his love and in his pity he redeemed them; and he bare them, and carried them all the days of old." Edom gladly points out how they repaid this mercy. "But they rebelled, and vexed his holy Spirit: therefore he was turned to be their enemy, and he fought against them." As pointed out earlier, Israel's track record has been terrible. They continually left the narrow path that leads to life set before them by God, and fall away after lies and false gods. It is true of us today.

But even with this Edom complains, "Then he remembered the days of old, Moses, and his people saying, 'Where is he that brought them up out of the sea with the shepherd of his flock?'" This is a reference to Christ as Paul explains in chapter ten of Corinthians. Edom is somewhat exasperated. Even though Israel and Judah rebel and are punished, God is still there to help them. Edom continues ranting accusing God of doing this to make a name for himself. "As a beast goes down into the valley, the Spirit of the LORD caused him to rest: so did you lead your people, to make yourself a glorious name." Edom is accusing God that the only reason he saved Israel's derriere was to make a name for himself. This isn't exactly the Dale Carnegie School approach to making points. To say that Edom is very bitter about the turn of events is a dramatic understatement. Edom's bitterness towards Israel and fierce determination to fulfill their progenitor's vow to kill his brother Israel has grown with the centuries and millennia. It is due to reach its peak with the emergence of the sixth empire sometime in the days ahead of us. Edom's snare is closing around Israel daily.

Edom though is just getting started here with God. "Look down from heaven, and behold from the habitation of your holiness and your glory: where is your zeal and your strength, the sounding of your inward parts and of your mercies towards me? Are they restrained?" Edom is challenging God, where is this great zeal and mercies when it comes to Edom?

Edom's anger continues, but almost in a way that we'd describe today as 'sucking up,' "Doubtless you are our father, though Abraham be ignorant of us, and Israel doesn't acknowledge us; you, O LORD are our father, our redeemer; your name is from everlasting." Today, who is aware of or even knows Edom as Abraham's son?

Then Edom gets down to the real nitty-gritty. He reverses field and blames God for their predicament, and pops the question. "O LORD, why have you made us to err from your ways, and hardened our heart from your fear? Return for your servants' sake, the tribes of your inheritance."

You see God, it wasn't our fault, it was your fault. Why did you do this to us? Okay we'll let bygones be bygones, but just give us back the birthright. After all, "the people of your holiness [Israel] have possessed it just a little while: our adversaries [Israel] have trampled down your sanctuary. We are yours. You never were able to rule over them, they were not called by your name."[139]

This is true. Israel has not been a faithful servant of God. It is Israel's track record that we are not faithful, yet in our ignorance the day will come when we will ask, "What did I do?" Israel is so quick to wander off the path that God has set before us. Today is not any different. However Israel and Judah are about to find out what they did or didn't do with the advent of the sixth empire led by Edom. They will break that yoke from off their necks and gain the dominion. They still seek to slay all of Israel.

When we lose sight of the little things, we become fools for the greater deceits. Case in point, the House of Israel today does not even know they are Israel. They are not called by the name given to our father Israel. They don't understand that Christ came to save the lost sheep of the House of Israel, to redeem them. Over the past two millennia, Edom has ever so slowly pulled the wool over Israel's eyes, very much being the wolf in sheep's clothing, as we'll see.

The sixth empire actually first appeared in the days just preceding the Roman Empire before disappearing into the dunes of history's archives lying dormant until the theological winds of the arrow of time uncover its second coming. Our story of events now transition from the older historical perspective of the Old Testament [the Jewish Bible] and transform into the events chronicled in the New Testament. The first coming of Christ marks the fulcrum point of our story. It is an amazing transition that takes place although both the Houses of Israel and Judah have been unaware of its significance for two millennia, as has Edom.

Recall, we read about the five empires in the Book of Daniel in Chapter Five. Tucked away in the description of the fourth empire, there is a partial description of the sixth empire, Edom. This description is found in Daniel chapter seven. Verse seven begins the description of the Roman Empire. But in verse eight we have our first mention of the sixth empire.

Daniel is writing, "I considered the horns [a reference to Rome] and, behold, there came up among them another little horn [king or ruler], before whom there were three of the first horns plucked up by the roots: and behold, in this horn were eyes like the eyes of a man, and a mouth speaking great things."[140]

In this description of the Roman Empire, we are told another little horn, or little king arises. Next we are given a timing event. Before this little king rises up, three of the first horns or rulers of Rome were pulled out by the roots. That is, they no longer existed by this time. We are also told that this little king, or kingdom had eyes like the eyes of a man and it had a mouth speaking great things.

Who is this little horn that becomes the sixth empire and arises at this time in history? Let's look at the timing first. Who are first three horns or rulers that could be considered plucked up by the roots by the time this little horn rises up? The three horns of Rome is a reference to the first Triumvirate of Rome, an alliance of three men.

Pompey the Great became part of the first Triumvirate of Rome along with Marcus Crassus and Gaius Julius Caesar. Pompey married Caesar's daughter, Julia. This first Triumvirate officially lasted for seven years from 60 to 53 BC. Crassus was defeated in a battle in 53 BC by the Parthian general Surena. Captured, he was executed. Pompey's wife Julia died in 54 BC. The relationship between Pompey and Julius Caesar deteriorated. Six years later in 48 BC, Caesar defeated his former son-in-law in battle to take control of the Roman republic. Pompey was assassinated in Egypt in 47 BC.

Gaius Julius Caesar, the last member of Rome's first Triumvirate, held the title dictator until some senators assassinated him on the Ides of March in 44 BC. His death, for all intents and purposes, signaled the end of the Roman republic. His nephew, Augustus, later became the first Roman Emperor. This little horn emerged just after the Roman republic was "plucked up by its roots." The sixth empire will emerge at the end of another republic.

This leaves us with the question, who was that little horn or king that came up after the end of the first Triumvirate? It was Herod the Great. He was made king [a little horn compared to Augustus] of Judea, reigning in Jerusalem, by proclamation of the Roman Senate and was later affirmed in that office by Augustus Caesar, the first of the Roman emperors. The Parthians had invaded Judea about 40 BC causing Herod to flee for Rome at that point. Once in Rome, and with some political maneuvering, he was proclaimed king. Herod finally reigned as king of Judea in 37 BC, seven years after the death of Julius Caesar, when he triumphantly returned to Jerusalem after three of the first horns had been plucked up by the roots marking the end of Rome's republic.

Interestingly, Herod was an Edomite, not a Jew or descendant of Israel's son Judah. His father, Antipater, was an Edomite, but his mother, Cyprus, was the daughter of an Arab [Ishmael] sheik. His family was from Idumea the traditional land of Edom, which is south of Judea. Yet, he was now officially recognized as the king of Judea reigning in Jerusalem, the city of David. Judea was the geographic territory belonging to the House of Judah. Legally, at this point in time, the House of Judah was the only repository of the birthright blessings given by Isaac to Israel. The House of Israel had been divorced. How was it that Edom, who sold the birthright, was now in control of the House of Judah? It is a long story that takes us slightly away from the point of this chapter. You can read more about this turn of events in the two books of the Maccabees or other historical texts. Essentially, by 130 BC or so, John Hyrcanus, the Hasmonean high priest conquered Idumea. The Edomites were given two choices. Convert to Judaism and obey the "Jewish" law as given by Moses, or get out of town. Most of Edom were incorporated into the House of Judah. Thus it was that Edom came into possession of the House of Judah, and therefore the Genesis Birthright when Herod was made king just prior to Christ's first coming.

Let's stop a moment to take stock of our key characters once again. Ishmael, Abraham's son though Hagar, Sarai's handmaid, is father of the Arabs. Isaac, Abraham's son concerning the birthright, had Edom and Israel. Edom sold the birthright though vowing to kill his brother and get it back. Israel was divided into two houses, Israel and Judah. The House of Israel was divorced and no longer was eligible for the inheritance of the birthright. This left Judah as the sole legal heir now ruled over by Edom.

By the end of the first century BC, we have had some dramatic and significant changes that set the stage for Christ's first coming. The House of Judah had been legally taken over by Edom in the person of Herod, king of Judea, whose father was of Edom and his mother was of Ishmael. Edom's identity transformation was complete. By doing nothing more, they would be perceived as the House of Judah rather than Edom and heirs once again. Edom had completed a somewhat historical three-pointed symmetry. Heirs, then cast out, then heirs once again. Edom's identity had vanished, but only to the rest of the world. The House of Israel remains out of the picture concerning the birthright still being down and just about out at this point.

Now let's go back to Daniel chapter seven and pick up the prophecy later in the chapter. "And of the ten horns that were in his head [Rome], and of the other which came up, and before whom three fell; even of that horn [Edom] that had eyes and a mouth that spoke very great things, whose look was more stout than his fellows."[141] Stout here in Aramaic is rab and means great. Thus Edom's appearance and stature were greater than his companions or peers including those of Judah.

If we go to the Book of Revelation, we read about the deadly wound that was healed. This is the sixth empire. And we read an interesting description about this sixth head. "And there was given to him a mouth speaking great things and blasphemies; and power was given unto him to continue forty and two months. And he opened his mouth against God, to blaspheme his name and his tabernacle, and them that dwell in heaven."[142] We've already experienced Edom's mouth in his ranting wanting back the birthright and the tribes of the inheritance in Isaiah.

Going back to Daniel in chapter seven we pick up the story. "I beheld, and the same horn [Edom] made war with the saints and prevailed against them; until the Ancient of days [Christ's second coming] came...."[143] We go back to the sixth empire in Revelation. "Who is like unto the beast? Who is able to make war with him? And it was given to him to make war with the saints, and to overcome them: and power was given him over all kindreds, and tongues and nations."[144]

Edom came into possession of the House of Judah as Herod was king of Judea by 37 BC. We see from Daniel and Revelation that this little horn came up or had its beginnings at the time just after the end of the Roman Republic and at the beginning of the Roman Empire. And we see this same Edomite empire will be the sixth empire in Revelation. They are seen by the world as the House of Judah, Israel's brother, yet are a wolf in sheep's clothing. Judah and Edom today are mixed together in the House of Judah. This is what the parable of the tares is all about.

"The kingdom of heaven is likened to a man which sowed good seed in his field: but while men slept [given eyes of slumber] his enemy came and sowed tares among the wheat, and went his way. But when the blade was sprung up, and brought forth fruit, then appeared the tares also. So the servants of the householder came and said to him, Sir, didn't you sow good seed in your field? From where, then came the tares? He said to them, An enemy has done this. The servants said to him, Do you want us to go and gather them up? But he said, No, unless while gathering up the tares, you also root up the wheat with them. Let both grow together until the harvest: and in the time of harvest I will say to the reapers, Gather together first the tares, and bind them in bundles to burn them: but gather my wheat into my barn."[145]

In this parable the enemy is Satan and the tares are Edom. The landowner is Christ. The wheat is the House of Judah at Christ's first coming but includes both Israel and Judah at his second coming. The field is the world, kosmos or the pleasant and harmonious old covenant. The harvest is the second coming of Christ when a new covenant will be made with the House of Judah and the House of Israel. The sixth empire of Edom, Babylon the Great, will be destroyed, "utterly burned with fire."

"...and as the tares are gathered and burned in the fire; so shall it be in the end of this age."[147]

At the end of the first century BC, however, Edom appeared to be sitting in the catbird seat concerning the birthright and blessings. Yet, just when it appeared Edom had control, had broken off the yoke of Israel and gained dominion, Christ was born and everything began to change. Herod was the Edomite king of Judea, ruler over the House of Judah. Christ's lineage, as we read in the very first passage of the New Testament, traces itself back through the kings of Judah through king David through Judah through Israel through Isaac and to Abraham. Notice, of course, that Edom is completely omitted in this description. There couldn't be a stronger claim to the throne of the House of Judah than this. Therefore, there couldn't be a stronger threat to Herod's throne and Edom's regaining the birthright. Christ's first coming had profound implications for the Genesis Birthright.

Here we come to another quantum theology point. There is about to be a complete shift in the promises and Genesis Birthright. Ask a typical Christian, "What is the significance of Christ's return from Egypt at the death of Herod into the land of Israel rather than Judea?" and they won't know. They probably won't know the difference or that there is significance, much less what it means. Ask them "Why did Christ begin his ministry in Galilee?" and they won't know this either. Yet these two points are benchmarks for understanding Christianity. Without understanding them, we have an elephant described by blind men.

A tremendous upheaval takes place with Christ's first coming that greatly impacts all our key players and reverberates down to us today. Everything shifts in its focus. It's as if one team is at the goal line about to score, in a tied game, for the win. Then, it fumbles the ball, which is recovered by the other team who returns it for the winning score.

Let's start when the wise men from the east arrive seeking the young child who was the new king. They inquired in Jerusalem, asking, "Where is he that is born king of the Jews?" By now you should be clear that the true Jews are those descended from Isaac and Israel and Judah. Those descended from Judah are Jews the same as those descended from Benjamin are Benjamites. The wise men were asking for the king of Judah, and by extension Judea geographically. Keep in mind that the House of Israel is still out of the picture at this point. Therefore, seeking the king of Israel really meant seeking out the king of Judea. When Herod heard about this, "he was troubled and all Jerusalem with him." We can understand Herod's reaction. Those of Jerusalem would have various reasons for this. Prophecies of the Messiah were read in the temple. This would no doubt cause a huge buzz on the streets and in people's homes. Did this mean the end of the world was at hand? Others might have a more carnal concern. How would this affect their businesses and lifestyles if a new king were born to challenge the status quo?

The story is familiar regarding Herod's reaction. Whether or not he realized it from the birthright perspective of Edom vowing to kill his brother Jacob, Herod was not about to let his power and kingship be threatened. From reading the Prologue, we know the wise men showed up at a house when Christ was a young child, not a baby in a manger. The gifts were brought to him as the rightful heir and king to the throne of the House of Judah, at this point still the sole heir to the birthright and promises passed from Abraham to Isaac and then to Israel all of which has nothing to do with "Christmas."

When the wise men departed, the angel of the Lord appeared to Joseph. He was warned to leave for Egypt as Herod planned to kill Christ. This fulfilled a prophecy in Hosea. When Herod found out he was tricked, in his anger he ordered all the children in Bethlehem and all the borders of it killed that were "two years old and under according to the time he had diligently inquired of the wise men."[148] This fulfilled a prophecy in Jeremiah thirty-one.

After Herod's death was made known to Joseph, he was told to take the young child and his mother and "go into the land of Israel." This, of course, meant the land of the House of Israel, not into Judea or the land of the House of Judah. Joseph took the family and came to live in Nazareth. This fulfilled a prophecy in Isaiah fifty-three.

That Christ came back not into Judea but into the land of Israel is significant. For we are told, Christ was not sent but unto the lost sheep of the House of Israel, those ten nations descended from Isaac and Israel who, for their transgressions, were divorced and scattered among the strangers by the Assyrians. Christ's coming back to Israel rather than Judea marked the beginning of a tremendous change that was about to take place with the Genesis Birthright.

Before we look into the New Testament about this change, let's flip a few pages back from the first page of the New Testament back into the Old Testament Book of Zechariah. Here we find a prophecy of two staffs or rods. They are called Beauty and Bands. This is a very important prophecy to understand for it has direct bearing on what has taken place the last two millennia, or in the last days from the time of Christ's first coming until his second coming.

"And I took my staff, Beauty [Hebrew no'am, also meaning pleasantness], and cut it asunder, that I might break my covenant which I had made with all the people [all Israel]. And it was broken in that day: and so the poor of the flock that waited upon me knew that it was the word of the LORD. And I said unto them, If it is good in your eyes, give me my price; and if not, then leave. So they weighed for my price thirty pieces of silver. And the LORD said to me, 'Give it to the potter, the goodly price I was valued at [sarcastic comment obviously that the savior of Israel was found to be worth only that of a slave killed by an ox].[149] And I took the thirty pieces of silver and gave it to the potter in the house of the LORD."

"Then I cut asunder my other staff, Bands [Hebrew, chabal meaning to bind] that I might break the brotherhood between Judah and Israel."[150] While the scholarly Biblical commentaries often suggest this refers back to the dividing of all Israel into the House of Judah and the House of Israel, at the time of Solomon's death, Zechariah one of the twelve minor prophets of the Old Testament, wrote the book after the Babylonian Captivity close to 400 years after the split between the Houses of Israel and Judah. It is considered one of the three restoration books along with Haggai and Malachi. Rather, this prophecy in Zechariah is tied into the death, and subsequent resurrection of Christ.

For indeed, Christ's death broke the covenant with all Israel, the Houses of Judah and Israel, as well as their brotherhood. The bond between Judah and Israel was broken. Even today, our Bible, while really one book written to the same people, is symbolic of this break in the brotherhood of the Houses of Judah and Israel. This break, too, had great implications for Edom. This is what the apostle Paul explains in his letter to the Romans in chapters nine through eleven. And as it turns out in the end, it sets in motion events that result in a restoration of both the Houses of Israel and Judah.

Paul explains this fundamental change that took place at Christ's first coming. Christ broke or nullified the first covenant with Israel now solely residing in the House of Judah in the first century AD under the dominion of Edom and transferred the birthright and promises back to the lost House of Israel. This fundamental point has been lost on Christianity for nearly two thousand years. This is the primary purpose in Christ's first coming. And it had to happen.

Edom had legally become part of the House of Judah when John Hyrcanus conquered Edom and caused them to be circumcised. Edom was a different manner of people than were those of Judah. However, they had a legal claim to Israel's birthright inheritance under the Law as legal descendants through the House of Judah. From the time between Christ's first coming until his second coming, Christ broke the legal bond of brotherhood between Judah, including those descended from Edom, and Israel because of Edom. Yet today, there still exists an unaccountable attraction between Israelites of Israel and the Jews of Judah.

## The Genesis Birthright

Let's peruse Paul's letter to the Romans with these very critical chapters. "I say the truth in Christ, I don't lie, my conscience also bearing me witness in the Holy Spirit, that I have great heaviness and continual sorrow in my heart that I could be accursed from Christ for my brothers, my kinsmen [House of Judah] according to the flesh: who are Israelites; to whom pertains the adoption, and the glory and the covenants, and the giving of the law, and the service of God and the promises:…. "[151]

Paul here is referring to those of Judah, who indeed are Israelites, Paul's kinsmen in the flesh. Keep in mind again that Christ said he was sent but unto the lost sheep of the House of Israel, not the House of Judah. He was going to break the bonds of brotherhood between the two. Israel was divorced. Those of Judah were children of the flesh according to the adoption, as it were, by God. "And you shall say to the Pharaoh, 'Thus says the LORD, Israel is my son, my firstborn."[152] Prior to Christ's death and resurrection, legally, the House of Israel was still out of the picture. But God would not adopt Edom who had become part and parcel of Judah according to the law.

Paul realized his brothers in the flesh, those of the House of Judah, at the time he wrote this epistle, were broken off from the brotherhood with Israel. Paul was saying he was willing to be cursed if it meant Judah could be part of the redemption brought to Israel through Christ at that point in time.

Paul continues, "Not as though the word of God has not taken effect, for they are not all Israel which are of Israel: neither because they are the seed of Abraham, they are all children: but in Isaac shall your seed be called."

This is a reference to Edom at the time of Christ's first coming. Remember, Edom was legally part of the House of Judah, the sole heir to the birthright and the promises. But they really are not Israel. This is why Paul says in Isaac shall your seed be called. Isaac passed the birthright to Israel not Edom. But Judah is only one part of Israel. Ten other nations were also from Israel plus the Levitical priesthood. Edom has a claim back to Abraham. And they have a claim back to Israel through the House of Judah, Judah being one of Israel's sons, but they don't have a claim back to Isaac. Thus the birthright and the seed of God, his children are through Isaac.

As Paul explains, "That is, they which are the children of the flesh, these are not the children of God: but the children of the promise are counted for seed." In other words, even though Edom may have legally become part of the House of Judah, and they are fleshly descendants of Abraham, they are not the children of the promise, the birthright. All Israel is.

Paul continues in Romans, "For this is the word of promise. At this time will I come, and Sarah will have a son. And not only this; but when Rebecca also had conceived by one, by our father Isaac; [for the children not yet being born, neither having done any good or evil, that the purpose of God according to election might stand, not of works, but of him that calls] it was said to her, 'The elder shall serve the younger. As it is written Jacob have I loved, but Esau have I hated.'"[153]

God loved Jacob or Israel, but Esau or Edom he has hated. Therefore, the birthright and the promises will not be attained by Edom. However, legally, according to the law and the covenant,

Edom had met the requirements for inclusion into the House of Judah, and therefore to the birthright. But Paul is explaining here that it is in Isaac that the children of the promises are counted for seed or heirs. Edom doesn't qualify. As we'll see here shortly, Edom snatched defeat out of the jaws of victory yet thinking they have succeeded.

Next we'll skip over to chapter eleven of Romans to pick up our story line. "I say then, has God cast away his people? God forbid. For I also am an Israelite, of the seed of Abraham, the tribe of Benjamin." Paul explained in chapter ten of Romans that the Law was a stumbling block for Israel. Works of the flesh cannot obtain righteousness. Righteousness is attained by faith, as are the promises. Because of Israel's failure with the Law, is God throwing away his people? Obviously not. But as we read in Zechariah, he was breaking the old covenant and the bond of brotherhood between Judah and Israel. When Paul wrote to the Romans here, it was an accomplished fact. God wasn't throwing his people away because they failed rather he was changing the way they would be saved. Salvation could not be attained through the works of the flesh under the Law. It had to be of the spirit through faith. Paul is explaining then how this affects Israel and Judah.

"God has not cast away his people which he foreknew. Don't you know what the scripture says of Elijah? How he makes intercession to God against Israel, saying, Lord, they have killed your prophets, and torn down your altars: and I am left alone, and they seek my life. But what did God say in answering him? I have reserved to myself seven thousand men who have not bowed the knee to Baal. Even so then at this present time also is there a remnant according to the election of grace.

"And if by grace then it is no more of works: otherwise grace is not grace. But if it be of works, then it is no more of grace: otherwise work is no more work. What then Israel has not obtained that which he seeks for: but the election has obtained it, and the rest were blinded. [According as it is written, God has given them the spirit of slumber [parable of the tares], even eyes that they should not see, and ears that should not hear:] to this day. And David said, Let their table be made a snare, and a trap, and a stumbling block, and a recompence to them: let their eyes be darkened that they may not see, and bow down always."[154] This is another quantum theology point.

Paul is leading up to what the prophet Zechariah spoke of concerning the breaking of the staffs. The bond of brotherhood was to be broken. The House of Judah was to remain blind to the first coming of Christ and salvation through faith rather than the Law and the flesh. God gave Judah the spirit of slumber that seeing they wouldn't see and hearing they wouldn't hear. This is for their protection and salvation, as we'll read. And it is this way to this day. Christ was sent but unto the lost sheep of the House of Israel until his second coming.

Speaking of the House of Judah, Paul continues, "I say then, have they stumbled that they should fall? God forbid. But through their fall salvation has come to the Gentiles to provoke them to jealousy." As we read in the Prologue, Biblically the Gentiles are the lost sheep of the House of Israel. What Paul is telling us is there has been a switch made at Christ's death and resurrection. The former covenant is broken. The bond of brotherhood is broken. Salvation and the promises are of the spirit and faith through Christ and the House of Israel not through the flesh and the House of Judah whom Edom now controls. Edom has indeed snatched defeat from victory. They are holders of the repository of the Law. All have come short of perfection under the Law. All therefore are guilty under the Law. And the penalty is death. Only through Christ, who sits on the throne of Israel as its king, is salvation possible. In other words, if Edom wants the birthright, they have to go through Christ to get it. It is of faith not of the flesh or through physical lineage or control of the House of Judah. Christ had just changed the rules.

Those descended from Edom in the House of Judah were also called Jews. Christ made the point to them, "If you continue in my word, you are my disciples indeed: and you shall know the truth, and the truth shall set you free." Those Jews answered Christ, "We are Abraham's seed and were never in bondage to any man: how can you say, you shall be made free?"

Now concerning Israel and the House of Judah, controlled by Edom, which "Jews" would and could make a claim that they had never been in bondage? Obviously, the House of Israel was taken captive by Assyria and before that they were slaves in Egypt as were those of Judah. That leaves Edom. Even when David put garrisons in Idumea, all the males had been slain and Hadad fled for Egypt so that the king of Edom was free and not in bondage to Israel. And who was it that would chaff at the very idea of being a servant, who wouldn't want to acknowledge the terms of the blessing that Israel would be lord over him? Who is it that wouldn't want to remember their brotherly covenant? Only one fits the bill here. It's Edom.

Edom was in control of the House of Judah, but as such, Edom had placed themselves under the Law. Therefore, they will be judged of the Law. The only way to be free of the Law and its penalty would be for them to acknowledge Christ and follow him as the savior of Israel. This would be a tough pill for them to swallow, one they are not willing to take.

"Jesus answered them, Truly, truly I say to you, whosoever commits sin is the servant of sin." Now Edom did not want to acknowledge they were anyone's servants. Yet Christ told them they would forever remain servants unless they followed him. As sin is the transgression of the Law, Edom had put themselves into a no-win situation. They would break the Law. They would sin. Therefore, they would be servants to sin.

"And the servant lives not in the house forever, the Son lives there forever." In other words, the birthright goes to the son, Christ by faith through the Spirit, not the servant, Edom, through works of the Law. While Edom has furiously sought to be the son, to have the birthright, Christ just told them that even though they had gained control legally over the House of Judah, they bought the wrong real estate. In effect, that house was sold. The bond of brotherhood was broken as was the former covenant. The Genesis Birthright now goes through Christ and it is of faith, not of the Law. The Law only serves to make you a servant of sin. The end of sin is death. You want to be free of death and being a servant and be considered a son? "If the Son therefore shall make you free, you shall be free indeed. I know you are Abraham's seed, but you seek to kill me [Edom vowed to kill his brother Israel] because my word has no place in you."

A very important quantum theological point needs to be made here, The Jews, those descended from Judah in the House of Judah, did not seek to kill Christ. It was those of Edom in the House of Judah who legally could be called Jews too who sought to kill Christ. Edom vowed to kill his brother Israel. King Herod, an Edomite had tried to kill Christ. The true Jews of Judah did not. Edom and those of Judah today are still mixed together as we saw with the parable to the tares. Perhaps it should be pointed out now that the "antichristos" as it reads in Greek, meaning the adversary of the Messiah, is not an adult, Jewish [House of Judah] male. The true head of the sixth empire will definitely be a descendant of Edom.

Christ continued to tell these Edomite Jews, "I speak that which I have seen with my Father: and you do that which you have seen with your father. They answered him and said Abraham is our father. Jesus said to them, If you were Abraham's children, you would do the works of Abraham. [Abraham being the father of the faithful while Moses is the father of the Law] But now you seek to kill me, a man that has told you the truth, which I have heard of God: this Abraham didn't even do. You do the deeds of your father…Why don't you understand what I am saying? even because you cannot hear my word. You are of your father the devil. He was a murderer from the beginning [Cain, Chapter Two], and lived not in the truth, because there is no truth in him. When he speaks a lie, he speaks on his own: for he is a liar and the father of it." Remember, in the description of the sixth empire in Revelation, it is the dragon, Satan that gives his power to this beast or empire. And who is it that Christ says is Edom's father?[155]

Let's go back to Paul's narrative in Romans. "Now if the fall of them be the riches of the world, and the diminishing of them the riches of the Gentiles: how much more their fullness?"[156] First let's look at the word world here. It is kosmos. It means a harmonious and orderly arrangement. It doesn't mean people. The word for people is anthropos. The word covenant, diatheke means arrangement. It is the same word as covenant or testament as in Old Covenant or New Testament, or old arrangement or new arrangement. In Zechariah when it is said that "I will break my covenant," this is what it is referencing. Remember this staff was called Beauty or pleasantness. A beautiful, harmonious arrangement was broken. This goes to the heart and core that Christ was sent only to the lost sheep of the House of Israel at his first coming

When the often quoted verse in John three sixteen says, "For God so loved the world..." it is kosmos. It is saying for God so loved that harmonious and pleasant agreement he had with Israel. But with the House of Israel divorced leaving only the House of Judah of which Edom legally was now a part, the covenant, the arrangement had to be broken and a new one put in its place. To break an agreement, or testament, it requires the death of the testator. Christ, at his first coming, therefore came to save the lost sheep of the Hose of Israel to redeem them back into what will be a new harmonious and pleasant agreement eventually including both the Houses of Israel and Judah.[157] Christ, therefore gave his life that Israel and Judah will have a new life. Edom's killing of Christ unwittingly closed their loophole and access to the birthright in the flesh.

The reference to "the fall of them" refers to the House of Judah not all twelve nations of Israel as they were the only legal heir to the birthright at Christ's first coming. The Gentiles refers to the divorced House of Israel. So we can read the verse "Now if the fall of the House of Judah be the riches of the harmonious and pleasant arrangement [because there will be a new covenant or agreement] and the diminishing of the House of Judah is the riches of the House of Israel: how much more the House of Judah's fullness [at Christ's second coming]?" Remember, the House of Judah were given eyes that they should not see, ears that they should not hear. They are intentionally made blind to the portent of Christ's first coming for a reason as Paul is about to explain to the House of Israel.

"For I speak to you Gentiles [House of Israel], inasmuch as I am the apostle of the House of Israel [Gentiles] I magnify my office: if by any means I may provoke to emulation them which are of my flesh, and might save some of them, for if the casting away of them [House of Judah] be the reconciling of the harmonious and pleasant agreement, what shall the receiving of the House of Judah be, but life from the dead?"

Paul has concerns here for those of the House of Judah, his brothers in the flesh. Paul understood what Christ's coming meant for the House of Israel, but it changed the status of the House of Judah due to the fact that Edom was now legally part of it and therefore could make a legal claim on the birthright meant only for Israel. In essence, the House of Israel and the House of Judah changed places with each other. The House of Israel was out, but now is in and vice versa for the House of Judah. However, Paul is telling the House of Israel, who are now saved by Christ, redeemed back into their place before God at the expense of the House of Judah, not to get a high and mighty attitude about it. The House of Judah remains their brothers in the flesh. And if God broke Judah off for the benefit of Israel, he could very well break them off again.

Paul explains this by way of an analogy. "For if the firstfruit be holy, the lump [as in dough] is also holy; and if the root be holy so are the branches. And if some of the branches be broken off, and you [House of Israel] boast, you bear not the root, but the root you. You will say then, the branches were broken off that I might be grafted in. Well, because of unbelief they were broken off, and you stand by faith. Be not highminded, but fear: for if God spared not the natural branches, take heed lest he not spare you. For if you were cut out of the olive tree which is wild by nature, and were grafted contrary to nature into a good olive tree: how much more shall these, which be the natural branches, be grafted into their own olive tree?"

Most Christians read this and see this as concerning the Jews, which they believe to be all Israel and not just the House of Judah. And, of course, the Gentiles here are thought to be anyone other than a Jew or Israelite. But this is not what is taking place here. We have a major shift in where the birthright and promises go. They do not go to Edom. But under the terms of the Old Covenant, Edom legally had a claim to the Genesis Birthright. Thus, in order to change this, the old agreement needed to be broken and, for a time, the bond of brotherhood between Judah and Israel was to be broken. Indeed today, who considers the Jews, those descended of Judah, their fleshly brothers? Israel cannot because the House of Israel thinks they aren't related. They think they are Gentiles! But the House of Israel is no longer divorced. They are no longer Gentiles or scattered among the nations. The

House of Israel has been reinstated into their arrangement with God through Christ who was sent but unto the lost sheep of the House of Israel that both the House of Israel and the House of Judah might receive the riches of God's goodness. All the nations of Israel are real. They have national identities once again as we can read in Genesis chapter forty-nine.

Let's let Paul explain the current situation of both the Houses of Israel and Judah. "For I would not, brothers, that you should be ignorant of this mystery, so you won't be wise in your own conceits; that blindness in part [slumbering eyes of Judah] is happened to Israel, until the fullness of the Gentiles be come in [or until all the House of Israel has entered]. And so all Israel shall be saved: as it is written, There shall come out of Sion the Deliverer, and shall turn away ungodliness from Jacob: for this is my covenant to them, when I shall take away their sins."[158] Paul's logic is simple, if blindness of a part of Israel plus Gentiles equals all Israel, then the Gentiles are a part of Israel too. As we have seen, they were the lost sheep.

Christ came to make a major change in the status of our key players and, in a sense, the rules. Prior to Christ's coming to the lost sheep of the House of Israel, they were odd man out concerning the birthright. Edom was odd man out from the get go. The birthright and inheritance belonged only to the House of Judah. But then Edom was legally incorporated into the House of Judah. By time of Christ's birth, Herod, an Edomite, was king of Judah ruling over the House of Judah and the priesthood. All Herod thought he had to do was kill Christ and Edom was home free with the birthright and promises. He did not realize that by Christ's death and resurrection Edom's destiny was sealed.

Christ, therefore, had to break the covenant, which required his death and resurrection to create a new covenant or agreement. "Neither by the blood of goats and calves, but by his own blood, Christ entered in once into the holy place having obtained eternal redemption for us. For if the blood of bulls and goats and the ashes of a heifer sprinkling the unclean, sanctifies to the purifying of the flesh: how much more shall the blood of Christ, who through the eternal Spirit offered himself without spot to God, purge your conscience from dead works to serve the living God? And for this cause he is the mediator of a new testament [harmonious and pleasant agreement] that by means of death, for the redemption of the transgressions that were under the first testament [the lost sheep of the House of Israel and the House of Judah are the only two peoples that were under of the first covenant] they which are called might receive the promise of eternal inheritance."[159] In this case, it is the promise of an eternal birthright.

As Edom was mixed in with those of Judah, it was necessary for the House of Judah to be broken off. The House of Israel was grafted in to the olive tree although being divorced they were a wild olive, or prodigal olive. This is why Christ was sent only to the House of Israel or the wild olives of the House of Israel.

With the death and resurrection of Christ, the birthright and promises were of faith available to the seed of Isaac meaning only Israel. Blindness happened to a part of Israel, the House of Judah part until all those of the House of Israel part [the Gentiles or lost sheep of the House of Israel] would enter. Once this is accomplished all Israel will be saved. Both the House of Judah and the House of Israel, but not Edom! "...he [Christ] is the mediator of a better covenant which was established upon better promises.

For if that first covenant had been faultless, then should no place have been sought for the second. For finding fault with them, he says, [referencing Jeremiah chapter thirty-one] Behold the days come when I will make a new covenant with the house of Israel and the house of Judah: according to the covenant I made with their fathers when I took them by the hand out of the land of Egypt...for this is the covenant that I will make with the house of Israel after those days says the Lord; I will put my laws into their minds and write them in their hearts: and I will be to them a God and they shall be to me a people."[160] Today, the House of Israel has access to that new covenant and promises by the Spirit of God. The House of Judah's time is to come at Christ's return.

The staff called Bands in Zechariah was cut apart that the bands of brotherhood between Israel and Judah would be broken. As we just read there will be a new covenant with both the House of Israel and the House of Judah. The symbolism of the staff told us what Christ's first coming would do. It's also used to show us what Christ's second coming will do. "The word of the LORD came again to me [Ezekiel] saying, Moreover, you son of man, take you one stick, and write upon it, 'For Judah and for the children of Israel his companions' then take another stick, and write upon it, 'For Joseph, the stick of Ephraim, and for all the house of Israel his companions': and join them one to another into one stick, and they shall become one in your hand."[161] From Joseph came the kings of the House of Israel. The brotherhood of Judah and Israel will be restored at Christ's second coming. This account in Ezekiel is parallel to Paul's comment in Romans chapter ten that "all Israel will be saved" as well as in the book of Hebrews chapter eight when a new covenant or agreement will be made with both the Houses of Israel and Judah.

A new covenant exists today with the House of Israel as the promises now go through them. It is not made with the House of Judah as they have eyes that see not and ears that hear not. But this lasts only until the second coming of Christ when both houses will have a new covenant. Christians and the Christian nations today comprise the House of Israel. Those Jews who are descended from Judah of the House of Judah are our brothers regarding the birthright. Edom is not. And Edom today is mixed into the House of Judah. Remember Esau and Jacob were two different manners of people as they are to this day. Edom still seeks the birthright. But they also have vowed to slay their brother Israel, all Israel including those of Judah. And according to Isaac's blessing, Edom dwells in the same land as does Israel, all Israel. And when they break off the yoke from their necks, Edom shall have the dominion. This is what the sixth empire is all about, Edom getting Israel's yoke off their neck. They are seeking to destroy Israel. From their point of view, only the slaying of all Israel could the birthright and the inheritance fall to the next heir in line, Edom. Their downfall lies in the fact that Israel's king is Christ. He was killed by their hand once. At the second coming, it is Edom and the sixth empire that shall perish.

To recap, at Christ's first coming, the birthright, the inheritance, the promises were broken away from the House of Judah. With Christ's death and resurrection, we have a new agreement or covenant, which now goes through the House of Israel, formerly the lost sheep of the House of Israel or Gentiles. Our relationship with our Father is not by the works of the flesh any more, but by faith through Christ. The House of Judah is blinded for their own sake, during the time between Christ's first and second coming, so as not to be held accountable while Edom rules over the House of Judah and emerges as the sixth empire of the apocalypse. Christ will return to destroy the sixth empire, and all of Edom, at his second coming establishing a new covenant with both the House of Israel and the House of Judah thereby establishing the kingdom of God here on earth.

This brings us up to our current day. While we have painted a picture here, it is no more than a stone skipping across the surface of the water. The Biblical record, the last two thousand years of history and current events fill in the details. For those of you wondering who are the nations today that comprise the House of Israel, read Genesis chapter forty-nine. "And Jacob, [Israel] called to his sons, and said 'Gather that I may tell you what will happen to you in the last days. Gather yourselves together, and hear, you sons of Jacob: and listen to Israel your father." Read also chapter forty-eight when one of the sons of Israel, Joseph has two sons, Ephraim and Manasseh. In them is the House of Israel to be blessed at least until the time when Edom gains the upper hand.

Prophetically, the last days refer to the time from Christ's first coming until his second coming. It should not be a surprise then that during the last two millennia each generation of Christians believed they were living in the last days or end times. The first two verses of the book of Hebrews says, "God who at sundry times and in diverse manners spoke in times past to the fathers by the prophets, has in these last days spoken to us by his Son....". Also, the period between the first coming and the second coming of Christ is the Great Tribulation which reaches its peak with the sixth empire whose "deadly wound was healed." A careful reading of Matthew twenty-four and the first five seals of Revelation chapter six show that false prophets, wars, famines, pestilence and descendants of Israel being killed for the testimony of Christ all occurred within a short time of Christ's first coming and have continued on to this day. History will one day show Edom's hand in this.

But what of Edom? Recall that Isaac blessed Israel with the dew of heaven and the fatness of the earth, and plenty of corn and wine. In other words, Israel would be blessed with an abundance of the wealth of the earth. Edom will dwell in the same place as Israel and Judah. But they won't have the inheritance. They will live in their brother's house, but never have it as their own. They are reminded daily of what could have belonged to them. The days are coming when they will throw off their brother's yoke and openly take control of the physical inheritance that is the kingdom of man. The promises of Christ are of the kingdom of God. In the meantime, Edom has imperceptibly, yet firmly grasped control over every vital element of the inheritance. It doesn't take much looking to discover Edom's hand in current events. They are a different manner of people than Israel and Judah. All Israel one day will wake up to realize he is his brother's slave. Edom's prophetic vow to kill his brother will hold true.

Edom's emergence as the sixth empire started back in the days just prior to Augustus Caesar's fourth empire with Herod being proclaimed king of Judea. The inheritance shifted at Christ's first coming to the House of Israel. Therefore, Edom is to be found predominantly in the nation of Joseph, between his two sons, Ephraim and Manasseh today. As noted, the nation of Joseph was the kingly line when Israel was split into the Houses of Judah and Israel. Judah, by Rehoboam, reigned over Judah. And Joseph, by

Jeroboam, reigned over Israel.

This sixth empire is described as "exercising all the power of the first beast [or empire which was Babylon] and causes the earth and them that live therein to worship the first beast whose deadly wound was healed." In other words, Babylon, the head of gold, the first empire of the image in Daniel has long since disappeared and gone from the earth as we read in Chapter Five. But this sixth head, this sixth empire will be as great as the original Babylon. And there are prophetic references to both the first and the second Babylon, the sixth empire, which is referred to prophetically as Babylon the Great.

Of course, the question in everyone's mind is who is this sixth empire today? How can we tell where it is? Where is its seat of power? As we mentioned earlier, Edom dwells in the land given to all Israel, which includes both the House of Judah and the House of Israel today.

In Ezekiel beginning in chapter thirty-five, we read that Ezekiel was to "set his face against mount Seir [the land of Edom] and prophecy against it." God said he will stretch out his hand against Edom because they have "a perpetual hatred, [a hatred stemming back to the days when Edom lost the birthright] and have shed the blood of the children of Israel by the force of the sword in the time of their calamity, in the time that their iniquity had an end... because you [Edom] have said, 'These two nations and these two countries [Houses of Judah and Israel] shall be mine, and we will possess it; whereas the LORD was there."

Note that Edom will possess both Judah and Israel as if the

LORD was there. Since the days of Christ's first coming, Edom has possessed the House of Judah. Until now, Edom has not openly possessed the House of Israel. Under the veneer that these nations are of the Jewish and Christian faiths is the reality that Edom is gaining dominion, control and possession of the physical birthright, unknown to the Houses of Judah and Israel today. In fact, religious leaders today are unwittingly playing into the hands of Edom through their ignorance of the true purpose and events of Christ's first coming. It is truly the blind man's elephant.

The Western [Wailing] Wall is considered the holiest site in Jerusalem by most Jews. The Romans totally and completely destroyed the entire temple in 70 AD. King Herod of Edom built that temple and according to current day sources the wall allegedly was part of the second temple wall ["...we [Edom] will possess it; as if the LORD was there"]. It is this second temple referred to by Christ in Matthew chapter twenty-four, "And Jesus went out and departed from the [Herodian] temple: and his disciples came to him for showing him the buildings of the temple [wherein the Ark of the Covenant was never in residence]. And Jesus said to them, You see all these things don't you? Truthfully I say to you, there shall not be left here one stone upon another that shall not be thrown down." Not only is this a prophesy concerning the physical temple built by Edom, it is a secondary reference to the Edomite sixth empire which will not stand past its appointed time. It is also a reference to Christ, [I am able to destroy the temple, and to build it in three days], who died and was resurrected, restoring the Genesis Birthright to the House of Israel. The apostle Paul queried the men of Israel in Corinth saying, "Don't you know that you are the temple of God and that the Spirit of God dwells in you?" The temple of God is no longer made of stone.

Christ refers to the complete destruction of Jerusalem including the demolishing of the temple and its foundation stones by the Romans as the abomination of desolation as spoken of in the book of Daniel in chapters nine and eleven. It marked the end of Edom's outward kingdom [the little horn] until its re-emergence as the sixth empire. The Arch of Titus, completed in 81 AD, located just outside the Colosseum in Rome today is a tribute to the emperor Titus for his victory in the Jewish wars [66-70 AD]. It depicts his triumphal return to Rome with many of the sacred objects from the temple built by Herod. In 130 AD, Hadrian arrived in "Jerusalem" and found it completely destroyed except for a few houses. After the second war with Jews in 132 to 135 AD, a new Roman city was built on the site of Jerusalem named Aelia Capitolina partly in honor of the emperor Hadrian. According to accounts, a sanctuary to Jupiter was built on the former site of the Herodian temple.

Ezekiel continues to Edom, "And you shall know that I am the LORD, I have heard all your blasphemies which you have spoken against the mountains [nations] of Israel, saying, "They are laid desolate, they are given us to devour...as you did rejoice at the inheritance [birthright] of the house of Israel, because it was desolate...Aha, even the ancient high places are ours in possession...all Idumea, which have appointed my land into their possession with joy in their heart, with despiteful minds to throw it out for a prey [as in the spoils of war]."[162] Make of it what you will, but the Western Wall Plaza in Jerusalem that now can accommodate tens of thousands people to the Wailing Wall was created as a spoil of war.

Edom today dwells in the land and for all intents and purposes possesses that which was given to Israel and Judah. When the sixth empire fully emerges, this will become very apparent, although, it will be a tad late. How do we know where this sixth empire is, where its seat of power is located? First, let's take a look at the first five empires and their common characteristics.

The first thing we note about these empires is that they were, indeed, empires. That is to say, they were not just a single, powerful country as China may be viewed today. There were no democracies or even republics. Although the Roman Empire began as a republic, it is the nature of empires to replace republics and therefore the two are mutually exclusive. They extend control far beyond their own borders. Secondly, they were very militaristic in nature. Respectively, their militaries were the most powerful in the world at the time. Which nation annually spends more on its military than all other nations of the world combined? Thirdly, powerful individuals led all these empires. They were kings, or conquerors like Cyrus or Alexander and his four generals or were caesars or sultans. There were no democratically elected officials in this group. Fourthly, their guiding religious principles would be contrary to the quantum theological points found in either Judaism or Christianity. In the case of Edom's sixth empire, which will rise up out of the sea of Judaism and Christianity, its religious underpinnings are Babylonian. And perhaps most tellingly, all these empires encompassed territory that included both Babylon, or its ancient site, and Jerusalem. Iraq prophetically is very significant in this regard. Perhaps the most up-to-date terminology we can use to describe the sixth empire is idolatrous fascism incorporating both the religious and political aspects of this empire. The existence of Christian "democracy," much to the chagrin of religious leaders, will disappear when the sixth empire fully emerges.

Today, just take a look at the world and see who fits this description. You will begin to see your answer although it is not yet complete. We do have some additional specifics regarding this head of the sixth empire that are found in Daniel eleven. "And the king shall do according to his will [without regard to any law]; and he shall exalt himself and magnify himself above every god, and shall speak marvelous things against the God of gods [same description as we've read in Daniel chapter seven and Revelation chapter thirteen], and shall prosper until the indignation be accomplished: for that that is determined shall be done [forty and two months].

We also find out that "neither shall he regard the God of his fathers, nor desire women, nor regard any god: for he shall magnify himself above all." It is Satan that gives his power to this sixth empire as we read in Revelation thirteen. This individual will exalt himself above all gods, and blaspheme God in heaven. Where is this motivation coming from? "How are you fallen from heaven O Lucifer, son of the morning, you are cut down to the ground, which did weaken the nations [Israel], for you have said in your heart, I will ascend into heaven, I will exalt my throne above the stars of God: I will sit also upon the mount of the congregation in the sides of the north: I will ascend above the heights of the clouds: I will be like the most High."[163]

And we are warned "For we wrestle not just against flesh and blood, but against principalities, against powers, against the rulers of the darkness of this world [age], against spiritual wickedness in high places."[164] Satan is projecting his desires through those who lead this sixth empire.

Daniel continues the description of the head of this sixth empire, "But in his estate shall he honor the god of forces, and a god whom his fathers knew not shall he honor with gold, silver and with precious stones and pleasant things. Thus shall he do in fortresses of his munitions [military bases] with a strange god whom he shall acknowledge and increase with glory; and he shall cause them to rule over many, and shall divide the land for gain."

We see we have a two-edged sword with Edom and Satan. On the fleshly level, Edom is throwing off Israel's yoke to gain possession of the birthright. Satan is rebelling against the authority of God directing his anger through Edom towards the Houses of Judah and Israel. Remember Edom's boast in Isaiah, "For I [Edom] will tread them [Israel] in mine anger, and trample them in my fury: and their blood will be splattered upon my garments, and I will stain all my clothing. For the day of my vengeance is in my heart, and the year of my redeemed [birthright] is come."

The questions can be asked, "Why does God allow it? What did we do?" The answer of course is the same as it always has been for Israel and Judah. We never stay on the path our Father has set before us. We prefer the wide gate. We haven't learned from the mistakes of our fathers because in the case of the House of Israel, we don't know who we are much less the identity of our fathers. As was pointed out in the Prologue, which nations today are the "indigenous" nations of Christianity, the lost sheep of Israel?

A simple little logic exercise will narrow it down greatly just by looking at the big picture. Would the continent of Africa be considered indigenously Christian? What about Asia? South America? From the opposite point of view, from which nations was Christianity dispersed even from before the time of the printing of the King James Version of the Bible until our present day? Israel has national identities again. Look to the formation of nations considered Christian beginning in the early 15th century. One could make the argument that the Peace of Westphalia in 1648, which marked the end of the Thirty Years' War between the Holy Roman Empire and the Germanic Protestant princes, was the defining event that marked the beginning of what has become the sovereign, secular nation state we know today. The formation of these sovereign nations is a fulfillment of the theological arrow of time mentioned in Genesis 49 that stated the sons of Israel once again will have national identities in the last days. When you decipher this, you will know where the House of Judah and the House of Israel are today.

What then is the status of our key characters now? Since the first century AD, we can follow the history of Ishmael and his descendants as the father of the Arab nations. And, not so coincidentally, the Arab nations make up the nations of the Middle East where tens of trillions of dollars worth of oil is deposited under the sand. Also, we can follow the history of Judah's descendants as well from the first century through today. The House of Judah is, in part, those descended of the Judah or the Jews, who live in the nation-state of Israel. The others of the House of Judah are found in many countries of the world, but mostly in those nations that comprise the House of Israel.

However, if you ask most folks today where are the nations of the House of Israel and Edom, they won't know. While the world is focused on the Arabs and Jews, from the first century onward, we sort of lose track of Edom and the House of Israel. Yet from the perspective of the Biblical record, they are the two key players today in our four millennia long drama. The peoples of the House of Israel are those we think of traditionally as being the Christian nations of the world today. Edom, who is masquerading under the mantle of Judah as the "wolf in sheep's clothing," today has maneuvered Israel and Judah and Ishmael into hating each other to varying degrees, fighting each other, spilling their blood for the spoils that will become the riches of Edom's empire. Israel and Judah's blood is staining Edom's garments. The focal point of world events, driven currently by geo-poilitics if you will, is that the children of Abraham are at war with each other over the Genesis Birthright passed down from Abraham to Isaac. These events will culminate in the apocalypse. Simply stated, it's a family feud.

Recall the blessing Isaac gave to Esau at the time of passing the birthright to Jacob. Let's read it again. "And Isaac his father answered and said to him, Behold your dwelling shall be the fatness of the earth, and of the dew of heaven from above." What was the blessing by birthright given to all Israel? "Therefore God give you the dew of heaven, and the fatness of the earth." Therefore, we will find Edom today in the nation-state of Israel and among the Christian nations of the world.

But the key portion of the blessing Isaac gave Edom followed. "And you shall live by the sword, and shall serve your brother."[165] Edom throughout the ages has lived in the shadow of the House of Israel, but they have earned their wealth profiting from wars involving the House of Israel and the House of Judah. Edom has been the downstairs tenant while the House of Israel has been the upstairs landlord. This relationship was to continue up to a point. It is this point that has provided Edom with its motivation for millennia. "...and it shall come to pass [it will happen] when you shall have the dominion, that you shall break his yoke [Israel's] from off your neck."

When this day happens, Edom will openly fulfill the Genesis prophecy that began with Christ. "...then I will slay my brother Jacob [Israel]." This will be the first day of the sixth empire we read about in Revelation known as the apocalypse. It is the same little horn that came up at the time of the Roman Empire, the fourth empire. It is the same empire described in Daniel seven. "And when he opened his mouth in blasphemy against God...and it was given to him to make war with the saints, and to overcome them: and power was given him over all kindreds, and tongues, and nations."

Remember back to the Prologue and the fifth question we asked, Christ came to bring peace on Earth? True or false? Christ's answer was, "Don't think that I have come to bring peace, but rather a sword and division." Christ broke the two staffs, Bands and Beauty. He caused division between the brothers of Israel, specifically Judah and Joseph. He changed the covenant or agreement with Israel so that it is of faith not of the Law. Edom was excluded from the Genesis Birthright. And since Christ's birth, Edom has sought to destroy Israel by the sword. It was Edom not Judah who was behind Christ's crucifixion while laying the blame on Judah. Their quest continues to this day with all Israel totally unaware of what is taking place around us daily. When Edom finally gains dominion, the monolithic sixth empire will emerge for the world to openly see. Meanwhile, the blind man's elephant, Christianity, is divided into 30,000 denominations making it much easier to be deceived and thus conquered.

Concerning the terrible events to be brought on Israel and Judah and the world at large by Edom's sixth empire, is there nothing we can do? There is. But to know what the solution is to a problem, we need to understand its causes. At the most basic level it boils down to ignorance and foolishness. We, the House of Israel in this case, are ignorant of our heritage. We don't even know who we are. We have been deceived into believing we are some ethereal group of gentiles that sort of came from somewhere, but that we have nothing to do with the peoples of the Biblical record much less the House of Israel and the Genesis Birthright. This despite the fact that Christ says he was sent only to the lost sheep of the House of Israel. It's true, sheep are not the brightest of critters. If indeed, Christians consider themselves just gentiles, and the House of Judah, the Jews are all Israel, then where in the world are these nations today that possess the riches of the world especially when it comes to the wealth of the earth? Which nations are considered the breadbasket of the world? Which nations have been blessed abundantly in agriculture to the point that their surpluses of food help feed the nations of the world? Which nations have been the direct beneficiaries of the mineral wealth of the earth?

The House of Israel is ignorant of who they are even though they profess to be Christian. But as a statement that made the rounds on the Internet says, "Going to church doesn't make you

# The Genesis Birthright

a Christian anymore than going to a garage makes you a car." It's time for the House of Israel to connect the dots. Because we have been ignorant, we have acted foolishly by running after fables in place of the truth. We teach for doctrine the commandments of men. We don't even teach that Christ was a child living in a house when the wise men visited. How simple a point this is. We foolishly celebrate days rooted in pagan superstition and whose ways we are told not to follow after, rather than the days set aside for Israel, to the delight of Edom. Why? Because it takes us off the narrow path we were chosen to walk on. We are gullible to every falsehood and deceit that comes our way. And, of course, Edom would have it no other way. The greatest deceit is the least truth unknown.

For from Edom's perspective, he lost the birthright by deceit [even though he won't acknowledge he sold it], therefore deceit is the greatest tool he has to get it back. Edom has learned how to play his brother Israel. The day is coming when we shall be taken to task. The House of Israel and the House of Judah will stand alone in this world, reviled by those we thought loved us, exposed in our collective shameful ignorance, the most foolish of people.

As God tells us, "All your lovers have forsaken you; they seek you not; for I have wounded you with the chastisement of a cruel one for the multitude of your iniquity: your sins were increased. Why do you cry in your affliction? Your sorrow is incurable for the multitude of your iniquity: your sins were increased. I have done these things to you."[166] This is exactly the opposite of what most religious leaders believe. They believe they are leading the way to Christ when, in effect, it is just the opposite.

God is telling us the painful lessons we will experience nationally at the hands of the sixth empire in the apocalypse that are detailed for us in the Book of Revelation will, in fact, be done to us by God. He is causing this to happen. Why? It is, as Pogo said, "Because we have met the enemy and he is us." It's because we have become wise in our own deceits. How tragically ironic it will be that the Houses of Israel and Judah will cry out to God for help when it is God who is chastising us!

God gave advice to our ancestors. "But this thing I commanded them saying, Obey my voice and I will be your God and you shall be my people: and walk you in all the ways that I have commanded you, that it may be well to you." Why is it that Israel never chooses wellness? We are wise in our own deceits. We prefer the falsehoods to the truth even when they are pointed out to us.

But the end of chapter three in the Book of Revelation gives advice to Christianity in the end of this age. "I know your works, that you are neither cold nor hot: I would that you were cold or hot. So then because you are lukewarm, and neither cold nor hot, I will spit you out of my mouth. Because you say, I am rich, and increased with goods, and have need of nothing; and don't know that you are wretched, and miserable, and poor, and blind, and naked:

"I counsel you to buy of me gold tried in the fire, that you may be rich; and white raiment, that you may be clothed, and [that] the shame of your nakedness do not appear; and anoint your eyes with eye salve, that you may see. As many as I love, I rebuke and chasten: be zealous therefore, and change your ways. Behold,

I stand at the door, and knock: if any man hear my voice, and open the door, I will come in to him, and will sup with him, and he with me. To him that overcomes will I grant to sit with me in my throne, even as I also overcame, and am set down with my Father in his throne."

So, what did our ancestors do upon hearing similar advice? As noted earlier, "But they listened not, nor inclined their ear, but walked in the counsels, in the imagination of their evil heart and went backward not forward." This is the history of Israel. And the history of Israel is one of suffering and pain instead of blessings and peace. But with us being so modern and sophisticated, the richest nations in the world with all our technology, with access to a panoply of knowledge, the greatest in the history of the world, one would think we should be smarter than our forefathers. Rather we bombard ourselves daily with sexually suggestive ads to sell us everything under the sun. Nearly everyone is taking some sort of pharmaceutical for some malady including, ironically, sexual dysfunction while we go about of our daily business. We're techno-zombies with ubiquitous cell phones fastened to our ears when not text messaging someone. We're inundated 24/7 by high def cycloptic eyes with repeated shallow sound bites passed off as meaningful news. MP3 players channel the most up to date noise down our ear canals invading our thought process. What would we do with our waking moments if we were left alone in silence...for a day... a week...or a month? How would we react if we were alone with just our minds to occupy us?

The cliché notwithstanding, we've become a society that glorifies violence and honors celebrity hypnotized by a steady stream of "sex, drugs and rock n' roll." All our mind-numbing, quantitative techno-digital diversions, however, come with a blowback.

"Weep loudly, for the day of the LORD is at hand; it shall come as a destruction from the Almighty. Therefore shall all hands be faint, and every man's heart should melt: and they shall be afraid, pangs and sorrows shall take hold of them; they shall be as a woman in labor: they shall be amazed among each other [shocked that this is happening to them]; their faces shall be as flames. Behold the day of the LORD comes, cruel both with wrath and fierce anger, to lay the land desolate: and he shall destroy the sinners thereof out of it. For the stars of heaven and the constellations thereof shall not give their light: the sun shall be darkened and the moon shall not cause her light to shine. And I will punish the world [inhabitable earth] for their evil and the wicked for their iniquity; ...therefore I will shake the heavens and the earth shall remove itself out of her place [moved off its axis] in the wrath of the LORD of hosts and in the day of his fierce anger."[167] This description in Isaiah thirteen is the same as we find in Revelation chapters nine and eighteen when the sixth empire falls in one hour. And except that God shorten these days, all flesh on earth would die. You can read the details, if you so choose, beginning in chapter seven of Revelation.

This book is not meant to be another abject doom and gloom end of the world warning from the patron St. Sooy [Scare The S**t Out Of You]. Rather it is like that mountain we talked about in the Prologue. We can choose to hike, unplugged, through the fog-filled valley caused by erosion of the facts over millennia and climb to the summit and check out the view... or not. The choice is ours.

# The Genesis Birthright

Most definitely, I am not saying, "The end of the world is here!" No one knows when this will happen except for our Father in heaven. Although one would have to say the leaves are beginning to fall from the trees. What is being talked about here is that we have lost sight of the big picture that is who we are and how we should be conducting ourselves regardless of any concern for the timing of events, the apocalypse in particular. When we don't know our true history, when we don't know our heritage, we can't see the big picture. We can't interpret and fit the pieces of the puzzle together properly. Therefore, we make choices that take us off that narrow path. In short, we are deceived. That's why the title of this book is "The Blind Man's Elephant." We are and have been living a deception with just enough perception of light in it to keep us following after it. One day we will come to realize we have been following a clever decoy. What we really don't realize yet is that what we think is the right path is really the wrong path. And this path of deception we've been walking for the better part of two millennia has given Edom its hope. Edom is performing the greatest sleight of hand in history and the House of Israel is none the wiser. Christians are not an amorphous group of religious orphans. Christians are the lost sheep of the House of Israel. Jews are those descended from the House of Judah. Edom is the wolf in sheep's clothing living among the Houses of Israel and Judah.

So what do we do? If we are wise, we will consider our choices for the path to the summit. If not we won't. For millennia people have been thinking or saying the end of the world is at hand, and all have been wrong. One thing is for certain. There will be a sixth empire. It involves the House of Israel and the House of Judah and Edom. It pivots around Ishmael's and Israel's historical lands that include ancient Babylon and Jerusalem as have all the empires described in Daniel that preceded it including the Roman Empire. However, the sixth empire is described as Babylon the Great in Revelation. The first head or empire's seat of authority was the city of Babylon. As Babylon the Great, the sixth empire's seat of authority will be that "great city" Jerusalem, a spiritual Babylon.[168]

As we said at the beginning of this chapter, our story is the metamorphosis of brothers into families, then into nations and ultimately into one world empire. It is a saga worthy of a Harold Robbins novel perfectly suited for the big screen. But when the complete story is known, the saga is reminiscent of a Shakespearean tragedy from one point of view and a psycho horror drama on the other. It is a story of devastation, imposed humility and ultimately triumph. It is a classic battle of evil versus good, self-righteousness versus blatant rebellion, determinism versus ignorance. Its climax is one of death and annihilation when victory seems assured and victory when all appears lost but at an appalling cost. And what makes this so intriguing on the one hand, and utterly terrifying on the other, is the fact that this is real. It is not a movie, it isn't Shakespearean theater; it isn't a best selling mystery thriller. It is 24/7 news. The Genesis Birthright is a story that is shouted from satellite to satellite across the Internet every minute of the day. It's there for us to see and hear. It is a truth, "...five are fallen...one is."

## Postscript: Seeing The Elephant

God it is said is in the details. But God is also in the big picture. This holds forth both in science and theology on the microscopic and macroscopic levels whether it is our past, our present, our future or in a singularity. Growth in our knowledge and understanding of our world, the kosmos, theologically speaking, is a process often punctuated by trial and error. However, if we are going to make the effort towards growth and understanding, then we need to make sure we see our goal clearly. In order to stay on the narrow path set before us, we need to know the landscape we are traversing. Thinking an elephant looks like a rope or a tree trunk means we got something wrong in the communication. It sends us off in the wrong direction. Continually acting on incorrect theological and scientific information means we walked off the path that leads to where we need to be. We end up searching for the elephant that only looks a rope or wall or tree trunk or a snake. If what we discover doesn't fit this pattern, then, we conclude incorrectly, it can't be an elephant. At some point, we need to make the decision to find the big picture. Spiritually, it means it's time we grow up. Else, we will forever wander the kosmos in the dark, blind.

Living our life in pursuit of quantum theological points that we can use as our solid foundation to build on then are much like the pieces of a puzzle in a box. The individual pieces of a puzzle are the details. Fitted all together, they form the big picture that is the elephant. To many, the Biblical record is exactly like a puzzle broken into little pieces in a book rather than in a box. Our adventure is powers of ten more difficult if we have a false view of the elephant when we begin putting the puzzle together.

Where do we begin?

Imagine someone handing us a puzzle box with ten thousand pieces in it and a picture of a tree trunk on the box. We set out to assemble the puzzle with this picture in mind. What happens if the puzzle inside the box is really the picture of our elephant? Well, we're like our blind men. As we attempt to fit the pieces of the puzzle to make a tree trunk, we won't have a clue of what we're really doing. We end up puzzled.

While a single piece of the puzzle may not seem important in and of itself, it can send us off in the wrong direction if we have the wrong big picture in mind. But it can also send us in the right direction if we have the correct big picture. We may think that not knowing that the wise men visited Christ in a house as a young child with gifts for a king not a birthday boy is not important, or that Christ was sent "but unto the lost sheep of the House of Israel" is not important, but we would be wrong. Correcting false leads provides us with a picture of reality. Otherwise, we will spend our time and energy walking down dead-ends. It probably won't be long until we reach the point of frustration ready to give up on the puzzle of life because none of this makes any sense to us. Our traditional beliefs therefore lack the very real relevancy they should provide us.

This is exactly the difficulty facing Christians today. The traditional Christian worldview is much different from what we find in the Biblical record. Thus putting the pieces of the Biblical record puzzle together has been frustrating. Many wrong conclusions have been made because we're thinking tree trunk or snake rather than entire elephant.

Now if someone deliberately wants to throw us off the path, then of course, they will keep telling us the puzzle is a tree trunk or rope or wall. They don't want us to discover the correct image of the elephant. Even knowing that one single piece of puzzle is part of a head with large ears is important. It changes our worldview. We ask questions. What is a head and ears doing on a rope or a tree trunk? So it is with even a little piece of truth. It helps us see the big picture. It helps us find the right path.

This book has provided a glimpse of the big picture to you so you can get a better feel for where the pieces fit. You still have to do the work to put the puzzle together in your own life. And everyone may put the puzzle together differently. Some may start at the corners. Others may want to start in the middle and work their way out. Some take longer than others. We need to be tolerant of others who may be at differing stages of putting their puzzles together. Our goal is the completed puzzle, the entire elephant. We should all be seeking the kingdom of God and helping each other along the way.

This book has intended to show you the incredibly complex, big picture contained in the Biblical record. We have discovered a different worldview than what we are probably used to experiencing. We started off looking at just the smallest pieces of the puzzle, five simple questions with their more than likely unexpected answers. These pieces suddenly look much different when they match the picture on the box. And if we are strong of spirit, we discover that putting these pieces together is actually fun and exciting, not something from which to run away. As the pieces of the puzzle begin coming together, we see more of the big picture, a glimpse of an ear, perhaps part of the head and the eye. We begin to see things we never knew were there. And it helps us to begin thinking about what else might be there too.

By combining the pieces of the Biblical record with science and history, we discovered some wonderful things about time in our universe, and the history of five world empires that now have a bit more significance and relevance in our lives especially concerning the Biblical record. Finally, we saw the biggest feature of our puzzle take shape as groups of pieces began connecting with each other in our mind's eye.

We see an empire that began forming millennia ago that now is transforming into the increasingly strong presence in our world today. Our puzzle is not just science and history. It's also current events.

Certainly, this is an adventure in discovering the many points of quantum theology, those marker pieces of the puzzle that we thought were just a rope or a wall but are much more. The task is not yet complete. The last chapter of this book is actually the Prologue, our base camp where we first took a look at those five simple questions. We need to connect our littlest detail ends together with our big picture ends to form a unifying circle. Remember what Edmund Hillary said. It's not the mountains that we conquer, but ourselves. And the person who returns from the top of the mountain is different from the one who began the journey. We've seen the elephant.

When examining our puzzle for the authenticity of its big picture, we need to be critical in its examination. If we just take someone's word for it, including this one, we may find ourselves never being able to get a clear picture. What's worse is if we spend our life living a false reality based on someone else's beliefs. When it comes to matters of theology and the spirit, everyone needs to be a professional. Everyone needs to ask their own "how can it be like that?" questions. There aren't any piggyback rides into the kingdom of God.

As we noted, God is in the details. Now that we should have a better understanding of the big picture, look at those details in the Prologue by reading it again. Then measure your knowledge and understanding against the feelings and experience you had the first time you read them. The details, those five little points should be much clearer to you now. At some level, you may even ask yourself, how it is that I never noticed them before? Big pictures can do that for you. There are lots more pieces out there for you to discover too that need some fitting together.

The search for pieces that fit together is very exciting if you are not afraid of the adventure. On your path to discovery, you probably will have some questions not answered to your satisfaction in the book or others may arise that are not addressed in the book. For this purpose, go to our website site www.redshoe.com to email us any sincere questions and thoughts you may have concerning your own adventure. Your questions, concerns and experiences will help us formulate future books.

The apostle Paul wrote in the first century to the House of Israel in Thessalonica, "Prove all things; hold onto those which are good" or of God whether they are the little pieces of the puzzle or the big picture on the box. Fitted together they lead us to truth. And as Christ said, the truth shall make us free.

**Appendix: Chapter Endnotes**

## Chapter One Endnotes

[1] This chapter does not include discussion on the scientific hypotheses concerning the origin of life, only evolution or change at the species level. However, indicative of the adversarial mindset in this battle between science and religion is this anecdote from the religious perspective.

> God is in heaven when a scientist prays to Him, "God, we don't need you anymore. Science has finally figured out a way to create life out of nothing. In other words, we can now do what you did in the "beginning."!
>
> "Oh, is that so? Tell me..." replies God.
>
> "Well," says the scientist, "We can take dirt and form it into the likeness of you and breathe life into it, thus creating man.
> God answered, "Well, that's interesting...show me."
>
> So the scientist bends down to the earth and starts to mold the soil.
>
> "No, no, no," interrupted God, "Get your own dirt."

The scientific perspective is that the Earth was formed out of the elements of the universe **billions** of years ago, which of course would rebut the point of the story. In turn this would lead us back to the genesis argument of something coming from nothing.

It is reminiscent of the familiar story in Hawking's *A Brief History of Time*. A well- known scientist gave a talk about the origin of the earth and the solar system. Then at the end of the lecture a little old lady stands up and says, "What you have told us is rubbish. The world is really a flat plate supported on the back of a giant tortoise." The scientist gave a superior smile before replying, "What is the tortoise standing on?" "You're very clever young man, very clever," said the old lady, "but it's turtles all the way down!"

2    In Darwin's final edition of his "Origin of the Species," in his lifetime [6th ed. 1872] he concludes, "There is a grandeur in this view of life, with its several powers, having been *originally breathed by the Creator* into a few forms or one,…" Even Darwin's choice of title "Origin of the Species *by Means of Natural Selection*…" implies that species evolve or change from a few forms or one, created by God, all within the laws of genetic mutation. Darwin continues, "Authors of the highest eminence seem to be fully satisfied with the view that each species has been independently created. *To my mind it accords better with what we know of the laws impressed on matter by the Creator,* that the production and extinction of the past and present inhabitants of the world should have been due to secondary causes, like those determining the birth and death of the individual." *Origin of the Species,* Charles Darwin, Chapter 14, Recapitulation and Conclusion.

The point made here by Darwin about the laws impressed

on nature by the Creator actually meshes very well with the six major events of creation chronicled in Genesis chapter one. Creation on "days" five and six describe the basis of life as we know it, life in the sea, birds of the air and creatures on land. Chapter Three discusses the nature of these "days."

The principle that organisms change, mutate or evolve is common to our experience on Earth. Why could the Creator not set in motion laws impressed on complex creatures that would allow for species to change albeit in time frames of greater scale? There is precedence for this principle in creation. A simple example is that each year society experiences a flu virus that has evolved, adapted or changed in some manner from the previous year. Last year's vaccines have no effect on them. In principle then, why is this not possible with more complex organisms?

This concept is called preadaptation. "…every feature of an organism, in addition to its obvious functional characteristics has others that could become useful in totally novel ways under the right circumstances." Scientists refer to the process God created as evolution. It can "innovate in ways that cannot be prestated [by man] and is non-algorithmic by drafting and recombining <u>existing entities</u> for new purposes—shifting them from their existing function to some adjacent function—rather than inventing features from scratch." Stuart A. Kaufmann, November 2006, Scientific American, p. 44. Parentheses and underline author's.

# Endnotes Chapter One

Think of this process like a bunch of building blocks that you formed into a large cube upon which you display your mint collection of Susan B. Anthony dollar and Canadian Loonie dollar coins. One day a friend stops by to see your mint coin collection. He turns and says to you, "Let's make a hendecagon!" Puzzled, you ask why change the cube? Your friend replies that both the Canadian Loonies and the Susan B. Anthony dollars are eleven sided coins.

Now you may not have thought to make an eleven-sided geometric shape called a hendecagon. But the existing building blocks are constructed such that you can change the cube into a hendecagon better suiting the function of displaying your eleven-sided Anthony and Loonie coins. When this type of change takes place biologically, it is called evolution.

Within the forms or "kind after kind" are the building blocks of living organisms. This is our DNA. Within the DNA, God has set forth the ability of life forms to make changes within the parameter of their form or kind down to the species level. It is only after the basic forms or kinds are established that we find evidence of evolution in fossils. Thus, creation deals with the origin of life as a primary cause, while evolution deals with the origin of species as a secondary cause.

There is no reason for this not to be possible. It should be noted, though, that man was created essentially as we are today as we read further on in this chapter.

3   Romans, chapter 8, verses 11 and 14.

4   Matthew, chapter 3, verses 16 and 17.

5   Acts, chapter 2.

6   Genesis, chapter 1, verse 20.

7   Dust of the earth. The Hebrew word for dust here is *aphar* and means dry earth. While there are variations depending upon which source is used, humans are approximately 70%, 60% or 50% water depending on whether you are talking about infants, young men or women and about 45% if you are talking about old men with less muscle mass. Our blood is about 80% water as is the heart and lungs.  So the recipe for man is for every two cups of dirt add five to six cups of water.

8   Genesis, chapter 2, verse 5.

9   Genesis, chapter 2, verse 6.

10  Genesis, chapter 4, verses 16 ff.

11  Ecclesiastes, chapter 3, verses 19 and 20.

12  Romans, chapter 8, verse 5.

13  Genesis, chapter 2, verse 7. The Hebrew word soul here is *nephesh* and means a <u>breathing</u> creature. It is not a reference to a spirit.

[14] Ecclesiastes, chapter 12, verse 7 and chapter 3, verse 21. Italics & bold are the author's. The word beast is *b'hamah*, a living breathing animal, which is a narrower definition than that of living breathing creature or *nephesh*. Beast is also translated as meaning "every living thing" using the Hebrew word *chay*. While use of the word nephesh or chay could include mankind, b'hamah specifically excludes mankind. By the time the author of Ecclesiastes wrote these verses, mankind was the only remaining hominid.

The point is that **all** living breathing bodies are created from the dust of the earth, and are flesh. When the fleshy body dies, that is the end of the physical body. It decomposes, it returns to the dust of the earth from which it originated to be recycled. This is the first death. Mankind however has a spirit that lives on after the first death. This spirit, the spirit of man, goes upward and returns to the Creator who gave it. Those not of adamkind, all other living creatures have or had a spirit that returned to the dust of the earth along with their bodies at death.

[15] The Human Genome Project in 2000 claimed mankind is 99.9% genetically alike although a recent study, Global variation in copy number in the human genome published in the 23 November 2006 issue of Nature has called this number into question. Mankind has 3 billions gene pairs. Using the 99.9% number to illustrate our point, what if mankind today and our genetically similar creaturekind were just 99.89% alike? This would

allow for 300,000 gene pairs, and their markers to be different. While this is pure speculation, even a .01 % difference could allow for a marker or markers that would physically distinguish man from creature. Time may tell us whether or not this is so. In either case, the discerning difference is of the spirit. While genes is what makes us alike, Genesis tells us what makes us different, in spite of the poor grammar.

[16] Revelation, chapter 20, verses 12-15.; verses 4-6. There is a second death mentioned in the Biblical record. Just as the spirit of a creature dies with the death of the physical body, the spirit of man does not mean immortality. It simply means that the spirit of man returns to God upon death of the physical body. There is a judgment in which "every man is judged according to his works." Then death, the grave and whosoever wasn't found written in the book of life were cast into the lake of fire. "This is the second death." This is not to an eternal torment, but a cessation of life or existence. It is the death of death so to speak. For those found written in the book of life, death will no longer have any hold on them. For it is the third creation of life, life given by the Spirit of God that gives us immortality in the spirit and on such the second death has no power.

[17] Daniel, chapter 4, verses 16 and 33. For those keeping score, this was *not* a change in his DNA, but in his spirit. It was not a literal heart transplant either anymore than when someone says, "he stole my heart," it's a human sacrifice. A case could be made here that

Nebuchadnezzar became the first, albeit temporary, Homo sapiens creature since the flood.

[18] *Species* is the most specific of the nine categories of the natural science classification system when including *Life and Domain*. *Kingdom* is followed by *Phylum* then by *Class* then *Order* then *Family* then *Genus* and finally *Species*. Using a tree as an analogy, *Kingdom* would be the trunk, *Phylum* the biggest of the branches, etc. Species would be the very ends of the tiniest branches.

Science is merely making the point that Homo sapiens as a species was not the only species of the family Hominidae. Our *Kingdom* is Animalia; *Phylum* is Chordata; *Class* is Mammalia; *Order* is Primates; *Family* is Hominidae; *Genus* is Homo and *Species* is Homo sapiens. Mankind today is the only living member of the *Genus* Homo. And until recently, scientists classified mankind as the only living member of the *Family* Hominidae.

When God said "Let the earth bring forth the living creature after his kind," it does not necessarily mean this included every *species* currently alive today. Creature here is *nephesh* in Hebrew. It means breathing, hence a living, breathing creature in very broad terms. This is what God called Adam when he breathed life into him. Its Latin equivalent is *anima* from which we get animal. Kind here in Hebrew is the word *miyn*. It means *form*. Thus the statement In Genesis could read, "Let the *earth bring forth* every breathing animal after his form."

Thus the classification of *animal* would place us in *Kingdom*, the broadest category. *Form* applied to mankind would mean that we could actually go to the fourth level of classification, *Order*. This classifies primates with two arms, two legs, standing upright. This is our form or basic appearance.

Remember, God created all the *forms or kinds* so we would have to give Him credit for intentionally making *form or Order* the cut-off point initially. Changes from this point down to species would be due to secondary causes as Darwin noted. From form up to *Kingdom*, these were primary causes created by God. Thus primary causes are creation from *Kingdom* to Order and secondary causes are evolution from *Family* to Species.

At one time religious teachings said the Sun revolved around the Earth because, it was reasoned, God would make man and the Earth the center of the universe. But such is not the case. Today, religious teachings say God created man physically and genetically different from any other species because mankind is the centerpiece of creation. But, perhaps we should be a bit more open-minded and give God credit for knowing what he's doing as our forefathers should have done in the 1600s. It might be good for us to consider that the spirit is the important defining factor for God, not the flesh.

New *Species* can come about from the Genus's available gene pool. In this sense, a new species is a new combination of <u>available</u> genetic material from the *Genus*. In mankind's case today, we Homo sapiens are the only members of our Genus in existence. Think of it as having a clothes closet with clothes for every imaginable occasion from a black tie royal affair down to camping in the outback. What we wear is dependent on the environmental conditions, hot, rainy, freezing, dry, etc. as well as the occasion.

All our clothes will have a certain form to them. All our coats will have sleeves only for two arms not three. Likewise any slacks will have two pant legs and not four legs. A shirt will have a collar for one head not two, but it could be a pullover or a button down, a small or extra large, blue or pink. Theoretically, we could combine our wardrobe into thousands of outfits to create new looks. The fashion industry is built on this premise of basic form. Any fashion designer who seriously brought out a line of dresses for six-armed women would soon go broke.

The wardrobe in our analogy is the gene pool. A new combination of clothes would be a new species. But we could never create anything other than what our wardrobe allows us to put together unless we somehow were able to add to our wardrobe. Genetic anomalies notwithstanding, our wardrobe, even if added to, would always being comprised of clothes of the same form... two arms for sleeves, two legs for pants, etcetera.

As we know, just a .3% genetic difference can make a world of difference. Genetically mankind is only 99.9%

alike not 100%. Given that we, Homo sapiens, have 3 billion gene pairs, a .3% means about 10 million gene pair differences occurring between us and chimps, our physical body's closest living genetic *Family* member. Between mankind we have about 3 million gene pair differences. One tenth or three tenths of one percent difference is pretty tiny considering the size of the wardrobe.

Thus when it comes to the physical containers, our bodies, the significant defining factor that makes mankind and ancestral Homo sapiens alike is found in our DNA. The significant *difference* is of the spirit.

## Endnotes Chapter Two

[19] Offaly Historical & Archeological Society www.offalyhistory.com The First Settlers- Mesolithic and Neolithic Offaly

[20] Archaeolink Prehistory Park www.archaeolink.co.uk/Neolithic-Age.html; Neolithic Age from 4000BC to 2200 BC

[21] Innovations Report, Earth Sciences, www.innovations-report.com/reports/html/reports/earth_sciences/report-20033.html Largest archeological excavation throws light on last 8,000 years at Heathrow 18 July 2003

[22] Gravegarder et Pramauvoir le Patrimaine et culturel du Pays de Retz www.museepaysderetz.free.fr/anglais_musee_archeo.html; The Ancient Past of Pays de Retz

[23] Archeological Research at Oslonki, Poland, www.princeton.edu/~bogucki/oslonki.html; Peter Bogucki, School of Engineering and Applied Sciences, Princeton University

[24] Lithuanian Cultural Heritage, Archeology, neris.mii.lt/heritage/archeol.html

[25] English.eastday.com/eastday/englishedition/features/userobject1ai1764022.html

26   Science, 20 December 1996, Vol. 274, no. 5295, pp. 2012- 2013

27   Archeology of Maize, Mesoamerica, www.geocities.com/CapeCanaveral/Hangar/3288/ARCHAEOLOGY.HTM

28   Fermilab, history.fnal.gov/archaeology.html

29   History of the Native People of Canada, www.civilization.ca/archeo/hnpc/npvol04e.html;   Early and Middle Archaic Complexes

30   A Canal Chronology, home.eznet.net/~dminor/Canals.html

31   Inventions 10,000 to 4000 BC, www.krysstal.com/inventions_02.html

32   Ancient Civilizations, library.thinkquest.org/C004203/science/science02.htm; Invention of the Wheel

33   Genesis, chapter 4, verse 13, 14. All Biblical record references are King James Version unless noted otherwise.

34   Genesis, chapter 3, verse 5.

35   Genesis, chapter 4, verse 16.

36   Genesis, chapter 3, verse 16.

[37] Genesis, chapter 4, verse 25.

[38] Genesis, chapter 4, verse 1, 2.

[39] Genesis, chapter 4, verse 25.

[40] Genesis, chapter 4, verse 16.

[41] The Epistle Dedicatory, KJV, Oxford University Press

[42] Genesis, chapter 5, verses 1-4.

[43] Genesis, chapter 4, verses 1-24.

[44] 1 Corinthians, chapter 15, verse 50.

[45] Jeremiah, chapter ten, verse 8. Chapter ten describes a tree that pertains to Christ. "...one cuts a tree out of the forest...they fasten it with nails and with hammers that it move not. They are upright as the palm tree...they deck it with silver and with gold...the tree is a doctrine of vanities...who would not fear you of King of nations...at his wrath the earth shall tremble [as in earthquake and the nations shall not be able to abide his indignation." Verses 1-10.

[46] Italics are author's emphasis.

[47] Genesis, chapter 1, verses 24-31.

## Endnotes Chapter Three

[48] http://www.newadvent.org/cathen/09238c.htm, Life

[49] http://www.newadvent.org/cathen/01046b.htm, Abortion

[50] http://www.newadvent.org/cathen/01046b.htm, Abortion

[51] Judges 13:3 All Biblical references are the King James Version unless noted otherwise.

[52] 1 Chronicles 7:23.

[53] Hosea 1:3.

[54] Luke 1:35.

[55] Isaiah 7:14.

[56] 1 Corinthians 15:45.

[57] BBC World News on-line edition, Saturday, 26 February 2005, David Willey, BBC Rome Correspondent, <u>Gossip rules at the Vatican</u>, "Could he [the Pope] not resign, the cardinal was asked. That would be a matter for the Pope's own conscience, the cardinal replied, implying that resignation was still on the cards, despite the Pope's frequent insistence that he intends to carry

on "while there is breath in my body."

[58] 1 Corinthians 15:45ff.

[59] John 3:3.

[60] Exodus 21:22, 23.

[61] Ezekiel 37:5-14.

[62] <u>On Size and Life</u>, 1983, TA McMahon, JT Bonner, Scientific American Library

[63] <u>Physiological changes at birth</u>, March 2005, Professor John Wyatt, University College of London, on-line posting, parentheses and underline are author's

[64] <u>On Size and Life</u>, 1983, TA McMahon, JT Bonner, Scientific American Library

[65] <u>http://www.law.umkc.edu/faculty/projects/ftrials/galileo/condemnation.html</u>, <u>The Trial of Galileo</u>, 2002, Douglas Linder

[66] Pope John Paul II, October 1992, Pontifical Academy of Sciences

[67] <u>http://www.dslnorthwest.net/~danwilcox/galileo.html</u>, <u>Vatican admits Galileo Correct</u>, 31 October 1992, LA Times

[68] John Heilprin, Scalia Rips Judges on Abortion, Suicide, October 21, 2006, Associated Press,

[69] Originally appeared in New York Times magazine, 9 November 1930

## Endnotes Chapter Four

[70] Planck Time. http://scienceworld.wolfram.com/physics/PlanckTime.html

[71] Planck Length, http://scienceworld.wolfram.com/physics/PlanckLength.html

[72] Schrödinger's Cat, University of Toronto, Department of Physics, http://www.upscale.utoronto.ca/GeneralInterest/Harrison/SchrodCat/SchrodCat.html

[73] Einstein's Special Theory of Relativity, Stanford University, Stanford Linear Accelerator Center http://www2.slac.stanford.edu/vvc/theory/relativity.html

[74] The three time references mentioned in the Bible are 1- time from instant of creation of the universe until creation of man; 2- time of creation of man until present day; 3- and a future point when time ceases to exist mentioned in Revelation 10:6 "And sware by him that lives for ever and ever, who created the heaven, and the things that therein are, and the earth, and the things that therein are, and the sea, and the things which are therein, that there should be time no longer…." This marks the end of what is called the space-time continuum. It marks the beginning of a "universe" that exists without time and by implication, without mass.

[75] 1 John 1:5, "This then is the message which we

have heard of him, and declare unto you, that God is light,....." Light here is *phos* in Greek. Literally, light as emitted from a lamp, but metaphorically as the nature of God. Perhaps, we could add a third definition: physics, meaning establishing the boundary for physical *matter/energy* in the space-time continuum at the speed of light.

As a side note, as God is light, what is the dark? Scientists have long suspected "dark matter/energy" existed. Using exploding supernovae, or white dwarf stars, they are now discovering dark *matter/energy* in the universe. It is this dark *matter/energy* they believe that has been responsible for the expansion of the universe as a counterforce to the universe collapsing due to gravity.

Looking at the creation account in Genesis, it says "God divided the light from the darkness." The word divided here is rather interesting as the one English word is two words in Hebrew. The first is *badal* which means to separate or to disjoin. This implies that dark and light were at one time joined together in the universe. The second word is *beyn* which means interval or space between. Thus light and dark were once joined together, but now have a space or interval put between them preventing their rejoining.

As a shot in the dark, pun intended, could it be then that the dark *matter/energy* is comprised of "skoteinons" [Greek for being *full of darkness*] while the photon is light? And could it be that the disjoining of photons from the "skoteinons" and the persisting space between them somehow is related to the expansion of the universe?

Regardless of what is the outcome, light was disjoined from the dark and a space currently exists between them [as mentioned in the fourth verse of the creation account], which fits in with what scientists are just now discovering.

[76]  Ecclesiastes 3:15.

[77]  Stephen Hawking, Public Lectures, The Beginning of Time, http://www.hawking.org.uk/lectures/bot.html

[78]  1 Corinthians 10:11 "Now all these things happened to them for examples, and they are written for our admonition, upon whom are the ends of the world are come." The word *world* used here is *aion* in Greek which means age as in the end of an age. This age is the time of the kingdom of man beginning with Adam and ending with the arrival of the Kingdom of God.

[79]  Richard Feynman, Nobel Prize physicist, [The Distinction of Past and Future, from The Character of Physical Law, **Richard Feynman**, 1965]

[80]  Gary Zukav, The Dancing Wu Li Masters, 2001, page 9, cited from Albert Einstein and Leopold Infeld, The Evolution of Physics, New York, Simon and Schuster,

1938, p.31. Underline mine.

[81] Ecclesiastes 3:11.

[82] http://www.infoplease.com/ce6/sci/A0857862.html The December 26, 2004 Indonesian earthquake may have made the Earth's bulge a little bit smaller making our day just a tad bit shorter according to Michael Schriber, a staff writer for LiveScience. http://www.livescience.com/forcesofnature/050112_earth_shape.html

[83] Romans 6:11, "Likewise reckon you also yourselves to be dead indeed unto sin, but alive unto God through Jesus Christ our Lord."

[84] Big Bang Nucleosynthesis, University of California at Los Angeles, Edward L. Wright, 2002-2004, http://www.astro.ucla.edu/~wright/BBNS.html
Periodic Table http://ccinfo.ims.ac.jp/periodic/

[85] Romans 1:20-22.

## Endnotes Chapter Five

[86] Ecclesiastes 3:15 states, *"That which has been is now; and that which is to be has already been; and God requires that which is past."*

That which has been, the past, is now or the present. That which is to be, the future has already been or is past. Thus this is saying, the past is the present and the future is the past. The past, present and future are all one or a singularity.

The same point has been made by Stephen Hawking, "The beginning of real **time**, would have been a **singularity**....." Hawking, Public Lectures - The Beginning of Time, www.hawking.org.uk/text/public/bot.html

We can only remember the past. Or as Ecclesiastes 3:15 puts it, "God requires that which is past." The word requires here is *baqash* [baw-kash'] a primitive root meaning to search out, but it can also be translated as requires. The word past is *radaph* [raw-daf'] a primitive root meaning to run after, figuratively, of time gone by. So the Creator, by implication, "requires" us to run after and search out the past, but we aren't allowed to do the same with the future even though time according to the laws of physics goes in both directions.

Richard Feynman, a Nobel Prize physicist, summed it up, "It may prove useful in physics to consider events in all of time at once and to imagine that we at each instant are only aware of those that lie behind us."

87   Aramaic is a Semitic language as is Hebrew. The book of Daniel has portions written in Aramaic and others written in Hebrew. Other Semitic languages include Akkadian which was the language of ancient Babylon and Assyria, and Arabic, currently the world's most widely used Semitic language. Christ spoke Aramaic. Perhaps the most recent popular use of Aramaic was the movie *The Passion of Christ*, which was spoken in Aramaic.

88   Isaiah 46:10, KJV [all Biblical quotes are KJV unless noted otherwise] "Declaring the end from the beginning, and from ancient time *the things* that are not done, saying, My counsel shall stand, and I will do all my pleasure."

89   "Science is reasoned-based analysis of sensation upon our awareness. As such, the scientific method cannot deduce anything about the realm of reality that is beyond what is observable by existing or theoretical means. When a manifestation of our reality previously considered supernatural is understood in the terms of causes and consequences, it acquires a scientific explanation. For example, God may choose to be hidden from this reality, hence making discussion over God's existence non-scientific." http://en.wikipedia.org/wiki/Science#Scientific_method

[90] Ockham's [Occam's] Razor is the principle of favoring simplicity over complexity involving answers to problems according to William of Ockham, a medieval philosopher in the 14th century. His premise is that when faced with numerous solutions to a problem, the simplest solution is the one that should be used. It's the "shortest distance between two points is a straight line" approach. Concerning the laws of the universe, the psychological arrow of time tells us mankind cannot know the future. Yet, the prophecy in Daniel let's mankind know the future. And God is telling man He can know the future and bring it to pass. Thus, Ockham's Razor would agree with God's existence as the simplest explanation for knowing the future.

[91]  Revelation 17:10, 13:1-3.

[92]  Daniel 4:25: "...seven times shall pass over you [Nebuchadnezzar], till you know that the most High rules in the kingdom of men, and gives it to whomever he will."

[93]  *ibid*

[94]  Daniel 2:28-30.

[95]  Terrible here is the Aramaic word, *tselem*, that implies to make one afraid or something dreadful. Strong's Concordance.

[96]  Daniel 2:31-36. The author, for clarification purposes,

has used modern terms such *you* for thee, etc. in quoting the KJV.

[97] Daniel 2:37-43.

[98] Daniel 2:44.

[99] Revelation 17:14.

[100] Daniel 2:45.

[101] Daniel 7:7 "After this I saw in the night visions, and behold a fourth beast, dreadful and terrible, and strong exceedingly; and it had great iron teeth: It devoured and broke in pieces, and stamped the residue with the feet of it; and it was diverse from all the beasts that were before it: and it had ten horns."

[102] Daniel 2:41-43.

[103] See list of Roman Empire Byzantine emperors, http://www.unrv.com/government/byzantine.php. Mahomet II even claimed for himself the title of Caesar.

[104] Daniel 2:41 "...the kingdom shall be divided, but there shall be in it of the strength of iron...."

[105] Daniel 4:16, 25b.

[106] Hexasegimal or sexagesimal system is a base 60

system. First used by the Sumerians, the system was adopted by the Babylonians. Our clocks use a base 60 system in that 60 seconds make up one minute, and 60 minutes make up one hour.

[107] Interestingly, the US military GPS satellite system as implemented inspired the Universal Transverse Mercator, which divides the Earth into 60 sections of 6 degrees each. Six times sixty. It is this GPS system that is capable of tracking every meter or less of the Earth's surface today. Thus the base sixty system, in addition to measuring minutes and hours, used by Babylon has other modern day applications.

[108] Daniel 5:25, 26.

[109] Babylonian years and our years using the Gregorian calendar are not exact matches as the beginnings of the years differ, as do the lengths of the years. The Babylonian calendar is lunar while our calendar today is solar.

[110] Daniel 2:28

[111] Last days, latter days. There has been much discussion about what constitutes the last days as mentioned in the Biblical record. Even the apostles in the first century believed they were living in the last days and Christ would return in their lifetimes. Using the analogy of a week of seven days, the millennium or the thousand years of peace portrayed by the seventh

day of the week, which is ushered in by the second coming of Christ, then the last days [plural, days five and six] would be approximately 2000 years. In our case, the last days would be the time between Christ's first coming and his second coming. A warning, this is not in any way intended to predict dates for a second coming. Live life passionately seeking first the kingdom of God daily and leave the rest to God.

[112] There is a general consensus among Biblical scholars that the stone here spiritually refers to Christ and his kingdom, the "...great mountain...filled the whole Earth." It is also a literal physical reference to the globe encompassing British Empire. Daniel chapter two, verse 35. The seeds of the kingdom of God were sown with Christ's first coming during the great images fourth beast, the Roman Empire. His second coming will culminate with the destruction of the sixth empire.

[113] Funk & Wagnall's Encyclopedia, 1949 ed., Ottoman Empire. "In 1918, following the fatal decision of the Ottomans to ally themselves with Germany against France and Britain in World War One, their once great empire was defeated and utterly destroyed." *Churchill's Folly*, p.15, 2004, Christopher Catherwood.

[114] Isaiah 46:9,10, Revised Standard Version.

## Endnotes Chapter Six

[115] Revelation 13:1.

[116] Revelation 13:3.

[117] Revelation 13:11-18.

[118] Gideon Bible Society, www.gideons.org/ freely distributes 63 million Bibles annually; International Digital Publishing Forum Top Selling Books in 2004, Zondervan Bible #6. Da Vinci #1.

[119] Genesis 25: 22, 23; See also 2 Samuel 8:14b

[120] Genesis 25: 23-25

[121] Genesis 25: 29-34

[122] Genesis 26: 35

[123] excerpts Genesis 27: 8-36

[124] Hebrews 12: 16,17

[125] excerpts Gen 27: 28, 29

[126] Genesis 16, 7-12

[127] Genesis 25:30

[128] Genesis 32: 24-28

[129] Genesis 27: 39, 40

[130] 2 Samuel 8:14

[131] excerpts 1 Kings, chapter 11:1-13

[132] 1 Kings 11: 28-43

[133] 2 Kings 15:29 While many historical accounts place the capture of the House of Israel in 722 BC, the reign of the Pekah, king of Israel, ended in 732BC. The Biblical record says that it was Tiglathpileser, whose reign in Assyria encompassed the time from 744 to 727 BC. However, the Biblical record says that Pekah reigned for twenty years beginning from the fifty-second year of Azariah, king of Judah. Azariah is thought to have begun his reign in 792. This would make it 740 BC. If Pekah reigned twenty years, then the captivity was in the year 720 BC. While the exact year may be important to some scholars, it is not critical to our story.

[134] excerpts Jeremiah, chapters 7 and 8

[135] Isaiah 48:4

[136] Psalms 137:7

[137] Obadiah, verses 13, 14

[138] Amos 1:9

[139] excerpts Isaiah, chapter 63

[140] Daniel 7:8

[141] Daniel 7:20

[142] Revelation, 13:5, 6

[143] Daniel 7:21

[144] Revelation 13:4, 7

[145] Matthew 13:24-30; See also Obadiah and Revelation chapter 17

[146] Revelation 18:8 ff

[147] Matthew 13:40b; see also Obadiah

[148] Matthew 12:16

[149] Exodus 21:32

[150] Zechariah 11:10-14

[151] Romans 9:1-4

[152] Exodus 4:22

[153] Romans 9:6-13

[154] Romans 11:1-10

[155] excerpts John 8

[156] Romans 11:12

[157] Hebrews 8:8

[158] excerpts Romans 11:13ff

[159] Hebrews 9:11-15

[160] Hebrews 8:6-10s

[161] Ezekiel 37: 15-17

[162] excerpts Ezekiel chapters 35-36; "[Titus] Caesar gave orders that they should now *demolish the entire city and Temple*, but should leave as many of the towers standing as they were of the greatest eminence; that is, Phasaelus, and Hippicus, and Mariamne; and so much of the wall enclosed the city on the west side. This wall was spared, in order to afford a camp for such as were to lie in garrison [in the Upper City], as were the towers [the three forts] also spared, in order to demonstrate to posterity what kind of city it was, and how well fortified, which the Roman valor had subdued; but for all the rest of the wall [surrounding Jerusalem], *it was so thoroughly laid even with the ground by those that dug*

*it up to the foundation, that there was left nothing to make those that came thither believe it [Jerusalem] had ever been inhabited." Flavius Josephus, The Wars of the Jews.* Thus, the western wall was part of the wall of Jerusalem [specifically Fort Antonia] and not the temple itself which was totally destroyed. The western wall left standing was a tribute to the Roman army.

It is also noteworthy to point out that when the Babylonians took the House of Judah captive in 586 BC, Edom was calling for Jerusalem to be razed to its foundation. While the walls of Jerusalem were broken down and the temple and palaces destroyed, it was at the end of the Edomite reign in Jerusalem in 70 AD that the city and the Herodian temple were utterly destroyed so that no one would "believe it had ever been inhabited."

[163] Isaiah 14:12-14

[164] Ephesians 6:12

[165] Genesis 27:40 Living by the sword is not only the use of weapons in war, but can be taken to mean making money on wars, either by the financing and sale of weapons, and by the financing of wars and the subsequent loans for reconstruction. Governments borrow money from international banks to finance their wars. These banks control the currency of nations including the Federal Reserve Bank which in everything but name is the Bank of the United States. One chart

shows the interrelationships of various banks although the author cannot vouch for its accuracy.

http://land.netonecom.net/tlp/ref/federal_reserve.shtml

President Eisenhower, upon leaving office in 1960 gave a warning, which has become a nightmarish prophecy fulfilled. "A vital element in keeping the peace is our military establishment. Our arms must be mighty, ready for instant action, so that no potential aggressor may be tempted to risk his own destruction.

*"Our military organization today bears little relation to that known by any of my predecessors in peacetime, or indeed by the fighting men of World War II or Korea. Until the latest of our world conflicts, the United States had no armaments industry*. [The 2008 fiscal year Bush administration budget figures are $623 billion, more than all other nations combined, with congressional estimates as high as multiple trillions of dollars including all the Afghan and Iraq war costs].

"American makers of plowshares could, with time and as required, make swords as well. But now we can no longer risk emergency improvisation of national defense; we have been compelled to create a permanent armaments industry of vast proportions. Added to this, three and a half million men and women are directly engaged in the defense establishment [1960 figure]. We annually spend on military security more than the net income of all United States corporations. [Now spending is more than equal to all other nation's combined military spending according to figures from the Stockholm International Peace Research Institute]

*"This conjunction of an immense military establishment and a large arms industry is new in the American experience. The total influence -- economic, political, even spiritual -- is felt in every city, every State house, every office of the Federal government. We recognize the imperative need for this development. Yet we must not fail to comprehend its grave implications. Our toil, resources and livelihood are all involved; so is the very structure of our society.*

"In the councils of government, we must guard against the acquisition of unwarranted influence, whether sought or unsought, by the military-industrial complex. *The potential for the disastrous rise of misplaced power exists and will persist.*

*"We must never let the weight of this combination endanger our liberties or democratic processes.* We should take nothing for granted. *Only an alert and knowledgeable citizenry can compel the proper meshing of the huge industrial and military machinery of defense with our peaceful methods and goals, so that security and liberty may prosper together."*

From the Public Papers of the Presidents, Dwight D. Eisenhower, 1960. Italics for emphasis. [ ] author's note.

[166] Jeremiah 30: 14,15

[167] Isaiah 13: 9-13

[168] Revelation, chapters 17, 18, 19. Chapter seventeen describes the "great whore," Babylon the Great, that "great city which reigns over the kings of the earth." This city represents the "one is" empire or the sixth empire as we read in verse ten. In Daniel chapter eleven, verse forty-five, "And he shall plant his tabernacles of his palace between the seas in the glorious holy mountain..." This great city is Jerusalem. All our main characters and all their religions are found in Jerusalem. Yet, the underlying basis for Edom's religion is Babylonian as will become apparent in time with the false prophet who deceives with miracles, the religious side of the coin, and the beast, the government side of the coin, mirroring the Old Testament prophets and kings.

In Revelation chapter eighteen, we read about the deeds of Babylon the Great, But in one hour the sixth empire will be destroyed ushering in the Kingdom of God at Christ's second coming described for us in chapter nineteen.

For an *excellent secular* understanding of the current events of the emerging sixth empire, read Chalmers Johnson's insightful trilogy, *Blowback, The Sorrows of Empire and Nemesis.*

***Note about the author, Michael J. Miller:***

The author has written numerous articles for newspapers and magazines, as well as television documentaries and award winning educational films on varied topics including local, national and international politics, economics, medicine, history, the marine environment and theology among others. He has degrees in political science, history and theology.

www.ingramcontent.com/pod-product-compliance
Lightning Source LLC
LaVergne TN
LVHW051823080426
835512LV00018B/2703